AF478228

FIRST STRIKE

MARK TOTTEN

First Strike

AMERICA, TERRORISM, AND MORAL TRADITION

Yale

UNIVERSITY PRESS

NEW HAVEN & LONDON

Yale University Press books may be purchased in quantity for educa-
tional, business, or promotional use. For information, please e-mail
sales.press@yale.edu (U.S. office) or sales@yaleup.co.uk (U.K. office).

Set in Scala and Scala Sans types by
The Composing Room of Michigan, Inc.
Printed in the United States of America.

Library of Congress Cataloging-in-Publication Data
Totten, Mark, 1974–
First strike : America, terrorism, and moral tradition / Mark Totten.
p. cm.
Includes bibliographical references and index.
ISBN 978-0-300-12448-4 (cloth : alk. paper)
1. Terrorism—Prevention—Government policy—United States.
2. Just war doctrine.   3. War—Moral and ethical aspects—
United States.   I. Title.
HV6432.T69   2010
172'.42—dc22   2010004735

A catalogue record for this book is available from the British Library.

This paper meets the requirements of ANSI/NISO Z39.48-1992
(Permanence of Paper).

10 9 8 7 6 5 4 3 2 1

CONTENTS

Acknowledgments   vi

Introduction   1

PART ONE. AMERICA

1 The Turn Toward Prevention   11

2 "Against Our Traditions"?   35

3 Just War at Home in America   74

PART TWO. TRADITION

4 Early Modern Rivals   99

5 Anticipation in a State of Nature   112

6 Evolution and Eclipse   129

PART THREE. REVISION

7 Behind Webster's Rule   149

8 Beyond Webster's Rule   161

Conclusion   184

Notes   187

Index   217

ACKNOWLEDGMENTS

My debts are many. I am grateful to those who gave my text a close reading at various points: Gene Outka, James Turner Johnson, Thomas Ogletree, Margaret Farley, Harry Stout, Paul Kahn, and several anonymous reviewers from Yale University Press. The circle widens with others who discussed ideas important to this project, such as George Weigel, John Noyes, Stephen Carter, Chris Ganski, Scott Dolff, Betsy Perabo, Jesse Couenhoven, and Corey Beals. Christopher Rogers, Executive Editor at Yale University Press, was encouraging throughout this project, and Larry Kenney and Kate Ganski provided invaluable editorial help. And supporting me at every turn was Kristin, my wife.

Several institutions generously supported my work, as well. The Mustard Seed Foundation, through a Harvey Fellowship, and the Michigan State University College of Law both provided financial assistance. The Sterling Memorial Library at Yale University, the Morgan Library in New York City, the Library of Congress, and the Burns Law Library at George Washington University Law School, where I was a research scholar in 2006–07, all provided research services.

I wrote much of this book from a desk overlooking 16th Street in the center of Washington, D.C., where Kristin and I lived for a few years thanks to the kindness of our friends Phil and Linda Lader. The nation's capital has no shortage of inspiring scenes, including the view from my desk. One block to the north, the Pullman Mansion, now the residence of the Russian ambassador but until the early 1980s the Soviet embassy. Three blocks to the south, the White House. The imagery of weighing these urgent matters between the symbolic poles of the Cold War was not lost on me.

Introduction

IN STANLEY KUBRICK'S BLACK COMEDY from 1964, *Dr. Strangelove,* a deranged General Jack Ripper, commander of the Burpleson Air Force Base, orders a wing of B-52s to drop nuclear bombs on targets across the Soviet Union. The order comes as "Plan R," allowing a commanding officer to order nuclear retaliation in case of surprise attack that disrupts the normal chain of command. However, no such attack had occurred. With the planes racing toward their targets and unable to turn back without a three-letter code only General Ripper knows, President Merkin Muffley and his inner circle meet in the Pentagon's War Room.

Blithely unaffected by the crisis, Air Force General Buck Turgidson advises the president to wage all-out nuclear war before Russia tracks the approaching planes and counterattacks. Turgidson cites a study he commissioned on this very scenario—"World Targets in Megadeaths"—showing that the United States could destroy 90 percent of the Soviet's nuclear arsenal "and suffer only modest and acceptable civilian casualties" from the remaining strike capacity:

> *President Muffley:* General, it is the avowed policy of our country never to strike first with nuclear weapons.
> *General Turgidson* (chuckling): Well, Mr. President, I would say General Ripper has already invalidated that policy.
> *President Muffley:* That was not an act of national policy and there are still alternatives left open to us. . . . You're talking about mass murder, General, not war.

General Turgidson: Mr. President, I'm not saying we wouldn't get our hair mussed. But I do say . . . no more than ten to twenty million [Americans] killed, tops. Uh, depending on the breaks.
President Muffley: I will not go down in history as the greatest mass murderer since Adolph Hitler!
General Turgidson: Perhaps it might be better, Mr. President, if you were more concerned with the American people, than with your image in the history books.[1]

In an otherwise absurd exchange, Kubrick's commander in chief expressed a conviction deeply held in the United States throughout the Cold War and beyond: Americans do not strike first. On this point, the logic of the military strategist and the morality of the average American agreed. Qualifying this conviction was an understandable exception, recognized by states for decades: facing an *imminent* armed attack, a state can strike first in self-defense.

During a press conference in March 1959, against the backdrop of the Berlin crisis following the Soviet demand that the United States withdraw from the city, President Dwight Eisenhower was asked whether the nation would ever "strike the first blow against a possible aggressor." The president answered, "No," but went on to say, "If we know we are, at any moment, under a threat of attack, as would be evidenced by missiles or planes coming in our direction, then we have to act just as rapidly as possible, humanly possible to defend ourselves. . . . The reason we have very great and expensive intelligence forces is to keep us informed as well as they possibly can." The next day Secretary of Defense Neil McElroy elaborated. A Soviet attack capable of destroying the ability of the United States to retaliate would require heavy communication traffic and movement of forces, giving notice and creating the grave situation the president described. With his statement, Eisenhower reflected the Cold War consensus against striking first.[2]

The attacks of September 11, 2001, and the new threat of global terrorism, however, challenged this conviction. Unlike past adversaries, this enemy lacks a sense of measured risk, seeks to effect maximum devastation, has or is seeking the means to do so, and can easily evade detection in executing its plans. This shift poses severe challenges to traditional strategies for managing risk, like deterrence and containment. The enemy has nothing to lose and the warnings Eisenhower described may never come. After 9/11 it became plausible to think that using force against a less-than-imminent threat might be a last resort to prevent an attack of unacceptable magnitude. In a narrow range of circumstances, unyielding commitment to the imminence rule is no longer possible. As Secretary of State Elihu Root remarked in 1914, every state has a right "to protect itself by preventing a condition of affairs in which it will be too late to protect itself."[3]

The past several years have witnessed a profound transformation in the nation's attempt to prevent future attack. Although the means of prevention took shape in a thousand ways, the symbol of this transformation at home and abroad was the government's expressed willingness to use preemptive force against emerging threats. The underlying judgment that in some situations waiting until a threat is imminent may be too late was correct. No party has a claim to this conclusion. But the claim as articulated and applied raised significant challenges to the task of rethinking the rules to reflect the new security environment. These challenges remain under a new administration. Thoughtful attention to the matter now—outside the heat of crisis and by policy makers, military officers, and morally responsible citizens—is an urgent task.

The work of revision faces at least two challenges. The first is to develop a narrow doctrine that defines when states can strike first in self-defense. What became known as the Bush Doctrine was vague on paper and flawed in practice. The most complete statement of the doctrine came in the *2002 National Security Strategy* and offered only loose generalizations: "The greater the threat, the greater is the risk of inaction—and the more compelling the case for taking anticipatory action to defend ourselves, even if uncertainty remains as to the time and place of the enemy's attack. . . . The United States will not use force in all cases to preempt emerging threats, nor should nations use preemption as a pretext for aggression. . . . We will always proceed deliberately, weighing the consequences of our actions. . . . The purpose of our actions will always be to eliminate a specific threat to the United States or our allies and friends. The reasons for our actions will be clear, the force measured, and the cause just." The only limit, it seems, was an assurance of America's good intentions.[4]

The danger of an open-ended right was realized in the invasion of Iraq in

2003, insofar as it was a preventive war. While also justifying the war on a string of Security Council resolutions dating back to the First Gulf War, the administration of George W. Bush cast the invasion as an act of preventive force against a regime possessing and seeking more weapons of mass destruction (WMD), which it would pass along to its terrorist friends. Iraq became the poster child for preventive war. Beginning in 2004, as evidence accumulated that the president's case was seriously flawed, criticism turned to the idea of preventive war more generally. Headlines appeared to this effect, for example, "Shooting First: The Preemptive War Doctrine Has Met an Early Death in Iraq" and "Preventive War: A Failed Doctrine." The debate over striking first turned into a debate about Operation Iraqi Freedom. But surely on a matter where the stakes are so high, judgment on that conflict cannot be the final word on preventive force.[5]

The challenge is to craft a framework that identifies the rare conditions under which striking the first blow is acceptable. Such a framework is crucial for facilitating shared expectations. An ambiguous doctrine opens the door to conflict. Where international norms are relatively settled, widely accepted, and generally upheld, America is more secure. And this doctrine must take into account not only substantive constraints but procedural ones as well. The Bush Doctrine branded preventive force as foremost a unilateral measure and gave scant consideration to multilateral institutions. Not only does this weaken institutions important to American security, but it grants a dangerous allowance to states eager for some pretext to mask aggression. We cannot rule out that the United States might have to go it alone, but doing so should be the exception rather than the rule.

The second challenge is to make the moral case for preventive force. The Bush administration's claim to a seemingly unbounded right to strike first left many Americans worried that the nation had abandoned its ideals in the name of security. Although scholars have made some contributions toward sketching a new framework, with few exceptions this second challenge remains unmet and more often than not unnoticed. And yet the importance of moral legitimacy is difficult to underestimate. It's not that advocates of revision have failed to describe the enemy in moral terms. Few presidents taking the nation to war have missed an opportunity to depict America as battling evil—and indeed much evil lies behind this new menace. The moral case I have in mind, however, concerns not the moral standing of the enemy —no one should doubt that terrorism reflects the depths of human depravity—but the moral status of the U.S. response. Specifically, it is the case that revision can uphold long-standing underlying moral principles that have shaped the law of force in the past and guide Americans' understanding of war today. As I will explore later, Americans have such an understanding, it's widely shared, and it's rooted in our identity as a nation.

To borrow the language of Joseph Nye, hard power is often dependent on soft power. That is to say, when achieving our ends requires coercive military force, the successful use of such force will in part depend on the degree to which publics at home and abroad deem such force morally legitimate. Morality shapes power. As Nye states, "Postindustrial democracies are focused on welfare rather than glory, and they dislike high casualties. . . . The absence of a prevailing warrior ethic in modern democracies means that the use of force requires an elaborate moral justification to ensure popular support." Although this dynamic is truer today than ever before, it is not new. In 1513 Machiavelli counseled the prince to maintain a veneer of virtue, lest his subjects turn on him. As John Gaddis and others have observed, during the Cold War the demand to reconcile our actions abroad with our morality at home became progressively urgent.[6]

Yet so far advocates of revision have failed to take seriously that, in the words of Michael Walzer, "justice has become a military necessity." The case for revision is almost always limited to some argument from expediency: striking first, even before a threat is imminent, is necessary to provide America with the security it requires. This claim alone, however, does not provide all legitimacy demands. It appeals to our fears, not our principles. Casting preventive force as a necessary evil or calling for an emergency ethics will not do. The case for revision must appeal to a larger moral framework that accounts for the duties and limits in using force and is consistent with what America stands for and who it claims to be. Americans prize security—the cardinal task of government—but they also cherish justice. My primary argument is that accepting a narrow role for preventive force does not pit morality against security.[7]

A few distinctions are in order. While this book focuses on the use of armed force to prevent a coming attack, the spectrum of preventive strategies is much broader. In the larger scheme, striking first should be a last resort. The day-to-day fight against terrorism takes place through diplomatic channels, disruption of the streams that finance terror, law enforcement actions, intelligence gathering, enhanced border controls, sophisticated sensory technology, and myriad other means.

Although no consensus has emerged, I will use three terms to describe the use of armed force to strike first. Most generally, I will use *anticipatory force* or *anticipatory self-defense* to describe any act of using force first against a potential attack. Although international law scholars often use this term in a more narrow sense, it has an older lineage bearing the meaning I ascribe here. A further distinction, which emerged during the Cold War, draws a helpful line between *preemptive* and *preventive force*. The Bush administration, perhaps to soften the degree to which its newly asserted right departed from established norms, lumped everything under preemptive force. But this use misses an important nuance based on the temporal proximity of the attack. As I use the terms, preemptive force always responds to an imminent threat and preventive force to a threat that is emerging but not yet imminent. Although scholars debate what counts as imminent, this debate takes place within certain bounds. Imminence suggests nearness: the attack is about to happen. Because states have long recognized as a matter of customary international law a right to strike against an imminent threat, our attention is on preventive force.

As a final distinction, the uses of preventive force also fall along a spectrum. Onetime surgical strikes lie at one end. Although not described in these terms, the bombing of the El Shifa pharmaceutical plant in Sudan in 1998 might be one example. On the other end lie full-scale invasions, more often described as preventive wars. The Iraq War of 2003, insofar as the Bush administration employed a preventive force rationale, is the most recent example.

Although the twin challenges I described earlier concern our response to the threats before us, we cannot meet those challenges looking forward, alone. We must also glance behind to understand the genesis of the contemporary imminence rule and to account for our moral intuitions about striking first. Much of this book takes a backward gaze, with the end of finding a way forward. In addition to exploring the American experience with preventive war, I draw upon a body of reflections on the morality of war that have accumulated over several centuries. Beginning at least with Augustine in the late fourth and early fifth centuries and over the course of fifteen hundred years in the context of diverse political arrangements and particular conflicts, a body of moral wisdom about war and its limits evolved. From a bird's-eye view, these reflections were the rudiments of a tradition: a socially embodied, historically extended argument about the occasion and conduct of war, commonly known as the just war tradition. Although the tradition developed a basic framework governing war, it did not address the issue of anticipatory force until much later. Beginning in the sixteenth century a sustained conversation on the use of preventive force ensued that today shapes not only our moral perceptions of war but also the legal norms we recognize.

Part I begins at home. I write as an American and focus on the relationship between preventive force and the nation's moral identity. The subject of this book, however, has global reach, and my use of the pronouns *we, our,* and *us* to refer to Americans is for the sake of expediency and is not meant to exclude readers who do not share this status. I begin by placing the announced willingness of the United States to strike first in the context of the imminence rule, recognized since at least the end of World War II and classically expressed by Daniel Webster in a fascinating but forgotten uproar in 1837 following a skirmish on the Canadian border. While the Bush Doctrine broke new ground, America had confronted the question of striking first before. On three separate occasions during the twentieth century the nation considered but rejected the prospect of preventive war. At least under the circumstances presented, the nation concluded such an act would be against our traditions. I close part I by asking why this might be so. The moral qualms Americans felt, at least by that point in time, reflected a shared intuition that the nation should use force only as a last resort. This intuition had roots in the moral tradition of the just war, which came to provide the grammar for how most Americans talk about war. The triumph of the moral tradition, however, is not happenstance. Rather, it reflects a deep affinity between the moral tradition and the nation's understanding of itself, its moral identity.

In part II I consider what this moral inheritance has to say about the issue of striking first. Beginning with a monk named Francisco de Vitoria in the sixteenth century, the tradition developed a nuanced standard governing when states could anticipate a coming harm. At the same time, I trace developments within a rival tradition that counseled striking first on the mere basis of fear, as the rational response of states coexisting in a state of nature. The most forceful account was that of Thomas Hobbes, which is still felt today.

Finally, in part III I bring this historical narrative directly to bear on the twin challenges we confront today: the challenge of moral legitimacy and the challenge of developing a narrow framework governing the use of preventive force. Contrary to the snap conclusions of most commentators, not only did the just war tradition not repudiate preventive force, it insisted that the differences between individuals and states demand that states have a limited right to strike first, even against a less-than-imminent threat. This allowance, however, was not open-ended. It followed a carefully circumscribed standard for when such a rare occasion might arise. Not only does this narrative provide a principled case for preventive force and identify the marks of just prevention, but it also provides a larger context for understanding the contemporary imminence rule, perhaps easing the absolute grip it has upon us. The moral tradition developed in a world very different from our own and does not provide simple answers to the challenges we confront. Any proposal, for example, has to take account of the institutions in place since World War II. Nonetheless, the tradition points a way forward that does not sacrifice American ideals on the altar of security.

PART ONE

AMERICA

1

The Turn Toward Prevention

America's announced willingness to strike the first blow against emerging threats marked a decisive shift in the nation's plan for protecting itself. One bold announcement at a West Point graduation ceremony cast off a consensus on the rule for striking first that nearly all nations, including the United States, had recognized since World War II. This rule limits the first use of force to cases of self-defense against an *imminent* threat: a coming attack so near in space and time that to prohibit a state from striking first would require it to take the first, and perhaps fatal, blow. To grasp the dimensions of this turn one needs a better understanding of where this rule came from, what it means, and why the balance it once achieved between security and restraint is questionable today. While consensus around the imminence rule emerged only during the past five decades under the UN Charter, its origins lie much earlier, in an 1837 attack on American soil that captured headlines for five years and nearly swept the young republic into its third war with Great Britain: the steamship *Caroline* was torched by Canadian loyalists and loosed into the churning rapids above Niagara Falls.

The *Caroline* Uproar and Webster's Rule

Although America's second war with Britain, the War of 1812, had officially ended with the Treaty of Ghent signed on Christmas Eve 1814, ill feelings between the Crown and its former colonies festered in the decades that followed. Many in the British ruling class still held a firm skepticism about the American experiment and a disdain for democracy. Furthermore, the two nations were at odds over borders. A long-standing dispute lingered over the northern boundary of Maine, which boiled over in the bloodless Aroostook War of 1838–39. Both nations also asserted conflicting claims over the Oregon Territory, a region rich in natural resources and lucrative grounds for the fur-trading industry.[1]

In addition, the British cast a suspicious gaze at the rapid pace of American expansion. President Thomas Jefferson, seizing an opportunity opened up by Great Power politics abroad and overcoming Federalist opposition at home, doubled the size of the United States with the purchase of the Louisiana Territory in 1803 for a pittance of three cents an acre. The military tact of General Andrew Jackson mixed with the political skill of Secretary of State John Quincy Adams to again extend the Republic's boundary in 1819, this time to the tip of southern Florida. And many British leaders believed the voracious nation would plant the Stars and Stripes on Canadian soil if given their druthers—a hope that animated many patriots shouldering muskets in 1812.[2]

Also a source of national resentment was the Royal Navy's practice of searching American ships to suppress the slave trade. Britain had outlawed the trade in 1807 and similar measures followed in the United States, including an Act of Congress of 1820 that made trading in slaves punishable by death. Although Adams had come close to negotiating a treaty with Britain in 1824 that would have established a mutual right of search, domestic politics interfered and the Senate killed the treaty. Not until 1862 did the two countries recognize such a right. Boasting the mightiest navy in the world, Britain continued to search ships flying the American flag off the western coast of Africa, treaty or not. While views on slavery in America during the 1830s and 1840s ranged from fierce abolition to ardent support, most Americans viewed Britain's practice as a brazen slight to American sovereignty. An editorial in the *Boston Recorder* in 1841 concluded, "We hear, likewise, of British cruisers on the coast of Africa reviving the odious claim to search our vessels, and committing insults and outrages well calculated to exasperate our national pride. The enforcement of such a claim occasioned our last war; and it certainly would not be strange if a renewal of the provocation should lead to another."[3]

Against this backdrop of resentment and suspicion, the sinking of the *Caroline,* an otherwise minor skirmish, fueled a national furor. The occasion was the Canadian Rebellion of 1837. Although the revolt proved short-lived, its leaders envisioned North America's second revolution. They demanded representative government reflecting the interests of Canadians and not the dictates of the Crown. While the colonists had an elected body, the British governors retained the power to ignore the assembly and rely instead on councils they appointed. At the same time, many Canadians resented the feudal land system imported from England.

Leading the movement in the province of Upper Canada was the firebrand William Lyon Mackenzie, an emigrant from Scotland who crossed the Atlantic in 1820 and established a reform newspaper called the *Colonial Advocate* (and whose grandson, William Mackenzie King, would later distinguish himself as the longest-serving prime minister in the history of the British Commonwealth). Mackenzie entered politics in the late 1820s as an elected member of the provincial assembly. Although expelled in 1831 for libeling his political opponents, he was later reelected and in 1834 became mayor of Toronto. Following the lead of American rebels some six decades earlier, Mackenzie helped draft a "Declaration of Grievances," published in July 1837. At the same time, he conspired to seize Toronto's city hall, capture the provincial lieutenant governor, and declare a provisional government. In early December, Mackenzie and his minions gathered at Montgomery's Tavern on the outskirts of Toronto and a few days later marched on the city. Government soldiers chased the ill-equipped rebels back to the tavern and fired cannon shot inside, scattering the insurgents and with them the once-grandiose aspirations for revolution. At least for the moment.

Like many of his rebel followers, Mackenzie fled for the American border. On December 11 he arrived to a hero's welcome in Buffalo, a frontier settlement which had not forgotten the flames that razed all but one of its buildings at British hands during the War of 1812. Resentful of British rule, eager to seize economic opportunities to the north, and far from federal control, frontier patriots intoxicated with democracy rallied to Mackenzie at a Buffalo coffeehouse and gathered arms and supplies to continue the rebellion. Among the recruits was Rensselaer Van Rensselaer, perhaps goaded to join the expedition by the offer to become Mackenzie's general and maybe earn something of the fame his Uncle Stephen had accrued during the War of 1812.

After less than a week of preparations, the band of twenty-four mostly Americans marched with Mackenzie and General Van Rennselaer north along the Niagara River. They occupied Navy Island, a small, densely wooded Canadian possession a few miles upstream from the falls. According to one account, Mackenzie announced the Republic of Canada, foisted a twin-starred flag representing Canada's two provinces, and issued a proclamation calling on American patriots to follow the "illustrious example of Lafayette" and other freedom fighters from abroad who had sought to throw off the "yoke of foreign oppression."[4]

Inspired by the cause of freedom—and drawn by Mackenzie's promise to give every recruit three hundred acres of land and one hundred silver coins—patriot sympathizers answered Mackenzie's call and streamed to Navy Island. Although accounts differ, it appears the force came to number several hundred musket-wielding men. The island was naturally suited for defense, skirted by strong currents racing toward Niagara Falls and flanked by steep sides jutting ten to twenty feet above the water's edge. Trees choked the interior of the island, providing cover and ample wood for fire, building defenses, and other needs. Armed with at least one cannon, the militants hurled several leaden balls across the few hundred yards separating the island from the Canadian shore and the nearby village of Chippewa. The only casualties were a few pierced roofs and, newspapers reported, an ill-fated horse.

To aid the transport of men, arms, and supplies from the American mainland to Navy Island, the rebels hired the *Caroline*, a forty-six ton, seventy-one-foot sidewheel steamer. William Wells, a Buffalo businessman, had recently acquired the vessel and agreed to the deal after wisely receiving surety in the event of loss. On the morning of December 28 the crew loosed the boat from its icy fetters along the Buffalo shore and the vessel steamed north toward Navy Island. Skippering the boat was Captain Gilman Appleby, a steamship master who had ferried passengers and goods across Lake Erie for years. After unloading provisions at the rebel outpost, the *Caroline* paddled supplies between the island and nearby Fort Schlosser on the New York side of the river. Fort Schlosser was a British outpost before the Revolution that was torched by the Crown during the War of 1812 and now boasted only a single house, a small tavern with some lodging, an old storehouse, and a dock.

Eyeing the steady buildup on Navy Island, Allan MacNab assembled at Chippewa several thousand Canadian militiamen loyal to the queen. Aware of the new role played by the steamer and believing the growing force might use the boat to invade Canadian shores, MacNab determined to capture or destroy the vessel. After sunset on the evening of Thursday, December 28, a small skiff manned by Commander Andrew Drew of the Royal Navy and Alexander McLeod, a deputy sheriff from Kingston, glided into the waters off Chippewa and made its way toward Navy Island. While drawing a chorus of whistling musket fire, the scouts managed to glimpse the steamer alongside a temporary wharf on the eastern side of the island.

The next day the *Caroline* continued to ferry passengers and supplies between the island and the American mainland. That evening MacNab called for sixty volunteers with experience rowing and wielding a cutlass, the short curved sword used by sailors. He placed Drew in command but revealed nothing about the mission's purpose or plan to anyone else. Galled by the occupation of Canadian soil and frustrated by idleness, the queen's men lined up at once. Around nine o'clock the raiding party pushed off from shore in seven or eight rowboats, and then Drew announced their task: to destroy the *Caroline*. As the night was especially dark, one of the men held a small flame behind the stern of the lead boat, guiding the rest as they rowed upstream against an aggressive current. Rounding the southern end of Navy Island, Drew discovered that the steamer was not at the wharf. Assuming the ship had docked at Fort Schlosser for the night and following his orders to destroy the vessel, Drew crossed into American waters.

The *Caroline* was chained to the dock, serving as a floating hotel for the night because the sole tavern in Fort Schlosser was unable to house the swarm of oglers drawn by the specter of war. Cloaked in darkness, the rowboats glided toward the steamer unnoticed until they were only a few strokes away. Catching sight of the approaching boats, the ship's watch commanded the party to announce itself and issue the password. "Friends" was the only reply Drew offered, and the watch sounded the alarm. By that time, however, the Canadians, led by Commander Drew, were boarding the boat. Aroused from slumber, the Americans managed to fire off a few musket balls, and the clash of cutlasses briefly dinned the air, but they were unprepared and fled.

Following Drew's orders, one of the Canadians scampered below deck and, finding the ship's furnace, spread its glowing coals and set the *Caroline* aflame. Others loosed the chains that bound the vessel to the dock. Returning to their rowboats, the soldiers heaved the vessel into the racing current and with three cheers for the young Victoria—as some American accounts have it—set the steamer loose, a silhouette of flames careening toward the cataract.

The news took about five or six days to reach the American press, but when it did a national squall ensued. The *Buffalo Daily Journal* of December 30, 1837, headlined, "GROSS OUTRAGE AND INVASION OF OUR TERRITORY BY THE BRITISH ROYALISTS!!!—AMERICAN BLOOD SHED!!!"—reprinted in papers across the nation a few days later. The *New York Herald,* one of the most widely read papers of the time, offered this account: "The first signal those on board [the *Caroline*] had of the proximity of danger, was from the shots, pikes, and cutlasses of the assailants, and as our informant states, were massacred unresistingly, before they had time to leap ashore. The Caroline was then towed into the stream, set on fire, and (to cap the climax of horrors, and make the narrative complete,) propelled into the maddening current, and, with upwards of thirty killed and wounded citizens, hurried over the Falls of Niagara!" The next day, the *Herald* all but issued a call to war: "The loyalist troops have made an assault upon our territory. They have murdered in cold blood our citizens. They cannot escape our vengeance. . . . Niagara's eternal thunders are sounding their requiem! and from the depths of that mighty flood come the wail of their spirits, calling for the blood of their murderers!"[5]

Early accounts of the "outrage at Schlosser" reported that loyalist militants killed between six and thirty Americans, based on the number of persons unaccounted for after the raid. In fact, many of the approximately ten crew members and the two dozen or so paying guests on board the *Caroline* that night fled without returning a fight, several popping out of portholes, jumping into the river, and swimming ashore. And despite the recurring account that the fiery boat plunged over the falls, it actually sank, and the fire was extinguished before it reached the precipice, although pieces of the boat did take the plunge.

The only confirmed death was that of Amos Durfee, whose body was found on the dock at Fort Schlosser the next morning. A few days later Durfee's body was taken to Buffalo for a public funeral, announced throughout town by posters shaped like coffins. Outside the Eagle Hotel organizers displayed Durfee's body for the hundreds of people who had descended on the city, muskets in hand and ready for a fight. As one reporter noted, Durfee's "corpse was held up—with its pale forehead, mangled by the pistol ball, and his locks matted with his blood! His friends and fellow citizens looked on the ghastly spectacle, and thirsted for an opportunity to revenge him." The spirit at Buffalo spread along the frontier to Cleveland, Detroit, and hundreds of other villages where Americans joined Patriot Lodges and prepared for war. As the *Daily Herald and Gazette* in Cleveland reported, "The whole frontier from Buffalo to Lake Ontario, now bristles with Bayonets." A few zealous patriots acted on their own. In May a group dressed as Indians wrested control of the Canadian steamer *Sir Robert Peel,* forced its occupants ashore, and set it aflame to cries of "Remember the *Caroline!*" In June, several hundred militia members crossed the Niagara and invaded Canada before British musketry reversed their march and sent them scuttling home. And in December a group of fervent patriots assembled in Detroit and crossed into Canada for a march on Windsor. The British militia drove them back but not before the Americans had burned the steamer *Thames* in revenge. While some papers such as the *Niles National Register* called for calm and a more subdued response, the frontier was not alone in demanding war with Britain. For many Americans, the *Caroline* outrage tapped a much deeper resentment.[6]

But President Martin Van Buren was unwilling to risk war and took several steps to calm the storm. He sent General Winfield Scott, the famed war hero from 1812, to the frontier on a mission of restraint. A presidential proclamation warned that the federal government would arrest and punish Americans violating the nation's neutrality laws. Van Buren called on Congress to give him, as president, authority not only to punish, but also to prevent violations of federal neutrality laws by citizens of the United States. At the same time, Van Buren demanded redress from Britain for a violation of national sovereignty.[7]

Although the diplomatic exchange continued for several years and the national appetite for war waned over time, tensions spiked again in early 1841 with the arrest of Alexander McLeod in western New York by state officials, who accused him of participating in the destruction of the *Caroline* and charging him with arson and the murder of Durfee. New York was determined to try McLeod in state court, where he faced execution, despite the international import of the issue and the later acknowledgment by the Crown that Drew and his comrades destroyed the *Caroline* under authority of the British government. Leading the states' rights cause in New York, ironically, was the Whig governor William H. Seward, later secretary of state under Abraham Lincoln and an ardent supporter of a strong national government. Faced with a popular outcry at home, however, politics bested principle. President Van Buren, an architect of Jacksonian democracy and defender of states' rights, was content to let the matter proceed in state court while attempting to assuage British consternation with lectures on American federalism.

When the Whig president William Henry Harrison came to office just a few months after McLeod's arrest, the *Caroline* controversy passed into the hands of Harrison's appointed secretary of state, Daniel Webster. His jet-black hair, deep-set eyes, and massive brow created an imposing presence. Webster first rose to national prominence as a lawyer in private practice. His legal acumen and silver tongue placed him behind the lectern of the U.S. Supreme Court for some of the most important cases of his day. In *McCulloch v. Maryland* (1819) Webster convinced the Court that Congress had the power to charter a national bank. Accepting Webster's argument in *Gibbons v. Ogden* (1824), the Court rejected New York's grant of a monopoly on steamboat operations between New York City and New Jersey, which the state had given to Robert Fulton and Robert Livingston of paddleboat fame. Congress, the Court ruled, had the power to regulate interstate navigation. Both cases were landmarks in the formation of a strong national government, a cause Webster later championed as senator from Massachusetts.

Against the doctrine of nullification defended by Senator Robert Hayne of South Carolina, which held that a state could nullify any act of the federal government it deemed unconstitutional, Webster delivered a harrowing rebuttal on the Senate floor that concluded with his famous proclamation, "Liberty and Union, now and forever, one and inseparable." Harrison's death one month after taking office could have brought Webster's job as chief statesman to an early end, but Vice President John Tyler kept him in the post. The *Caroline* affair afforded Webster another opportunity to steel the Union.[8]

During the lead-up to McLeod's trial, the drums of war reached a steady beat on both sides of the Atlantic. In violation of the Rush–Bagot Agreement of 1817, Britain began a naval buildup on the Great Lakes and moored two large steamers, the *Minos* and the *Toronto*, at Chippewa in case of conflict. Democratic senators pressured President Tyler to release correspondence between Webster and the British government regarding the trial and then harangued the secretary with accusations of making America look weak. Across the Atlantic both houses of Parliament discussed the crisis. The *Times* concluded that the execution of McLeod would be "an act of such atrocious and disgusting cruelty, that we suppose there are not three Englishmen living who would not insist on a prompt appeal to arms for redress."[9]

Congress had not yet given Webster power to remove the case to federal court—that grant came with passage of the so-called McLeod bill in late 1842, allowing an authorized federal judge to grant a writ of habeas corpus to any prisoner who claimed his alleged offense was committed under the law of nations or a foreign sovereign. Nonetheless, Webster did everything he could behind the scenes to ensure McLeod was not executed, making certain he had strong legal representation and for a spell taking up residence at the Astor Hotel in New York City to offer counsel. In addition, Webster pressed Britain to claim public responsibility for the attack on the *Caroline* to bolster his claim that responsibility for the incident was a matter of foreign policy capable of redress only at the diplomatic level. The British minister in Washington, Henry Fox, made this avowal on March 12, 1841, upholding the destruction of the *Caroline* as a necessary act of self-defense and demanding McLeod's release. To Webster's disbelief, Fox's public assertion of state responsibility failed to convince the New York Supreme Court to release McLeod. After a six-day trial in October 1841, however, a jury of nine farmers, two merchants, and one doctor needed only twenty minutes to conclude McLeod was not a member of the party that raided the *Caroline*.[10]

During the trial and for more than a year afterward, Webster continued to press the diplomatic case with Britain, unwilling to concede any ground on the consistent American claim that the British attack on the *Caroline* in neutral U.S. territory was a violation of the law of nations and an unjustified assault on American sovereignty. Webster wrote his most famous note—and the most important source for the evolving standard governing the use of anticipatory force—on April 24, 1841, in response to Fox's public acceptance of the *Caroline* incident as an act of the Crown. Webster agreed that an individual cannot bear responsibility for an act of state and, though lacking the power to end the state judicial proceeding, expressed confidence that the New York Supreme Court would agree.

As to the attack on the *Caroline*, Webster looked to the law of nations and announced a rule for the first use of force that would long outlive the skirmish at Schlosser. "It will be for that Government to show a necessity of self-defence, instant, overwhelming, leaving no choice of means, and no moment for deliberation." Furthermore, "it will be for it to show, also, that the local authorities of Canada, even supposing the necessity of the moment authorized them to enter the territories of The United States at all, did nothing unreasonable or excessive; since the act, justified by the necessity of self-defence, must be limited by that necessity, and kept clearly within it." What I will call Webster's Rule identified two criteria governing the use of anticipatory force: *necessity*, as measured by the presence of an *imminent* threat; and *proportionality*. Webster then described what this rule would have required on the night of December 29, 1837, and drew his conclusion on the facts:

> It must be shown that admonition or remonstrance to the persons on board the *Caroline* was impracticable, or would have been unavailing; it must be shown that day-light could not be waited for; that there could be no attempt at discrimination between the innocent and the guilty; that it would not have been enough to seize and detain the vessel; but that there was a necessity, present and inevitable, for attacking her in the darkness of the night, while

moored to the shore, and while unarmed men were asleep on board, killing some and wounding others, and then drawing her into the current, above the cataract, setting her on fire, and, careless to know whether there might not be in her the innocent with the guilty, or the living with the dead, committing her to a fate which fills the imagination with horror. A necessity for all this, the Government of The United States cannot believe to have existed.[11]

The British government, now under the leadership of Sir Robert Peel and his special envoy to the United States, Lord Ashburton, awaited the outcome of the McLeod trial before responding to Webster's letter. With McLeod quietly ushered across the Canadian border to resume life as a grocer, Lord Ashburton sent a note to Webster in July 1842 that brought an end to the long dispute. Most important, he accepted Webster's imminence rule for anticipatory self-defense: "It is so far satisfactory to perceive that we are perfectly agreed as to the general principles of international law applicable to this unfortunate case." Although Ashburton maintained the British position and argued that circumstances justified the attack on the *Caroline* under Webster's Rule, in an act of diplomatic wisdom he offered a word of peace: "Looking back to what passed at this distance of time, what is perhaps most to be regretted, is, that some explanation and apology for this occurrence was not immediately made." Accepting this salve for America's wounded pride, Webster laid the affair to rest.[12]

Webster's Rule since World War II

Also laid to rest and given only passing reference was Webster's Rule for when a state could strike the first blow. Only in the wake of World War II and with attempts to craft a new international order did the *Caroline* resurface. And when it did, Webster's Rule was cast in a new role. In his letter of April 24, Webster's demand for "a necessity of self-defense, instant, overwhelming, leaving no choice of means, and no moment for deliberation" was not an appeal to a general principle of law governing the decision to use force in that day. War was an accepted tool of international politics. While states in the nineteenth century gave some credence to a handful of norms governing armed force, the ultimate decision to wage war was a prerogative of state.[13]

Rather, Webster's Rule made sense against the backdrop of the law of neutrality, a norm increasingly recognized during his day that prohibited belligerents in a conflict from invading a neutral state. The young republic was an ardent champion of neutrality. Eager to secure the freedom of the seas, avoid entanglement in Europe's perpetual wars, and keep the colonial powers from interfering with America's neighbors to the south, America had every reason to support the doctrine. In 1837 the United States regarded itself as a neutral party in what it viewed as a Canadian civil war between rebels and loyalists. President Van Buren's proclamation, issued a few days after the *Caroline* was destroyed, had warned that "any persons who shall compromise the neutrality of this Government . . . will render themselves liable to arrest and punishment under the laws of the United States." Webster stated his rule directly after a lengthy discourse on the law of neutrality and his conclusion that America's commitment to that principle "has set an example not unfit to be followed by others"—a thinly veiled barb against British meddling in the republican revolutions of Latin America. Webster's Rule announced a narrow exception to the prohibition against invading the territory of a neutral state and for the next several decades received only passing mention in that context.[14]

When lawyers in the halls of learning and the corridors of state dusted off the *Caroline* correspondence more than a century later, they gave new meaning to Webster's words in a world that looked very different from that of 1841. The clash of swords was now governed by the UN Charter—at least in principle, if not always in practice. The transition from a largely unlimited right to use force that existed during Webster's day to the present era under the Charter took place over a span of at least fifty years. Developments after World War I included the formation of the League of Nations, finally discredited by its failure to prevent a second global conflict, and the utopian Kellogg–Briand Pact of 1928, providing for the "renunciation of war as an instrument of national policy" but allowing no exception for self-defense. The horror of a second world war, however, provided the impetus for ratification of the UN Charter in 1945.[15]

The shift inaugurated by the Charter was sweeping, especially compared to Webster's day. Article 2(4) announces a general prohibition on the use of force: "All members shall refrain in their international relations from the threat or use of force against the territorial integrity or political independence of any state, or in any other manner inconsistent with the Purposes of the United Nations." The prohibition bars the use of force in general, not merely war or the more narrow term used elsewhere in the treaty, "armed attack." This general disavowal, however, admits two exceptions. The first pertains to the Security Council. Under Chapter VII, Article 39, where the Council finds an "act of aggression" or even "the existence of any threat to the peace" or "breach of peace," it can use armed force "to restore international peace and security." The Council can take broad remedial action, presumably including the use of preventive force. Given the realities of Great Power politics and the interests of states, it comes as no surprise that the list of actions under Chapter VII is short.[16]

In addition, the Charter grants a second exception to individual states. Unlike the Kellogg–Briand Pact, the Charter allows states to use force for the limited purpose of self-defense. Article 51 reads, "Nothing in the present Charter shall impair the inherent right of individual or collective self-defense if an armed attack occurs against a Member of the United Nations, until the Security Council has taken measures necessary to maintain international peace and security." On its face, the plain language of Article 51 appears to rule out the use of anticipatory force, even against the most imminent threat. The exception applies "if an armed attack occurs." The Charter says nothing about coming attacks, and in the absence of comment the general prohibition against the use of force would seem to apply.

The Charter, however, must be read in the light of what jurists refer to as customary law. Rather than looking to the treaties states sign, this source looks to the actions states take. Customary law, then, is a body of norms that states have widely recognized and consistently followed in their past practice. Many scholars have concluded that the Charter's mention of an *"inherent* right" of self-defense incorporates customary law directly into the Charter. This was the conclusion of the International Court of Justice in 1986 in its *Nicaragua* decision. While not ruling on the issue, the court stated, "The United Nations Charter . . . by no means covers the whole area of the regulation of the use of force in international relations. On one essential point, this treaty itself refers to pre-existing customary international law; this reference to customary law is contained in the actual text of Article 51, which mentions the 'inherent right' . . . of individual or collective self-defence. . . . The Court therefore finds that Article 51 of the Charter is only meaningful on the basis that there is a 'natural' or 'inherent' right of self-defence, and it is hard to see how this can be other than of a customary nature."[17]

Events since World War II make clear that states do recognize a limited right to use preemptive force governed by Webster's Rule. No longer an exception to the law of neutrality in a world with otherwise few limits on war, Webster's Rule was now an exception to the law limiting force to self-defense against an armed attack. The earliest example lies in the judgment against leading Nazi officials after Germany's surrender, issued from the Palace of Justice at Nuremberg on October 1, 1946. Before a block of wool-suited defendants that included Hermann Goering, Rudolf Hess, and Ernst Kaltenbrunner, judges representing Britain, France, the United States, and the Soviet Union read their lengthy judgment. Reviewing Germany's aggression against neighboring states, the court turned to the invasion of Denmark and Norway on April 9, 1940.

Erich Raeder, commander in chief of the German navy, helped plan the invasion. Raeder's defense counsel had argued that Germany invaded Norway because of an imminent threat that Britain and France would do so first and then use Norway as a base of operations against Germany. Citing several treatises, Raeder's attorney framed the act as justified under international law. Quoting Webster, the court judged the rule correct but unmet. "It must be remembered that preventive action in foreign territory is justified only in case of 'an instant and overwhelming necessity for self-defense, leaving no choice of means, and no moment of deliberation'. . . . It is clear that when the plans for an attack on Norway were being made, they were not made for the purpose of forestalling an imminent Allied landing, but, at the most, that they might prevent an Allied occupation at some future date." Although the tribunal was applying international norms in effect before the formation of the United Nations, the invocation of Webster's Rule set the stage for its recasting under the Charter and was a seminal recognition in the middle of the twentieth century that states could strike first against an imminent threat.[18]

An acceptance of this right was also implicit in world response to the Israeli–Arab War of 1967. Since the Suez Canal crisis more than a decade earlier, a force of about six thousand blue-helmeted soldiers, the UN Emergency Force (UNEF), had served as a buffer between Egypt and Israel. In May 1967 Egypt asked the United Nations to withdraw UNEF. Because the force was present under Egyptian consent, Secretary U Thant complied. At once Egyptian troops occupied the buffer zone, bringing them face to face with Israeli forces. At the same time Cairo closed off the Strait of Tiran, blocking Israeli shipping from the south, and called for Arabs to unite against Israel. Early in the morning of June 5, 1967, both Israel and Egypt notified the Security Council that the other had begun an armed attack. Launching nearly two hundred jets at once, Israel made a decisive first strike, shredding tarmac and destroying almost the entire Egyptian air force. At the end of the conflict six days later, Israel had seized the West Bank, Gaza, the Sinai Peninsula, and the Golan Heights. Among other arguments, Israel justified the war as a legitimate act of anticipatory self-defense. Subsequent UN actions suggested that most nations accepted this claim. The Security Council demanded a cease-fire but never required Israel to return the occupied territory or even censured Israel's actions. Most states seemed to conclude that Israel's survival was at stake, and, faced with an imminent threat, it did not have to absorb the perhaps fatal first blow.[19]

Israel was again at the center of registering international opinion on the use of preemptive force in 1981, when it launched several F-16s in Operation Opera to destroy an Iraqi nuclear reactor at Osirak. Although Iraq claimed the reactor was for peaceful purposes, Israel justified the raid as a necessary act of self-defense. Iraq, it argued, aimed to produce atomic bombs to use against Israel. Since the reactor was to become operational in a few months, Israel argued that the action was necessary at that point in time to avoid the later risk of nuclear fallout and consequent injury to civilians. The international community, however, rejected Israel's claims. The Security Council unanimously adopted a resolution condemning the action as a violation of international law. As the resolution noted, Iraq was party to the Treaty on Non-Proliferation of Nuclear Weapons of 1968. The reactor at Osirak was subject to regular inspections by the International Atomic Energy Agency, which had never found any violations.

In condemning the action, several members of the Security Council made clear that circumstances did not give rise to the right of anticipatory self-defense. Jeane Kirkpatrick, U.S. ambassador to the United Nations, stated, "Our judgment that Israeli actions violated the United Nations Charter is based solely on the conviction that Israel failed to exhaust peaceful means for the resolution of this dispute." Ambassador Olara Otunnu of Uganda cited Webster's Rule and argued that Israel failed to satisfy it. Sir Anthony Parsons from Britain concluded "there was no instant or overwhelming necessity of self-defense." Webster's Rule was again affirmed.[20]

More recent events further evidence that the United States has recognized a right of preemption under the imminence standard. President George H. W. Bush invoked this justification for the invasion of Panama in 1989 that deposed Manuel Noriega. "The deployment of U.S. Forces is an exercise of the right of self-defense recognized in Article 51 of the United Nations Charter and was necessary to protect American lives in imminent danger." Two weeks after the bombing of American embassies in Kenya and Tanzania in 1998, President Bill Clinton ordered a surgical strike on a pharmaceutical plant in Sudan, allegedly an al Qaeda operation for producing chemical weapons. The government justified the attack as a legitimate act of anticipatory self-defense, invoking the now-classic test: "The United States acted in exercise of our inherent right of self-defense consistent with Article 51 of the United Nations Charter. These strikes were a necessary and proportionate response to the imminent threat of further terrorist attacks against U.S. personnel and facilities."[21]

Together these cases represent a widespread recognition by states since World War II of a limited right to use preemptive force against an imminent threat. Although Webster's language may represent the most stringent interpretation of what states require by way of an imminent threat, the sinking of the *Caroline* is the locus classicus for this narrow right. While the "outrage at Schlosser" was long ago laid to rest, Webster's Rule received new life.

Necessity, Proportionality, and Imminence

Having traced the evolution of the imminence standard from a national hullabaloo in 1837 to the close of the twentieth century, I want to examine more closely what Webster's Rule in this new context requires. As mentioned earlier, the rule stands for the twin principles of necessity (or last resort) and proportionality. Neither are mentioned in the UN Charter, but both are widely regarded as established norms of customary law governing the use of force in general and preemptive force in particular. The International Court of Justice's advisory opinion in *Legality of the Threat or Use of Nuclear Weapons* (1996) is instructive: "The submission of the exercise of the right of self-defence to the conditions of necessity and proportionality is a rule of customary international law. . . . This dual condition applies equally to Article 51 of the Charter, whatever means of force employed."[22]

When states have invoked the language of necessity to justify their recourse to force over the past few centuries, they have meant different things. Prior to the Charter, for example, the term often swept in a broad assortment of rationales that would hardly seem to fit the term today. For my concerns, however, the term refers to the customary law restraint on the decision to use force and is classically represented by Webster's statement: "a necessity of self-defense, instant, overwhelming, leaving no choice of means, and no moment for deliberation." Much confusion exists over the relationship between necessity and imminence, both expressed in Webster's Rule. Are they different requirements? Does one fall under the other?

As one definition rightly describes the requirement of last resort, "The State attacked (or threatened with imminent attack . . .) must not, in the particular circumstances, have had any means of halting the attack other than recourse to armed force." Webster's Rule stipulates that force is a last resort only when the threat is imminent. Although Webster does not employ the word *imminent,* his description of a threat "instant, overwhelming, leaving no choice of means, and no moment for deliberation" clearly points to it. Scholars have debated what counts as an imminent threat, with Webster's language representing a stringent interpretation of the word, but this debate goes on within certain limits. Few dispute that the imminence requirement rules out the use of force against an attack not nearing the point of execution. Lawrence Freedman's definition is helpful: a preemptive attack against an imminent threat takes place "at some point between the moment when an enemy decides to attack—or, more precisely, is perceived to be about to attack—and when the attack is actually launched." Threats merely emerging, outside the heat of a crisis, are not imminent. Traditionally it meant a visual mobilization of armed forces preparing for an attack. Such was the case in the Israeli–Arab War of 1967.[23]

Although the challenges to the contemporary rule primarily concern the principle of necessity, customary law and Webster's Rule also require proportionality. As in the case of necessity, states also mean different things when they use this term. The primary distinction here is between proportionality as part of the *jus ad bellum* (law governing the decision to use force) and the same judgment under the *jus in bello* (law governing the means of force). Proportionality under the *jus in bello,* sometimes called proportionality of means, assesses the means used to conduct war. Only *jus ad bellum* is of concern here. Again, the classic statement is Webster's: "The act, justified by the necessity of self-defense, must be limited by that necessity, and kept clearly within it."[24]

As the word suggests, proportionality concerns a judgment about the relationship between two things. One point of comparison is clear: the nature and extent of force used by the target state acting in self-defense. But to what is this compared? Some commentators have wrongly suggested that the use of force in self-defense must be proportional to the particular use of armed force that initiates the defensive response. If I have lined up a hundred nuclear-tipped missiles at your border and fire a small, conventional rocket into your territory, this view holds that you can respond only with a use of force proportional to my measly one rocket—even though the threat is more serious. The obvious problem with this view is that it threatens to undermine the underlying goal of self-defense.[25]

The better view measures the nature and extent of force used by the target state against the aim that justifies the use of force in the first place: self-defense. As one commentator has stated, "The requirement of *proportionality* of the action taken in self-defence . . . concerns the relationship between that action and its purpose, namely . . . that of halting and repelling the attack or even, in so far as [anticipatory] self-defence is recognized, of preventing it from occurring." In the context of my discussion, a judgment of proportionality is especially difficult because the target state must measure the proposed use of force against an armed attack that has not yet occurred. Nonetheless, proportionality here is a measure of the

amount of force necessary for self-defense, not a comparison with the perceived initial attack.[26]

Webster in an Age of Terror

After the attacks of 9/11, the nation that birthed Webster's Rule suddenly
disowned it. While strategies of deterrence and containment were not obsolete, they were deemed no longer sufficient. The security of the nation demanded a new paradigm based on prevention. This shift would register in
countless ways, but none more stark than the willingness to strike first
against a less-than-imminent threat.

The changes came rapidly but not without precedent. September 11 was
not the first day America woke up to a new world with new threats. December 7, 1941, was another. Disillusioned by the experience of World War
I and the diplomatic failures that followed, Americans during the 1930s
were eager to stay out of European affairs. An active peace movement blossomed in church halls and student unions, boasting twelve million members. An article in *Fortune* magazine in March 1934 entitled "Arms and the
Men," along with a Book-of-the-Month Club publication, *Merchants of Death,*
accused the arms industry of fomenting war for its own gain and fueled a
Senate investigation. More important, an even larger swath of the public,
uncomfortable with peace parades and pacifist pledges, was nonetheless
convinced that Europe's distant troubles were not America's.

Keenly aware of the nation's vulnerability but also aware that the pendu-
lum of a democratic government can swing only so far, President Franklin
Roosevelt took measured steps to convince America of the threat it faced.
With German troops in the Rhineland and Adolf Hitler having freshly re-
pudiated the Treaty of Versailles, Roosevelt began his efforts with a speech
in Chicago on October 5, 1937. Concluding that the "very foundations of civilization are seriously threatened" by a "present reign of terror" in Europe
and Asia, the president warned that "if those things come to pass in other
parts of the world, let no one imagine that America will escape." In December 1940, with German aggression now in plain view, Roosevelt's "Arsenal of Democracy" address crackled on American radios before a public
still lulled by the false security of oceans east and west. "Some of us like to

believe," Roosevelt said, "that even if Britain falls, we are still safe, because of the broad expanse of the Atlantic and of the Pacific. But the width of those oceans is not what it was in the days of clipper ships." With the bombing of Pearl Harbor on December 7, 1941, the last skeptic was aboard. America confronted a new vulnerability. And Roosevelt, followed by Harry Truman, oversaw a massive shift that extended American power not only across the Western Hemisphere but around the globe.[27]

On September 11, 2001, Americans awoke to a world changed once again. Now global terrorists, most representing a radical faction of Islamism, posed a grave new threat to American national security. As in 1941, the threat had been emerging for some time. Osama bin Laden had made known his intentions to attack America for several years, and a report from 1999 entitled *New World Coming,* prepared by a high-level government commission, predicted that over the next quarter century "terrorists will acquire weapons of mass destruction and mass disruption, and some will use them. Americans will likely die on American soil, possibly in large number." To understand the strain on Webster's Rule that 9/11 presented, I need briefly to review why this menace looks so different from what we faced in the past. A few distinctions are clear.

Global terrorists lack a sense of measured risk. They have no territory to preserve and no citizens to protect, and they are zealous to sacrifice their lives in the act of terror. Guiding their deeds is a radical religious ideology that glorifies death.

Global terrorists seek to effect maximum devastation. Unlike the Great Power rivalry of the Cold War, in which nuclear weapons and other WMD were tools of last resort, terrorists are eager and willing to use the most destructive weapons they can acquire and deploy. Death has become an end in itself, not a means to negotiate some other purpose.

These terrorists possess not only the will but unprecedented means to effect devastation. Nuclear, chemical, and biological weapons capable of wreaking wide-scale destruction are, or plausibly may be, available to nonstate actors. The government's sense of the new threat America confronts was made known in the draft "National Planning Scenarios," inadvertently released in early 2005. The Department of Homeland Security identified several possible terrorist strikes it deemed most plausible. Included was the blowing up of a chlorine tank, killing 17,500 people and injuring more than 100,000; an anthrax attack exposing 350,000 and killing 13,200; and the release of a dirty bomb, killing 180, injuring 270, and contaminating 20,000. The threat of terrorism is not new—from the Barbary pirates to Theodore Kaczynski (a.k.a. the Unabomber) and the Symbionese Liberation Army, America has faced terror in the past. What is new, however, is the terrorists' aim and capacity to effect such enormous harm.

These terrorists can readily evade detection. No troops massing at the border or ships steaming toward their targets. The warning signs Eisenhower described in 1959 may never appear. Small, mobile networks move undetected between states, following a plot that may climax with the deed of only a single person. A weapon capable of catastrophic harm slips quietly into a backpack, moving from one place to the next with little trace. Even lacking WMD, terrorists have proven adept at using means widely available in a free society—planes, cars, nails, and gasoline—to inflict devastating harm.[28]

Under this new threat, the United States rightly concluded that in some cases, waiting for a threat to become imminent may be too late. To understand why, one needs to consider Webster's Rule in relationship to the strategies of containment and deterrence, which together formed the backbone of American grand strategy after World War II. These Cold War doctrines first appeared in an eight-thousand-word so-called Long Telegram, dispatched from Moscow in 1946 by a little-known career diplomat named George Kennan, who offered a perceptive account of Soviet behavior and a convincing plan of response. Rather than appeasing Joseph Stalin and his successors or waging nuclear war, the United States would contain the spread of communism and Soviet influence by supporting noncommunist forces of resistance. This support would include military force, but it would also include other means, such as the financial assistance funneled to Western Europe under the Marshall Plan. The underlying belief was that an isolated Soviet Union would eventually collapse under its own weight. In addition, the United States increasingly relied on a strategy of nuclear deterrence: the credible threat of retaliation to forestall an enemy attack.[29]

Under this paradigm, preemptive force against an imminent threat functioned as an escape valve. Supported by all the tools of diplomacy, deterrence provided a reliable means to prevent attack. It shaped behavior before the actual use of force: weighing the risks of attack, the enemy would choose otherwise when faced with the consequences that would follow. Implicit in the deterrence paradigm is the possibility that a state may have to absorb the first blow if the deterrent is insufficient or misinterpreted or if the enemy does not act rationally. The paradigm recognizes one exception governed by Webster's Rule: faced with an imminent threat, the target state can strike first. Eisenhower described this exception in his press conference. A preemptive strike under these circumstances, however, is always a second-line defense when the first-line deterrent has failed. That the Cold War never turned hot is testimony to the effectiveness of deterrence when right conditions prevail.

For reasons mentioned above, however, the traditional strategy of deterrence is largely ineffective against the new terrorist threat. Deterrence requires an adversary who has something he is unwilling to lose and which a credible deterrent threatens to destroy, take away, or diminish. The new enemy, however, has no people to protect and no borders to secure and places his mission of terror above his life—even wishing to die in the act of carnage. Deterrence as the first line of defense is no longer reliable.

And the second-line defense—the right to use preemptive force against an imminent threat—is also compromised. When the adversary can surreptitiously transport WMD across porous borders and carry out his deed without warning, the demand to wait for an imminent threat becomes a demand to take the first blow. Webster's Rule reflected a consensus that striking first is a last resort only when directed against an imminent threat. The problem with this rule is that it is now possible to imagine a situation in which using force against a less-than-imminent threat could be a last resort to prevent an attack of unacceptable magnitude. In such cases, the balance represented in Webster's Rule between security and restraint is lost.

For this reason the new threat of global terrorism demands a shift toward strategies of prevention. While deterrence provides an incentive for the adversary to choose against inflicting the harm, prevention arrests the harm by incapacitating the adversary—and in the rare case, striking first against a threat not yet imminent. America is menaced by a multitude of threats, and for many of them the traditional strategies of deterrence and containment still have an important role to play. Arresting terror, however, demands a paradigm of prevention.

The United States asserted the right to strike first without waiting for an imminent threat soon after the attacks of 2001. President Bush hinted at this shift in his State of the Union address of January 2002 and made it clear in his commencement speech at West Point in June of that year. The primary statement appeared in the 2002 *National Security Strategy* in September under the heading "Prevent Our Enemies from Threatening Us, Our Allies, and Our Friends with Weapons of Mass Destruction":

> For centuries, international law recognized that nations need not suffer an attack before they can lawfully take action to defend themselves against forces that present an imminent danger of attack. Legal scholars and international jurists often conditioned the legitimacy of preemption on the existence of an imminent threat—most often a visual mobilization of armies, navies, and air forces preparing to attack. We must adapt the concept of imminent threat to the capabilities and objectives of today's adversaries. Rogue states and terrorists do not seek to attack us using conventional means. They know such attacks would fail. Instead, they rely on acts of terror and, potentially, the use of weapons of mass destructions—weapons that can be easily concealed, delivered covertly, and used without warning. . . . The United States has long maintained the option of preemptive actions to counter a sufficient threat to our national security. The greater the threat, the greater is the risk of inaction—and the more compelling the case for taking anticipatory action to defend ourselves, even if uncertainty remains as to the time and place of the enemy's attack. To forestall or prevent such hostile acts by our adversaries, the United States will, if necessary, act preemptively.[30]

Again, what the Bush administration called preemptive force is better called preventive force. Although the 2002 *National Security Strategy* says "we must adapt the concept of imminent threat"—the core requirement of Webster's Rule—it is clear here and elsewhere the president was rejecting the concept as a categorical rule. In an interview with Tim Russert on *Meet the Press* in February 2004, President Bush stated, "I believe it is essential that when we see a threat, we deal with those threats before they become imminent. It's too late if they become imminent." In late 2002, former president Clinton revealed that his administration had drawn up plans for strikes against several North Korean nuclear reactors. Although the U.S. government had considered the possibility of a first strike against less-than-imminent threats, it had always publicly committed itself to Webster's Rule since World War II. After 9/11, the United States for the first time announced its willingness to use force not only against imminent threats but against emerging threats as well.[31]

Despite the many failures of the Bush Doctrine, an uncompromising commitment to Webster's Rule asks too much in an age of al Qaeda. Winning support for a carefully expanded right to strike first, however, will depend on the degree to which this claim achieves moral legitimacy. And achieving moral legitimacy will depend on making the case that revision upholds core American values. The question remains, then: Is striking first —especially against a less-than-imminent threat—against our traditions?

"Against Our Traditions"?

THE UNITED STATES AND THE VAST majority of nations have long claimed a right to use preemptive force against an imminent threat. Despite the unbending language of the UN Charter, this allowance is hardly surprising. No state would recognize a rule that damned it to take the first, perhaps fatal, blow. America's sweeping claim to a right to use force against less-than-imminent threats, however, was a step on untrodden ground. Or at least terrain untouched in recent times—a closer look, and American footprints are faintly visible. Certainly since World War II and before 9/11 the United States never publicly embraced a right to use force in these circumstances. It joined the international consensus, which drew a line with Webster's Rule. During its first 150 years, however, the United States sometimes employed armed force to counter not an imminent threat, but the danger posed by possible European meddling in the Americas.

As colonialism waned, however, so did this rationale for preventive force. That is not to say policy makers and presidents from Franklin Roosevelt forward never considered striking first against emerging threats. They did. And for several years after World War II the issue was also a subject of intense public discussion in lecture halls, church pews, and opinion pages. In the end, however, Americans and their leaders rejected preventive force in those cases in which the question arose. The reasons were several, including sheer practical concerns: a first strike might fail to incapacitate the enemy and lead to a wider war. A consistent theme in American thinking, however, was

the worry and even conviction that striking first was "against our traditions."[1]

Prevention and the Young Republic

America's use of preventive force in the nineteenth century and the early
twentieth was part of a broader strategy for achieving security in a world in
which the nation's greatest threat was European imperialism. The path
America took was noticeably different from the system European states
adopted to protect themselves from each other. After Napoleon's defeat in
1814, Europe's leaders met to draft a new order and restore a balance of
power as the keystone of continental security. This system aligned political,
economic, and military force to ensure no state could accrue enough power
to threaten the sovereign independence of another. Prince Klemens von
Metternich, Robert Stewart Viscount Castlereagh, and other representatives
at the Congress of Vienna aimed to prevent another grab for empire at
home.[2]

The young American republic, blessed by the breadth of the Atlantic, pursued a very different path to security, one marked by two goals: keeping
America out of Europe's wars and keeping Europe out of the Americas. The
first goal it pursued through a commitment to unilateralism, that is, avoiding alliances with other states, especially European states. This commitment
was canonized in President George Washington's celebrated "Farewell Address," printed in newspapers on September 19, 1796, and announcing his
decision not to run for a third term: "Europe has a set of primary interests,
which to us have none, or a very remote relation. Hence she must be engaged in frequent controversies, the causes of which are essentially foreign
to our concerns. Hence therefore it must be unwise in us to implicate ourselves, by artificial ties, in the ordinary vicissitudes of her politics. . . . Our
detached & distant situation invites and enables us to pursue a different
course. . . . 'Tis our true policy to steer clear of permanent Alliances, with
any portion of the foreign World." Wary of "foreign influence" as a grave
threat to republican government, which could foster factionalism and im-
press the nation in service to interests not its own, Washington charted a
course the nation would follow for well over a century. Not until 1949 did the

United States enter its first formal alliance, reflecting a major shift in how America would secure itself.[3]

The United States pursued the second goal—keeping Europe out of the Americas—by seeking hegemony. This strategy rejected a balancing of powers in the New World, among the United States and Europe's colonial powers. Rather, America would seek to position itself as an unrivaled power in the Western Hemisphere. This strategy meant the exercise of power, at times military power, to remove the occasions for European intervention, accelerate the demise of colonial rule, and expand the national boundaries. Although not its first expression, this commitment was canonized in President James Monroe's address to Congress on December 2, 1823, most remembered for announcing the Monroe Doctrine and its spottily enforced claim that the Americas were closed to European colonization.

Preventing European footholds in the Americas was one end President Monroe had in mind when he finally came around to defend General Andrew Jackson's startling invasion of Florida in 1818. The conflict was the First Seminole War. Since the Revolution, the Floridas were divided into East and West, both under nominal Spanish rule. Faced with rebellion in its Latin American empire, Spain was left with scant resources to govern its claim. On several occasions the United States had witnessed the strategic vulnerability of not flying the Stars and Stripes over the peninsula and its panhandle—a vulnerability exacerbated by Spain's absenteeism. Napoleon's invasion of Spain created a French interest in the territory. And during the War of 1812 the British landed forces in West Florida, allied with the Indians, and attacked the republic from the south. Anyone looking at a map of North America "would have seen at once the vital significance of the Floridas to the security of the United States. In the hands of any foreign power they were a pistol pointed at the heart of the future Continental Republic. . . . Spain had been too feeble to load the pistol and pull the trigger, but not her ally England, nor her enemy Napoleon if he could lay hands on the weapon."[4]

In the interests of keeping France and Britain out of the Floridas and convinced that Spain's hold on the territory would continue to wane, Congress passed a "No-Transfer Resolution" in 1811. This declaration was an early statement of the republic's quest for hegemony in the Americas: "Taking into view the peculiar situation of Spain, and of her American provinces; and considering the influence which the destiny of the territory adjoining the southern border of the United States may have upon their security, tranquillity, and commerce: Therefore . . . the United States . . . cannot, without serious inquietude, see any part of the said territory pass into the hands of any foreign power; and that a due regard to their own safety compels them to provide, under certain contingencies, for the temporary occupation of the said territory."[5]

The First Seminole War, in 1817–18, resulted in such an occupation and provided an opportunity for the United States to secure its ultimate goal of possessing the Floridas, for which it had been in negotiations with Spain for several years. The occasion for the war was conflict with hundreds of Creeks, Seminoles, and fugitive slaves who had taken refuge in Florida. For several years General Jackson had campaigned against the Indians near the southern border of the United States. The Creek War of 1813–14 ended with the onerous Treaty of Fort Jackson, stripping the Creek nation of twenty-three million acres of land. Many Creeks fled to Florida and, joined by Seminoles and hundreds of escaped slaves, were intent on regaining their land. War ensued when an American military band attempted to enforce the Treaty of Fort Jackson in Fowltown, Georgia, against a group of Seminoles who were not party to the treaty. When they refused to leave, the Americans raided the town, killed several Indians, forced the rest to flee, and burned everything that remained. The Seminoles soon retaliated, killing several dozen Americans in a grisly raid on a supply boat traveling along the Appalachicola River in Florida.

The day after Christmas, Secretary of War John C. Calhoun ordered Jackson to "adopt the necessary measures to terminate" the conflict. A few days later, President Monroe sent Jackson a cryptic message about his new mission: the campaign against the Seminoles "'will bring you on a theatre where you may possibly have other services to perform. Great interests are at issue. . . . This is not a time to repose . . . until our cause is carried triumphantly thro.'" Jackson interpreted these words as a nod to accomplish something more than quelling the quarrel of the moment. Within six months, the general had razed several Indian villages by fire, seized the Spanish garrisons at Pensacola and St. Marks, and captured, court-martialed, and executed two British subjects convicted of inciting and supporting the insurgents. East and West Florida were suddenly in Monroe's hands.[6]

News of the Florida conquest startled the president, despite his seemingly open-ended grant of authority. He at once worried about the political fallout of either embracing or condemning Jackson's deeds. If he censured Jackson, he could isolate the military hero's wide following and make himself vulnerable to charges of abdicating executive authority to a rogue general. If he defended the invasion, he might face accusations of going to war without the approval of Congress. And he worried that the audience at home and especially abroad would view the act as pure aggression—Bonaparte redux—which could drive the nation to war. Facing the prospect of losing either way, Monroe and his cabinet were ready to condemn the general and return the territory to Spain. The one exception was Monroe's secretary of state, John Quincy Adams.

In his role as America's chief statesman Adams was the single most important architect of American foreign policy in the early years of the republic, and his influence is still visible today. An ardent supporter of keeping the United States free of any entangling alliances with foreign powers, he was also committed to expanding American hegemony. Jackson's victory in Florida afforded Adams an early opportunity to extend American rule to the southeastern tip of North America, inching Spain off the continent and preventing any other European nation from entering America's back door. Mustering every argument he could, Adams convinced the president and his advisers over the course of several days to defend Jackson while making a conditional offer to return the captured territory—a condition he knew Spain could not meet.

Adams made his case public in a letter to the Spanish government of November 28, 1818, released to the press weeks in advance and meant as much to sway the American public as to lay out the government's position to Spain. He argued that Jackson's invasion was a "necessary measure of self-defence" to protect the United States from enemies finding refuge in a lawless no-man's-land. Spain had forced the United States to act because it had abandoned its duty under a treaty of 1795 to restrain the Indians living within Spanish territory from menacing the nation. When Spain was willing to meet these obligations, the United States would return the territory. Adams concluded, "The right of the United States can as little compound with impotence as with perfidy, and . . . Spain must immediately make her election, either to place a force in Florida adequate at once to the protection of her territory, and to the fulfilment of her engagements, or cede to the United States a province, of which she retains nothing but the nominal possession, but which is, in fact, a derelict, open to the occupancy of every enemy, civilized or savage, of the United States."[7]

Adams's apologia, while concealing key facts which considerably weakened the government's case, was immensely successful at home, kindling patriotic fervor and sapping interest in a congressional investigation. So successful was Adams's argument in shaping American opinion that nearly two decades later, with the republic roiled by the sinking of the *Caroline*, American newspapers opposed to war likened MacNab's nighttime raid to Jackson's invasion of Florida. In less than a year after Adams wrote his letter, Spain was ceding Florida to the United States. While Adams justified Jackson's invasion as a necessary act of self-defense against stateless "banditti," it is also clear he accepted the seizure of East and West Florida as a preventive means to remedy the nation's long-standing vulnerability along its southern border.[8]

Five years later the Monroe Doctrine, announced in a speech drafted by Adams, enshrined the principles that guided his handling of the Florida crisis. Lying behind the address was the secretary's fear that members of the Holy Alliance—Russia, Austria, and Prussia—might try to reverse republican gains in Latin America as well as a concern that Russia might renew its territorial claims in the Pacific Northwest. The message restated the nation's twin foreign policy goals: keeping America out of Europe and Europe out of the Americas: "The American continents, by the free and independent condition which they have assumed and maintain, are henceforth not to be considered as subjects for future colonization by any European powers. . . . In the wars of the European powers in matters relating to themselves we have never taken any part, nor does it comport with our policy to do so. . . . With the movements in this hemisphere we are of necessity more immediately connected, and by causes which must be obvious to all enlightened and impartial observers."[9]

Although the Monroe Doctrine lay moribund for large stretches of time, keeping Europe out of the Americas would continue to mean sometimes using force against emerging threats that might create an occasion for intervention. In the First Seminole War this motivation mixed with American thirst for expansion to extend the borders of the United States to the south. Later presidents invoked the Monroe Doctrine in support of extending the western boundary as well, wrapping the American arm around Texas, California, and everything in between. An ardent expansionist, President James Polk argued that America needed to act soon if it was to prevent the California ports from falling into the hands of the British. The United States annexed Texas in 1845 and the Mexican–American War that followed concluded with Mexico ceding present-day California, Nevada, Utah, and New Mexico. The United States justified its expansionist policies in part on the basis of preventing European intervention, and the nation willingly entered the war with Mexico with this broader goal in mind.[10]

In the early twentieth century, Presidents Theodore Roosevelt, William Howard Taft, and Woodrow Wilson all claimed the legacy of Monroe to justify American economic and, sometimes, military intervention, especially in the Caribbean. In each case the United States acted to quell political instability, sometimes through occupation. And in each case, one rationale was consistent: to prevent European meddling in the Americas by removing any incentive or pretext for intervention.[11]

The Venezuela crisis of 1902–03 became the paradigm. Refusing to pay its debts to European creditors, Venezuela found its coasts cordoned off by British, German, and Italian warships, threatening war if Venezuela did not cooperate. Roosevelt sent more than fifty ships to the Caribbean supposedly for maneuvers under the command of Admiral George Dewey, a national celebrity who had destroyed the entire Spanish fleet at Manila in 1898. Although Roosevelt was less concerned about Britain and Italy, he worried the kaiser was hungry for land. The president warned Ambassador Theodor von Holleben of Germany at a private White House party that he was prepared to intervene by force if Germany took any steps toward acquiring a foothold in Venezuela. After several tense days, Berlin agreed to place the matter in international arbitration.[12]

While Roosevelt had no sympathy for states refusing to service their debts, he had no qualms about wielding the American stick to prevent European intervention. In an annual message to Congress in December 1904, he announced what later became known as the Roosevelt Corollary to the Monroe Doctrine: "Chronic wrongdoing, or an impotence which results in a general loosening of the ties of civilized society, may in America, as elsewhere, ultimately require intervention by some civilized nation, and in the Western Hemisphere adherence to the Monroe Doctrine may force the United States, however reluctantly, in flagrant cases of such wrongdoing or impotence, to the exercise of an international police power."[13]

Preventing European intervention did not always require military force. When revolution swept the Dominican Republic at the beginning of the century, its new government stopped payment on foreign debts in an attempt to negotiate better terms. Among other motivations, Roosevelt worried European governments might again steam their warships westward. To counter this threat he signed a treaty with the Dominican Republic in 1905 that created a customs receivership, ensuring that the nation paid its foreign creditors. Taft's "dollar diplomacy" followed this same path.

President Wilson also sent American troops south to stop political unrest in the Caribbean, this time to Haiti in 1915. Political upheaval infected Haiti more than any other Caribbean nation. Seven presidents had come and gone in the previous seven years, every one of them forced out of office. The most recent coup had left the former president and his police chief hacked to pieces in the streets of Port-au-Prince. German merchants controlled more than 80 percent of Haiti's foreign commerce, and the sight of the kaiser's navy in nearby waters raised the same concerns that confronted Roosevelt in Venezuela. The island flanked one side of the Windward Passage, the primary entrance into the Panama Canal which was so vital to American security. U.S. Marines landed on Haitian soil to protect American and foreign interests, and they did not leave for nineteen years. A year later similar concerns about German intervention led Marines to quash a political revolt and restore stability next door in the Dominican Republic. As the Haitian occupation shows, preventive action meant bullets and bayonets, but it also meant building schools and hospitals, constructing roads, and digging irrigation ditches. American motives were always mixed—Wall Street had interests as well—but preventive force was often followed with a dose of preventive medicine.

The use of anticipatory force, then—even against potential threats—is not new to America. Hackles occasionally were raised on the Hill, in the press, and elsewhere, but for at least a century and a half political will did not finally constrain the president from sometimes using force to prevent a distant threat. At the same time, preventive force was often a means not only to secure the nation's borders, but to extend them as well. Adams knew Spain could not keep peace in Florida, but by making this a condition for return he revived the stalled negotiations and soon walked away with the entire peninsula.

Moreover, preventive force was limited to countering European colonialism. The pond separating America from Europe diminished the possibility that a powerful nation might directly attack the United States; the real threat was that the European nations might augment their power elsewhere in the West. By ensuring stability among its neighbors and thereby removing any occasion for intervention, America could keep Europe out. This policy allowed the United States to achieve hegemony at home without directly confronting the real threats across the Atlantic, namely, Germany, Britain, Russia, and the other colonial powers of Europe. It lessened the possibility that the use of preventive force might precipitate a wider conflict or saddle the nation with the moral baggage of having started a war. In practice, preventive force was a child of the Monroe Doctrine and limited to the Western Hemisphere.

The Infamy of Pearl Harbor

With the gradual demise of colonialism, such use of preventive force largely came to an end by the mid-twentieth century. At the same time, advances in technology diminished the security America had long enjoyed because of the geographical lottery. The question now arose whether the nation might directly use force to prevent threats from abroad. More than any other event, President Franklin Roosevelt's refusal to strike first against the Japanese in 1941, and the "infamy" he ascribed to the Japanese for doing so at Pearl Harbor, shaped the nation's response to striking the first blow for the next sixty years.[14]

Focused on supporting the British in their fight against Germany, Roosevelt's stance toward events in the Pacific in 1940–41 was to seek peace or at least to delay any confrontation as long as possible. Fueled by imperial ambitions and short on natural resources, Japan had invaded Manchuria in 1931. For several years Japan and China engaged in intermittent fighting, but the conflict erupted into full-scale war in 1937. To counter the threat posed by Japan in the Pacific without pulling the United States into war, Roosevelt pursued diplomatic talks, made limited shows of strength, and provided aid to China.

This policy, however, did not keep Japanese aggression at bay. In September 1940 Japan formed a military alliance with Italy and Germany. With the German offensive against Russia beginning in early summer 1941, Japan contemplated either an invasion of Russia from the east or a move into Southeast Asia, where the British and the Dutch had significant colonial holdings and where the United States was caretaker in the Philippines. In July 1941 the Japanese opted to head south, with the aim of consolidating their hold on Indochina and Siam, closing the Burma Road as the major supply route for shipments of aid to China, and taking the Dutch East Indies.

The possibility of an aggressive push to the south was of great concern to the United States. Although Roosevelt had placed an embargo on shipments of oil to Japan in August, Japanese success in Southeast Asia would offer important war-making resources, such as rubber and oil. These gains, along with the effect of cutting off the Burma Road, might lead China to capitulate. Moreover, Winston Churchill was warning Roosevelt that an attack in the south would destroy Britain's lifeline to its Pacific possessions, perhaps a decisive blow to Britain in its war against Germany. And the Philippines, where the United States had a presence, would likely not escape Japanese aggression either.

Diplomatic talks continued from August to November 1941, including direct talks in November between Roosevelt and Secretary of State Cordell Hull and the Japanese ambassador Kichisaburo Nomura and a special envoy, Saburo Kurusu. Nonetheless, intercepted communications between Japan and Nomura, Japan's unwillingness to make any acceptable diplomatic offers to the United States, and the rise to power of General Hideki Tojo in mid-October signaling the beginning of a military dictatorship all led Roosevelt and his top advisers to believe war was inevitable and could come at any time. Roosevelt worried that if Japan chose to spare the Philippines to avoid a direct confrontation with the United States, he would have difficulty convincing a public still mesmerized by the false promise of isolationism to support the British and the Chinese through direct military action. Even after several incidents in which German U-boats had fired at American ships in the Atlantic, Congress had only narrowly reformed the nation's neutrality laws in November, allowing the president to arm merchant ships which supplied lend-lease goods to the Allies and to send such ships to friendly ports in combat zones.

On November 26 Roosevelt learned from Secretary of War Henry Stimson that a large Japanese naval force was heading south along the China coast. The president was furious and took the news as evidence of bad faith on the part of the Japanese, who were in the midst of negotiations with the United States that might include an entire withdrawal from China. The president was also aware through intercepted communications that the Japanese were pushing for a deal with the United States no later than November 29, after which time, the intercepted letter indicated, it would be too late. Roosevelt and Secretary Hull agreed to send a ten-point outline of a proposed agreement to Japan, but both concluded negotiations were effectively finished. During a War Cabinet meeting a few days later, Roosevelt and his advisers discussed the likelihood of an attack against Britain at Singapore, against the Dutch East Indies, or against the United States in the Philippines. No one imagined an attack on Pearl Harbor.

Pressed by Churchill, who was desperate to bring the United States into the war, to issue an ultimatum against Japan, Roosevelt agreed but first wanted to query the Japanese government about its intentions in Southeast Asia. After receiving an evasive response, Roosevelt sent his warning on December 6, telling the emperor that Japanese movements in Southeast Asia threatened peaceful relations with the United States and demanding withdrawal. He later remarked to some White House guests, "'This son of man has just sent his final message to the Son of God.'" That evening an intercepted communication containing Japan's reply to Roosevelt's ten-point proposal made it clear Japan would not yield.[15]

The next day at 7:55 a.m. Hawaii time, the first wave of Japanese dive bombers, torpedo planes, and fighters attacked the U.S. naval base at Pearl Harbor. The brass band of the *U.S.S. Nevada* was trumpeting the "Star-Spangled Banner" as the first wave arrived. In the end, the attack killed 2,403 Americans and almost totally destroyed the American fleet and the navy and army aircraft on the island. Japan also attacked the Philippines, Thailand, British Malaya, Guam, and Wake Island. Intent on pushing its empire into Southeast Asia and certain any attack on British holdings in the region would bring America into the conflict, Japan was highly successful in immediate military terms in its first strike against the United States. In the larger picture, however, the attack was a decisive blunder, creating in the United States what Roosevelt's countless appeals had not: a united America in support of war.

On the eve of the fateful December attack, Commander Lester Schulz sat in a small windowless office in the mail room of the Executive Office Building, adjacent to the White House. He was on temporary assignment as a communications assistant for the navy. Between nine and ten o'clock that evening Schulz was met by a naval officer delivering a locked pouch for the president. Inside was "Magic" material: the code name given to intelligence the military received by intercepting and deciphering Japanese communications. Commander Schulz walked the few steps to the White House and requested permission to go to the president's study on the second floor. Entering the office, Schulz found the president seated at his desk talking with Harry Hopkins, a close adviser who was living in the White House at that time. An architect of the New Deal, Hopkins was instrumental in putting the lend-lease program in place and traveled frequently with the president.[16]

Roosevelt was expecting the delivery. Schulz unlocked the pouch and handed over the papers inside: fifteen typewritten pages fastened together and containing a translation of the intercepted Japanese response to Roosevelt's ten-point proposal. Schulz remained in the room for several minutes while the president read the papers. Hopkins paced back and forth and then read them as well. Japan, they now knew, would reject their final offer. In testimony given during the congressional hearings on Pearl Harbor in 1946, after the war had concluded and both the president and Hopkins had passed away, Commander Schulz recalled to Congress the conversation that ensued: "The President then turned toward Mr. Hopkins and said in substance . . . 'This means war.' Mr. Hopkins agreed." Pressed to recall what Roosevelt and Hopkins said next, Schulz responded, "There are only a few words that I can definitely say I am sure of, but the substance of it was that —I believe Mr. Hopkins mentioned it first—. . . . that since war was undoubtedly going to come at the convenience of the Japanese, it was too bad that we could not strike the first blow and prevent any sort of surprise. The President nodded and then said, in effect, 'No, we can't do that. We are a democracy and a peaceful people.'"[17]

Roosevelt no doubt had several reasons to draw this conclusion, now less than sixteen hours before Japanese fighter planes would slice the still air at Pearl Harbor. Certainly the strong sentiment in the United States against going to war, resting on years of isolationist thinking, restrained the president. In testimony before Congress during the Pearl Harbor hearings, the former secretary of war Stimson described a meeting on November 25, 1941, that included, among other principals, Secretary Hull, Army Chief of Staff George C. Marshall, and the president: "The President said the Japanese were notorious for making an attack without warning and stated that we might even be attacked, say next Monday, for example. One problem troubled us very much. If you know that your enemy is going to strike you, it is not usually wise to wait until he gets the jump on you by taking the initiative. In spite of the risk involved, however, in letting the Japanese fire the first shot, we realized that in order to have the full support of the American people it was desirable to make sure that the Japanese be the ones to do this so that there should remain no doubt in anyone's mind as to who were the aggressors." Political considerations, then, constrained the president from striking the first blow that many of his military advisers thought best. Pragmatic concern, however, was not the only force at work. As Schulz's testimony demonstrates, Roosevelt's understanding of the nation's political and moral identity—America as "a democracy and a peaceful people"—held his hand as well.[18]

Even more than Roosevelt's decision not to strike first—the details of which were not known publicly for several years—his subsequent portrayal of Japan's decision to do so as an act of moral treachery shaped the nation's understanding of striking first in powerful fashion. In a brief, plainspoken speech to Congress the next day, Roosevelt declared with sober firmness,

"Yesterday, December 7, 1941—a date which will live in infamy—the United States of America was suddenly and deliberately attacked by naval and air forces of the Empire of Japan." The infamy Roosevelt ascribed to Japan's strike embedded itself in American memory for several reasons. Foremost was the deceit. Japan conceived and initiated the attack while presenting itself as being in good faith negotiations with the United States about the Pacific crisis. The accusations of deceit gained even more traction when the public learned that Nomura and Kurusu, their timing off because of a delay in preparing the encrypted text, arrived at Secretary of State Hull's office to deliver the now-intercepted memorandum an hour after the first bombs fell on Pearl Harbor. Although known for an otherwise steady temperament, Hull was undone. As Roosevelt concluded in an extended address to the nation on December 9, "No honest person, today or a thousand years hence, will be able to suppress a sense of indignation at the treachery committed by the military dictators of Japan under the very shadow of the flag of peace borne by their special envoys in our midst." The infamy of Pearl Harbor, however, was also due to the fact that it came as an act of sudden aggression, cutting off other means of easing tensions short of destructive force. Pearl Harbor, one of the most emotive images in American memory, became a symbol of how the nation conducts itself differently in the world. To remember Pearl Harbor was, in part, to remember that America does not strike the first blow, absent the most pressing threat to its security.[19]

Roosevelt's judgment that the United States could not strike first against the Japanese in 1941 was made on the eve of an enormous shift in how America understood its role in the world and what its security required—a shift Roosevelt had patiently urged for several years. Although technological advances in warfare, including the advent of steam power for transatlantic crossings nearly a century earlier, had diminished the security afforded by two oceans, it was not until the bombing of Pearl Harbor that Americans realized their vulnerability and assumed a greater role in world politics. A *New York Times* editorial headlined "Decade of Fame and Infamy" concluded on the ten-year anniversary of the attack, "At that moment the hurrying tide of history washed over the last pinnacles of our isolationism. It was no longer possible, and has not since been possible, for us to deny our historic mission in modern history."[20]

The sea change in public opinion that followed December 7 gave Roosevelt the support he needed to inaugurate sweeping changes in American grand strategy. Most important, as John Gaddis, Robert Dallek, and others have described, Roosevelt realized that American security depended on extending the nation's sphere of responsibility from the West to the world. It was no longer sufficient to achieve hegemony at home; the United States would directly have to confront threats across both the Atlantic and the Pacific. This new vulnerability might have pushed the United States toward a policy of preventive force, especially given the increasingly destructive nature of war. And certainly many earnest Americans thought it should. Nonetheless, presidents, more often than not constrained by what they knew the American people would accept, rejected striking first absent some imminent threat.

No one reason accounts for this national unease with preventive force. Most obvious, perhaps, was the end of American expansionism and the coming to a close of European colonialism. Both forces had given rise to the Monroe Doctrine and the use of preventive force as a means to extend America's boundaries and keep Europe out of the Americas. Congress's repeal of the Platt Amendment in 1934, which had announced the nation's intention to intervene in Cuban affairs when it deemed necessary, was a part of Roosevelt's broader Good Neighbor Policy and committed the United States not to intervene in the internal or external affairs of Latin American nations. The UN Charter, moreover, committed the United States to use force only in "self-defence if an armed attack occurs." While we have seen that states interpreted Article 51 to allow the customary right of anticipatory self-defense against an imminent threat, the same against an emerging threat was a very different situation. It did not take too many years for American leaders to realize the Charter would not provide all the international security it promised; yet the United States had a stake in upholding international norms as much as possible.

In addition, the peculiar marks of the Cold War, which followed on the heels of World War II, also made preventive force less attractive. Nuclear weapons exponentially increased the costs of war. Even before Stalin acquired the bomb, any preventive attack against his weapons development facilities would have left largely intact his vastly superior conventional forces, which could plausibly sweep all of Europe. Moreover, the national security policy Roosevelt put in place and Truman developed placed great importance on a multilateral framework, which a unilateral use of preventive force might have fractured. Most important, however, many Americans and their leaders came to believe after Roosevelt that, under the circumstances encountered, striking first was finally inconsistent with the nation's political and moral traditions. Two later episodes show that Roosevelt's handling of Pearl Harbor signaled an emerging conviction during the Cold War that striking first in those cases was somehow not American.

Russia and the Bomb

The first episode was already underway before the Japanese formally surrendered aboard the *U.S.S. Missouri* in early September 1945. It arose from the convergence of two factors, neither of which was known even a year earlier: the budding realization that America's ally during the war, the Soviet Union, would become its next greatest enemy and the American invention of and monopoly over the atomic bomb. The two nations had joined hands in World War II not because of ideological affinity but to defeat a common enemy. When the leaders of the Grand Alliance turned to the task of forging a postwar settlement, the unity fractured. While Churchill and Roosevelt shared a vision of an integrated Europe, balanced in power, politically self-determined, and secured under the United Nations, Stalin had very different ideas. He envisioned an extended western border and an even broader sphere of influence into Eastern Europe, all as a prelude to eventual domination over Europe hastened by the inevitable collapse of capitalism that Karl Marx had predicted. As Churchill did in the years leading up to World War II, he would again sound the early warning alarm. In the first few months of 1945, however, neither Churchill nor Roosevelt foresaw entirely what would follow.

While Stalin projected an outward image of apathy, the success of the Manhattan Project vastly altered the balance of world power and accelerated Stalin's efforts to possess the atomic bomb. Roosevelt had authorized the top secret project out of fear that Germany would develop the weapon first, although the United States did not successfully test "the Gadget" until July

1945, after Germany had surrendered. When Truman shared the news with Stalin at Potsdam, only days before mushroom clouds would rise over Hiroshima and Nagasaki, the president did not know that Soviet spies had penetrated Los Alamos and Russian scientists were already mining its secrets. While the prominent American journalist Walter Lippmann would not popularize the term *Cold War* until more than a year later, in his 1947 book bearing that name, a discernible chill was in the air.[21]

Together the onset of the Cold War and radical changes in the security environment brought on by the advent of the atomic bomb gave rise to a decade-long debate, behind closed government doors but also at American dinner tables, about whether the United States should launch a preventive war against the Soviet Union before Stalin cracked the American nuclear monopoly or, after 1949, before the Soviets achieved nuclear parity. Although the debate would conclude with a clear judgment against preventive war, the idea of striking first in peacetime reflected a certain logic not lost outside the Beltway, at once simple and fearfully alluring beyond the bellicose few.[22]

Several postwar circumstances lent credence to the idea of striking first. Although Stalin concealed his basest ambitions, in early February 1946 he delivered an address describing the recent war in Marxist terms "as the inevitable result of . . . capitalism" and bringing into question the postwar peace Churchill and Roosevelt championed. At the same time he expressed certainty that Soviet scientists "will be able not only to overtake but also in the very near future to surpass the achievements of science outside the boundaries of our country," which seemed a veiled reference to the Russian quest for the bomb. The significance of these statements was not lost on the United States. As a *New York Times* editorial warned a few days later, Stalin's words "demand careful scrutiny." Quoting Stalin's reference to inevitable conflict, the editorial cautioned, "When such doctrines and ideas are advanced by the all-powerful rulers of one of the greatest Powers, which has also been our ally, they cannot be lightly brushed aside." Against the backdrop of communist takeovers in Eastern Europe, American gratitude toward a nation that had sacrificed so much in the war against Hitler was now turning to fear.[23]

At the same time, a consensus among government leaders and the broader public was emerging that the policies of appeasement leading up to World War II had failed. Cities in rubble and millions of fresh white crosses testified to the failures of Munich. The strategic and moral question loomed large: should the free nations have acted sooner to prevent the horrors of the past five years? In addition, the devastation in Western Europe and the vast Soviet military machine at the end of the war left a power vacuum in Europe, with nothing but the might of the United States and its atomic bombs to check Russian aggression. No one believed, however, that the American nuclear monopoly would long endure. The United States confronted a narrow window of opportunity to strike first before its nuclear advantage was lost and the nation would have to face the possibility of an atomic Pearl Harbor. Moreover, the quick and decisive surrender of Japan forced by the dropping of just two bombs tempted some Americans to believe that the same action could achieve a simple victory against the Soviets as well.

The initial argument for a preventive war against the Soviet Union came in a top secret document approved by the Joint Chiefs on September 19, 1945, for transmission to President Truman, a little more than a month after Hiroshima. The document, JCS 1496, grappled with the radical new security environment the United States confronted at the dawn of the postwar world. The Joint Chiefs concluded that any future reach for world domination by one of the major foreign powers would almost certainly begin with a strike against the United States before it could mobilize its forces and productive capacity. The nation must be ready to defend itself alone. Finding that the American people would never accept the maintenance of "overwhelmingly strong forces in time of peace," the document concluded the nation should nonetheless be ready "to take prompt and effective military action abroad to anticipate and prevent attack." "When it becomes evident that forces of aggression are being arrayed against us by a potential enemy, we cannot afford, through any misguided and perilous idea of avoiding an aggressive attitude to permit the first blow to be struck against us. Our government, under such conditions, should press the issue to a prompt political decision, while making all preparations to strike the first blow if necessary." In a confidential memorandum of January 2, 1946, General Leslie Groves, who had led the Manhattan Project under Roosevelt, urged a limited preventive attack against Russia if a current attempt at international control of atomic weapons failed: "If we were truly realistic instead of idealistic, as we appear to be, we would not permit any foreign power with which we are not firmly allied, and in which we do not have absolute confidence, to make or possess atomic weapons. If such a country started to make atomic weapons we would destroy its capacity to make them before it had progressed far enough to threaten us."[24]

Beginning in early 1946, high military officials who supported this recommendation began seeping their views to the public. One member of the Joint Chiefs, the five-star general Henry Arnold, chief of the Army Air Forces, made remarks to the press that landed him a headline in the *New York Times* reading, "'Shoot First,' Arnold Declares on Defense." The word *defense,* he explained, can no longer capture the military's goal, since a purely defensive posture could render the nation vulnerable to a debilitating first strike by the enemy. Several months later, Lieutenant General Ira Eaker, deputy commander of the Army Air Forces, made similar comments before a conference of the National Air Reserve about the importance of striking the enemy first.[25]

At the same time, others outside the military began to express their support for a preventive war against Russia. The leftist English philosopher and popular writer Bertrand Russell was one such voice. By the middle of the twentieth century, Russell had a wide following and was a frequent activist on issues of war and peace. His political agitation during World War I had landed him in a British prison for six months, shorn of his post at Cambridge. During World War II, Russell lived in the United States and taught at several American universities. In October 1946 he published an article entitled "The Atomic Bomb and the Prevention of War." Although pacifist in his sympathies and confident that measures short of war could secure the Soviet Union's commitment to an American-backed plan for the international control of nuclear weapons, Russell contemplated that world peace might require the United States to wage a preventive war. A trip to Russia in 1920 and a one-hour meeting with Vladimir Lenin had squelched any attraction he might have had to communism. After the Soviet Union rejected the Baruch Plan, Truman's effort to place atomic weapons under international control, Russell was less hesitant, directly calling on the United States to start an atomic war against the Soviet Union as "the war to end wars."[26]

In early 1947, James Burnham of New York University made the case for preventive war in *The Struggle for the World*. A onetime communist and frequent correspondent with Leon Trotsky, Burnham's observations of developments in the Soviet Union pushed him steadily to the right until he took up a post in 1955 as senior editor for William F. Buckley's new serial National Review, a position he held for more than two decades. In *The Struggle for the World* and later works, Burnham urged the United States to take action before the Soviets developed a nuclear arsenal, including, if necessary, an air offensive against the Russians. Under these circumstances, a first strike would be not only prudent but also morally obligatory because it would prevent a greater harm.[27]

The well-respected science editor for the *New York Times* and foremost popular authority on atomic bombs, William Laurence, argued the United States might not be able to maintain a purely defensive posture. When Laurence learned in March 1940 that scientists had isolated uranium-235, capable of creating a nuclear chain reaction, he decided to warn the public of its implications in a story that ran on the front page of the *New York Times* in May and in a longer version published in the *Saturday Evening Post* in September—articles which perversely may have first alerted Soviet officials to the possibility of an atomic bomb. In April 1945 Laurence disappeared for a month, tapped by the government to be the official historian of the Manhattan Project. And when the U.S. B-29 Superfortress Bockscar dropped the bomb on Nagasaki, Laurence was on board. In an article in the *Saturday Evening Post* on November 6, 1948, Laurence said one of the gravest dangers facing the United States was that "while we possess the atomic bomb, we at the same time recoil from the very thought of ever using it except as a desperate, last-resort measure of retaliation against an unprovoked attack." While emphatically denying that America should fight a preventive war now, Laurence argued that the United States should confront the Soviet Union with an ultimatum: either accept international control of atomic energy or face an American attack against your bomb-making facilities.[28]

Although his calls for preventive war were less explicit, the much-revered Churchill was another early supporter of offensive action against the Soviet Union. Churchill had lost his post as prime minister in the landslide election for Labour in 1945, but his authority on world issues did not wane in the West. When Neville Chamberlain had proclaimed "peace for our time" to much applause, Churchill was an outspoken opponent of appeasing Hitler. Still recovering from his defeat, Churchill scheduled a vacation to the United States and received an invitation to speak at Westminster College in the small town of Fulton, Missouri. Accompanying the invitation was a personal note from the Missouri native Harry Truman offering to introduce the former prime minister if he would accept. Having traveled to Fulton by train from Washington with the president, Churchill delivered his speech on March 5, 1946. Most famous for its declaration that an "iron curtain" had descended across Europe, Churchill's speech likened events in Russia to developments in Germany during the 1930s. Rejecting the notion that war with the Soviet Union was inevitable, Churchill nonetheless called for decisive action by a united West. Although he carefully limited his public comments, after the Soviet Union's rejection of the Baruch Plan Churchill let American officials know he favored an ultimatum: the Soviets must withdraw from East Germany or else we will "raze their cities." In a speech at the Massachusetts Institute of Technology in 1949 Churchill had stated that he did not think "violent or precipitate action should be taken now" against the Soviet Union. The widely read journalists Joseph and Stewart Alsop, great-nephews of Teddy Roosevelt, discerned Churchill's veiled message in their *Washington Post* column a few days later. Churchill's real message was between the lines: "Here is the first serious public suggestion—dim and roundabout, to be sure—that preventive action may ultimately be necessary to counter the Soviet Menace."[29]

As talk about a preventive atomic war against the Soviet Union increased, so did opposition to the idea. Lippmann fired off an early condemnation in March 1946. His objections were entirely on expedient grounds, as they would be on repeated occasions in the future: any hint of an atomic attack and the vast Red Army would overrun all Europe, where Americans would never be willing to drop the atomic bomb. Several nuclear scientists who had contributed to the creation of the bomb and had formed the Emergency Committee of Atomic Scientists under the leadership of Albert Einstein spoke out vociferously against preventive war. Religious groups organized against the idea as well. The Catholic Association for International Peace, the

World Peace Commission of the Methodist Church, and the Board of Social Missions for the United Lutheran Church in America all issued early statements against talk of a preventive war with Russia. Gallup polls throughout this period repeatedly confirmed that the vast majority of Americans opposed the idea. Asked whether they thought the United States should declare war on Russia now, Americans consistently said no by large majorities: 87 percent in September 1946; 80 percent in July 1950; and 75 percent in 1954.[30]

Leaders within the administration also spoke out against the idea. Truman's secretary of commerce, Henry Wallace, vented his long-standing disagreements with the president's tough polices toward the Soviet Union in a speech at Madison Square Garden in September 1946. On September 18, 1946, the *New York Times* published a long letter Wallace had written to Truman earlier on the same subject. Wallace castigated realist military officers advising the president and accused them of advocating a preventive war. That same day, the Secretaries of War and Navy denied the accusation in a joint letter to the president, quickly shuffled off to the press: "We know of no responsible officer in the Army or Navy who has ever advocated or even suggested a policy or plan of attacking Russia." That same day Truman ordered Wallace to the White House and forbade him to speak on issues of foreign policy. Two days later Wallace was packing his bags and heading to the *New Republic,* where he would sling his criticisms in print.[31]

Some of the most important statements against the idea of a preventive war came from respected leaders who had worked for President Truman, but whose public statements the White House did not orchestrate: Henry Stimson, John Foster Dulles, and James Conant. Accepting but moving beyond Lippmann's narrow critique on practical grounds, all three concluded that a first strike against Russia would be at odds with America's moral and political identity. Stimson had enjoyed a long career in foreign policy, appointed secretary of war by Taft in 1911, secretary of state by Hoover in 1929, and again secretary of war by Roosevelt in 1940, where he served until the conclusion of the war. In an article published in *Foreign Affairs* in October 1947, two years after he had left the War Department, Stimson opposed "those who argue that Americans by strong-arm methods, perhaps even by a 'preventive war,' can and should rid the world of the Communist menace.

I cannot believe that this view is widely held. For it is worse than nonsense; it results from a hopeless misunderstanding of the geographical and military situation." This much Lippmann had said, but Stimson continued: "Worst of all, this theory indicates a totally wrong assessment of the basic attitudes and motives of the American people. Even if it were true that the United States now had the opportunity to establish forceful hegemony throughout the world, we could not possibly take that opportunity without deserting our true inheritance. Americans as conquerors would be tragically miscast."[32]

Dulles, appointed by Wilson to serve on the U.S. delegation to the Paris Peace Conference after World War I, emissary for Truman on multiple international missions, and future secretary of state under Eisenhower, sounded a similar note in a speech in New York City in January 1948. His audience was the Foreign Policy Association, and his speech was broadcast over the CBS Network and reported the next day on the front page of the *New York Times*. "It is unthinkable," he said, "that the United States should initiate a so-called 'preventive' war. That is contrary to the nature of democracy." Having argued that America's greatest weapon in the new war was being faithful to itself as a "free society," Dulles ended his speech by stating that "the moral quality of our response, more than any ingredient of the plan, will determine whether this time we win the peace."[33]

Finally, Conant, a chemist and the president of Harvard University from 1933 to 1953, wrote another widely read statement against preventive war. During the war, he left responsibility for the university in the hands of the provost and headed for Washington, where he played an important role in scientific research for the military, including the Manhattan Project. On July 16, 1945, he stood flabbergasted as a witness to the firing of the first atomic bomb in Alamogordo, New Mexico. In a cover story first published in the *Atlantic Monthly* in 1949 and later republished in the *Washington Post,* Conant pointed to what he described as a fundamental paradox in American thinking: "Freedom has often emerged from the successful use of force; yet we abominate war as intensely as we love freedom." Although war may give birth to liberty, he concluded, preserving liberty requires limiting the use of force. At the heart of totalitarianism, however, is a notion that the end justifies the means. The doctrine of preventive war, he went on to say, rested on this very notion inimical to America's democratic tradition: "For us to develop a Machiavellian foreign policy which would culminate in our launching a surprise attack on the Soviet Union . . . would negate the very premises on which our culture rests" and "would be the moral equivalent of dropping atomic bombs on a dozen of our own cities." Stimson, Dulles, and Conant all held a sober account of the Soviet threat and the need to check power with power. But each voiced a conclusion that would echo again and again well into the 1950s: beyond any strategic limitations of the moment, waging an atomic first strike against the Soviet Union to prevent it from developing the bomb would violate the deep character of the nation, so vital to America's struggle against totalitarianism.[34]

Although the case against preventive war was winning the day, proponents renewed their efforts when Truman announced to the American public on September 23, 1949, that the Soviets had successfully tested an atomic bomb. The news came as a shock, not because anyone doubted the Russians could develop the bomb—the end of America's nuclear monopoly was inevitable—but because they had acquired it so soon. Most estimates held the Soviet Union would need five to twenty years to reach the goal. Four years later the day arrived. As *Time* remarked in its first issue after the announcement: "Washington had known it was coming. . . . Nevertheless, the news hit the nation with the jarring impact of a fear suddenly become fact. The comfortable feeling of U.S. monopoly was gone forever. . . . What had been a threat for some time in the future, hard to visualize, easy to forget, had become a threat for today, to be lived with."[35]

No longer could Americans ask whether they should strike first before the Soviets acquired an atomic capacity. The question now was whether the nation should act before Russia obtained a significant stockpile of the weapon or, as the question evolved, whether the advantages of a first strike are so tremendous and the harms so catastrophic that Americans had little choice but to initiate war. With the outbreak of the Korean War in the early summer of 1950, less than a year later, a spate of public statements in support of preventive war grabbed headlines. Policy makers had worried that the new balance of power would embolden the Soviets to be more aggressive. Stalin's behind-the-scenes role in the Korean conflict, it seemed, confirmed this conclusion.

The most publicized and unsettling claim for striking the first blow came from Francis Matthews, Truman's secretary of the navy, speaking before a crowd of one hundred thousand people celebrating the 150th anniversary of the Boston Naval Yard in late August 1950. Invoking the nation's birth from revolution, Matthews feted the patriot soldiers as aggressors who "violated the peace of their time in a most holy cause." The liberty they secured, he warned, was in grave peril today. "A true democracy ordinarily does not seek international accord through resort to violence. . . . Never have we drawn the sword unless first attacked and so compelled to fight in self-defense." Nonetheless, he continued, the United States faces a wholly new kind of threat. Calling on Americans to become "the first aggressors for peace," Matthews declared, "To have peace we should be willing, and declare our intention to pay any price, even the price of instituting a war to compel cooperation for peace."[36]

Similar statements quickly followed. General Albert Wedemeyer, commander of the Sixth Army, wrote Matthews and extolled his speech, making a similar call in a lecture five days later at the National War College. Hanson Baldwin, the military editor for the *New York Times,* reported that Matthews's speech was a "trial balloon" floated for Secretary of Defense Louis Johnson, who many suspected was sympathetic to a preventive war against Russia. The controversy over Matthews's speech had hardly dimmed when Major General Orville Anderson, chief of the Air War College, embraced the cause, telling a reporter in Montgomery, Alabama, that "waiting until you're hit first" is un-American. A few voices from Congress entered the fray as well, including Senator John McClellan of Arkansas, who called for a "peace-or-war" showdown with Russia, and Senator Richard Russell of Georgia, who insisted that preventive war should remain an option.[37]

After Matthews's speech in Boston, Truman moved at once to quell the uproar that ensued and the image it cast of a foreign policy in turmoil. In coordination with the White House, the first move came from the State Department, which made clear the speech did not represent U.S. policy. Secretary of State Dean Acheson had on two occasions earlier that summer denounced the notion of a preventive war, telling a group at Southern Methodist University that such a war "is unthinkable for us" and "would violate every moral principle of our people," a statement he repeated to a group of congressmen a few months later. The White House followed the State Department press release with a statement affirming it had not cleared Matthews's address. In an interview broadcast by CBS, Ambassador-at-Large Phillip Jessup continued the administration's cleanup efforts: "Dropping atomic bombs on the Soviet Union now is not the way we act; it is not the way America does things." While both Acheson and Jessup recognized the practical problems of such a proposal—Jessup, for example, pointing to enormous problems posed by an occupation—their primary response invoked not strategic but moral obstacles.[38]

On September 1, 1950, in a speech on Korea broadcast via television and radio from the White House, President Truman finally made his first public statement against the idea of preventive war: "We do not believe in aggressive or preventive war. Such war is the weapon of dictators, not of free democratic countries like the United States." In his memoirs published five years later, Truman reflected on the incident: "I have always been opposed even to the thought of such a war. There is nothing more foolish than to think that war can be stopped by war. You don't 'prevent' anything by war except peace." Earlier that day the chief of the Air Force removed Major General Anderson from his post at the Air War College. When Secretary of Defense Johnson submitted his resignation to Truman less than two weeks later, Stewart Alsop concluded in his *Washington Post* column that the secretary's shrouded efforts to encourage a preventive war against Russia had cost him his job.[39]

One of the most important statements against preventive war during the decade in which Americans debated the issue lay concealed in a top secret document, NSC 68, adopted by the president on September 30, 1950, and laying out the administration's first comprehensive national security policy since Russia acquired the bomb. Its organizing principles would guide the nation through much of the Cold War, judging that America would win the conflict not only through political and economic means but through an imposing military that could contain Soviet expansion. Although NSC 68 remained classified until 1975, it reflected the unspun conclusion of Truman and many of his advisers that America could not wage a preventive war against Russia.[40]

The document begins by describing a fundamental opposition between the United States and the Soviet Union: while the United States exists to "assure the integrity and vitality of our free society, which is founded upon the dignity and worth of the individual" the Soviet Union seeks to retain and extend "absolute power." This leads to an asymmetry in the means each state is willing to employ toward its ends. Whereas the Kremlin is able to select "whatever means are expedient," the United States cannot do so without negating its very purpose—a point Conant had pressed earlier. NSC 68 continued, "The free society is limited in its choice of means to achieve its ends. Compulsion is the negation of freedom, except when it is used to enforce the rights common to all. The resort to force, internally or externally, is therefore a last resort for a free society. . . . [W]e have no choice but to demonstrate the superiority of the idea of freedom by its constructive application, and to attempt to change the world situation by means short of war."[41]

The final section of NSC 68 turns to several courses of action the nation might pursue to secure itself and counter the threat posed by a nuclear Russia, one of the options being preventive war: "Some Americans favor a deliberate decision to go to war against the Soviet Union in the near future. It goes without saying that the idea of 'preventive war'—in the sense of a military attack not provoked by a military attack upon us or our allies—is generally unacceptable to Americans." While the document envisions an atomic conflict, the exponentially more lethal hydrogen bomb was still more than two years down the road, and the costs of nuclear war, while staggering, were not yet unthinkable. The Red Army would almost certainly roll across the whole of Europe. These practical limitations, however, are not the decisive objection: "Apart from this, however, a surprise attack upon the Soviet Union . . . would be repugnant to many Americans. . . . [T]he shock of responsibility for a surprise attack would be morally corrosive. Many would doubt that it was a 'just war' and that all reasonable possibilities for a peaceful settlement had been explored in good faith." Affirming Webster's Rule, the document concludes as follows: "These considerations . . . rule out an attack unless it is demonstrably in the nature of a counter-attack to a blow which is on its way or about to be delivered. . . . [T]he only sure victory lies in the frustration of the Kremlin design by the steady development of the moral and material strength of the free world." NSC 68 offered the clearest statement during the Cold War that the nation must finally reject a preventive war with Russia as against its traditions.[42]

Over the next several months, Acheson denounced the idea of an aggressive war against the Russians on multiple occasions. In October 1950 he warned against "foolish talk about preventive war" in an address before Freedom House in New York City. A month later he told the National Conference of Christians and Jews, meeting in the plush halls of the Mayflower Hotel in Washington, that a preventive war would be self-destructive: "Unless we have a constant awareness that our purpose is to maintain the peace so that the democratic values we cherish may continue their fruition, we run the risk of allowing power to become an end in itself." A little more than a year later Acheson assured the North Atlantic Treaty Organization that the U.S. military buildup, a direct result of NSC 68, was not for the purposes of launching a preventive war. And condemnation from the broader public continued to mount. The Federal Council of the Churches of Christ issued a statement, produced by a commission that included the influential theologian Reinhold Niebuhr, upholding atomic weapons as a justifiable means of defense but repudiating talk of a preventive war as morally off-limits (a more restrained assessment than that of the Episcopal bishop of Washington, who, upon returning home from a meeting of the World Council of Churches in Switzerland, lectured the press on the "Satanic idea of a preventive war").[43]

When Eisenhower took office on January 20, 1953, the United States had successfully tested the first hydrogen bomb that past November, and Russia would do the same in less than eight months. While the atomic bombs dropped in 1945 could decimate three to four square miles, the new H-bombs could wipe out three hundred to four hundred square miles, with radioactive fallout even more devastating. Under these exacerbated circumstances, the logic of prevention could cut both ways. An effective first strike against the nation could result in unacceptable loss and perhaps eliminate any capacity for a second strike. This worry was already coming to the fore at the end of the Truman administration, as Paul Nitze, director of the Policy Planning Staff at the Department of State and the primary force behind NSC 68, worried aloud in a memorandum to Acheson. At the same time, a preventive war would invite the same loss if the Soviets could retaliate. Despite any strategic argument in favor of prevention, the public consensus remained firmly against the idea of the United States initiating war with the Soviet Union. As a young Henry Kissinger would conclude in 1954, "There has always been an air of unreality about a [proposal] so contrary to the sense of the country and the constitutional limits within which American foreign policy must be conducted."[44]

As Eisenhower's pick for secretary of state, Dulles continued to voice the same moral opposition to preventive war he had expressed in 1948. In January 1953 Dulles declared in his first address to the American public, broadcast on national television, that he and the president rejected the notion that war was inevitable and that the nation should therefore launch a preventive war. Rather, as he wrote a few months later in *Foreign Affairs,* the nation faces the "difficult task" of finding policies "which would be adequate for security and peace and at the same time compatible with its traditions." Neither now nor at any time in the foreseeable future, Dulles told reporters in 1954, would a first strike against Russia be a part of U.S. foreign policy—a view he affirmed in public as well as in private meetings with the National Security Council.[45]

As president of Columbia University following his retirement from the army and before his run for the presidency, Eisenhower had come out strongly against the idea: "There is no such thing as a preventive war. . . . [N]one has yet explained how war prevents war." He repeated the same theme in a major televised address from Denver during his presidential campaign in 1952 and again in a press conference in August 1954. At the same time, Eisenhower did not escape the alluring logic of striking first. In September 1953, in a letter to Dulles written from the summer White House in Denver, Eisenhower wondered aloud whether a democracy could for long maintain the means of massive retaliation in a bipolar world of ever-increasing nuclear stockpiles without either driving itself to war or sacrificing its freedom. "In such circumstances," he speculated, "we would be forced to consider whether or not our duty to future generations did not require us to *initiate* war at the most propitious moment that we could designate." Despite these questions, Eisenhower was finally convinced that the United States could not strike first. On January 23, 1956, he wrote in his diary what was a fitting close to a decade of earnest questioning by a nation threatened as it never was before: a "surprise attack against the Soviets," he concluded, would be "against our traditions."[46]

Thirteen Days in the Shadow of Infamy

From 1945 until 1955 the nation debated the use of preventive force against a threat distant but sure to grow. In October 1962, however, the discovery by U-2 surveillance of Soviet nuclear missiles under swift assembly on the island of Cuba forced President John F. Kennedy to consider whether the nation should strike first against a threat that within days or even hours might amount to a gun pointed at the nation's head.[47]

Unlike the earlier debate, this one would take place entirely behind closed doors, among the president and a small group of advisers, and would last only a few days. During that time those involved were vigilant to keep the matter secret until they formulated a response: exiting through back doors and secret tunnels, sitting on each other's laps in a crowded limousine to shuttle between the White House and the State Department to avoid the attention a long motorcade would draw, and ensuring that the lights went out as usual in the West Wing, even as meetings pressed late into the night elsewhere. In the crucible of decision, the president too worked hard at keeping up appearances. He traveled to Connecticut to stump for congressional candidates on the New Haven Green. He presented an award in the Rose Garden to Lieutenant Commander Victor Prather Jr., who had recently set a new altitude record for manned balloon flight. And he welcomed the Mercury 7 astronaut Wally Schirra and his family to the Oval Office, taking Schirra's youngest daughter out on the South Lawn to see Macaroni, Caroline Kennedy's pony, who had appeared with her on the cover of *Life* just that past month. In private, however, the president faced the most difficult decision of his presidency, aware that a misstep, a miscommunication, a mistake could trigger a nuclear World War III.

When the president and his advisers met for the first time in the Cabinet Room at the White House on Tuesday, October 16, the group quickly agreed the United States must do something to prevent a nuclearized Cuba, less than ninety miles from its southern boundary. Following the intelligence briefing, the president asked Secretary of State Dean Rusk to speak first.

Rusk said the group, later named the Ex-Comm, had two options: a surprise air strike to take out the missiles and perhaps other military targets, or political pressure backed up by the threat of military force to compel the Soviets or the Cubans to remove the missiles themselves. Following Rusk, Secretary of Defense Robert McNamara addressed only the first option and warned against such an attack if there was any worry nuclear missiles were already operational. The chairman of the Joint Chiefs, General Maxwell Taylor, however, strongly urged the president to strike first, as he and the Joint Chiefs would throughout the crisis. "We're impressed, Mr. President, with the great importance of getting a strike with all the benefit of surprise," to "take them out without any warning whatsoever." Within a few days the Joint Chiefs would be pushing for a full invasion of Cuba. During the rest of the meeting, the group inclined toward a surprise attack, and the president's comments suggest this response remained his leaning for at least another day. Only at the end of that first meeting did McNamara make a comment that pointed in the direction of where the discussion would head, asking the group to consider whether political action should precede military action to give Nikita Khrushchev a way out, the answer to which McNamara thought was "almost certainly yes."[48]

By 6:30 that evening, as Kennedy and his advisers gathered again in the Cabinet Room, McNamara had followed his earlier line of thought further and was ready to float another idea, short of a surprise air attack but combining military force with the opportunity for a political settlement: a blockade against all offensive weapons entering Cuba backed up by the threat of further military force. McNamara then began to press the group with two questions he would raise again and again: (1) what are the consequences of a surprise air strike? and (2) if the consequences include the possibility of setting off a general war with the Soviet Union, as McNamara was increasingly worried an air strike would, are there alternative means to remove the nuclear threat from Cuba that reduce the risk of a nuclear clash? In addition to developing a strike plan, "the second thing we ought to do," McNamara said, "is to consider the consequences. I don't believe we have considered the consequences of any of these actions satisfactorily. And because we haven't considered the consequences, I'm not sure we're taking all the action we ought to take now to minimize those. I don't know quite what kind of a world we live in after we've struck Cuba, and we've started it." Even two days later, on Thursday, McNamara was still warning the president that "what's lacking here is a real well-thought-out course of action, alternative courses of action." McNamara was not yet ready to argue for the blockade plan. All the options had strategic weaknesses, and this one did as well—for example, what to do with the missiles already on the island—but McNamara signaled, if not inaugurated, a shift that would move a majority of the president's advisers away from a first strike.[49]

In addition to McNamara, several members of the group began to think that a surprise air strike against Cuba carried not only strategic flaws but also moral ones. In the course of thinking out loud and then arguing to their colleagues, these advisers evoked the image of Pearl Harbor, with all the infamy Roosevelt ascribed to the attack of December 7. Who first evoked the image is uncertain. Perhaps it was difficult not to make the connection, barely twenty years after the attack which so radically shaped the world they now inhabited. Pearl Harbor brought the nation into World War II, but more than that, it brought the nation out of its isolationist slumber and into a position of world leadership. And it shaped what Americans thought of themselves: when a war should be fought and by what means.

The first mention of Pearl Harbor in the record was by George Ball, under secretary of state, a New Dealer, advocate of free trade, and later an early critic from within the Johnson administration of American involvement in Vietnam. As Kennedy's secret recording machine continued rolling after the meeting closed and a few advisers remained, Ball contrasted the blockade and air strike options: "[The blockade is] a series of single, unrelated acts, not by surprise. This coming in there, a Pearl Harbor, just frightens the hell out of me as to what goes beyond." The next evening, Ball passed a memorandum to the president expressing his personal views against a surprise air strike: "I think that—far from establishing our moral strength—we would, in fact, alienate a great part of the civilized world by behaving in a manner wholly contrary to our traditions, by pursuing a course of action that would [illegible word] directly thwart everything we have stood for during our national history, and condemn us as hypocrites in the opinion of the world. We tried Japanese as war criminals because of a sneak attack on Pearl Harbor."[50]

When the president returned from Connecticut and reconvened his advisers on Thursday morning in the Cabinet Room, Ball expressed his views to the full Ex-Comm. Describing a surprise first strike as "like Pearl Harbor," he stated, "It's the kind of conduct that one might expect of the Soviet Union. It is not conduct that one expects of the United States." A few minutes later President Kennedy suggested the possibility of military air strikes following an announcement of intentions. This course, he says, "isn't Pearl Harbor"—suggesting he was taking Ball's critique seriously. Following a brief discussion of the strategic value of such an announcement, Robert Kennedy—who was perhaps to press this point more than anyone else—broke in:

> *Robert Kennedy:* I think George Ball has a hell of a good point.
> *President Kennedy:* What?
> *Robert Kennedy:* I think it's the whole question of, you know, assuming that you do survive all this, . . . what kind of a country we are.
> *Rusk:* This business of carrying the mark of Cain on your brow for the rest of your life is something.
> *Robert Kennedy:* We did this against Cuba. We've fought for 15 years with Russia to prevent a first strike against us [unclear]. Now, in the interest of time, we do that to a small country. I think it's a hell of a burden to carry.

After another meeting of his advisers that evening, held in the Oval Room of the Executive Mansion to avoid attracting the attention of reporters, the president went to the Cabinet Room and noted for his recorder that the momentum was turning in favor of a blockade, backed up by the possibility of air strikes if the crisis was not resolved.[51]

Robert Kennedy made perhaps the most forceful argument against a surprise first strike the next day, Friday, October 19, at the State Department, where the president's advisers had gathered to develop the details of two alternative plans while the president traveled to the Midwest for a scheduled trip. The meeting began at 11 a.m. and lasted eight hours. The broad support for a blockade, however, evaporated when National Security Advisor McGeorge Bundy changed his direction and came out forcefully in favor of a surprise air strike, which he said he had expressed personally to the president that morning. Also present was former secretary of state Dean Acheson, whom the president had asked to join the group. Acheson expressed unwavering support for a surprise attack and little patience for alternatives. And the Joint Chiefs, represented by General Taylor, reiterated their support for the same, followed by a full-scale invasion of the island. Leonard Meeker, acting legal adviser at the State Department, described Robert Kennedy's response:

> The Attorney General said with a grin that he too had had a talk with the President, indeed very recently this morning. There seemed to be three main possibilities as the Attorney General analyzed the situation: one was to do nothing, and that would be unthinkable; another was an air strike; the third was a blockade. He thought it would be very, very difficult indeed for the President if the decision were to be for an air strike, with all the memory of Pearl Harbor and with all the implications this would have for us in whatever world there would be afterward. For 175 years we had not been that kind of country. A sneak attack was not in our traditions. Thousands of Cubans would be killed without warning, and a lot of Russians too. He favored action, to make known unmistakably the seriousness of United States determination to get the missiles out of Cuba, but he thought the action should allow the Soviets some room for maneuver to pull back from their over-extended position in Cuba.[52]

Writing in his memoirs, Ball recalled that several of those present were moved by Robert Kennedy's arguments, especially his statement "My brother is not going to be the Tojo of the 1960s." Later recounting that Robert Kennedy's argument that afternoon sealed his opposition to a surprise air strike, Ted Sorensen, a longtime friend of the president and special counsel, stated, "A sudden air strike at dawn Sunday without warning, said the Attorney General in rather impassioned tones, would be 'a Pearl Harbor in reverse, and it would blacken the name of the United States in the pages of history' as a greater power who attacked a small neighbor. . . . [A]nd the Soviets would entertain the very dangerous notion that the United States, as they had feared all these years, was indeed capable of launching a pre-emptive first strike."[53]

At 2:30 Saturday afternoon the Ex-Comm reconvened at the White House with the president, who had cut short his trip on the excuse of a bad cold. Various advisers made their case for the two alternative plans they had worked on the day before, Secretary McNamara making the case for a blockade. This path, he explained, had four advantages: (1) it would cause the least trouble with the allies; (2) "it avoids any surprise air attack on Cuba, which is contrary to our tradition"; (3) "it is the only military course of action compatible with our position as a leader of the free world"; and (4) it avoids a sudden move which might escalate into general war. After some discussion, Bundy made the case for a preventive first strike. Robert Kennedy and now Rusk again argued that this route would violate the nation's traditions and evoke the memory of Pearl Harbor.[54]

By the conclusion of the meeting, President Kennedy had said he was ready to go forward with the blockade, backed up by possible air strikes in the near future. Although he based his decision on several grounds—and indicated he could imagine a situation in which the nation might have to strike first in the future—the arguments made by his brother, McNamara, Ball, and others had impressed him that a preventive air strike would somehow violate the American character. Reflecting the tumble of principle and pragmatism that formed his decision, President Kennedy remarked on Monday, "I think we've done the best thing, at least as far as we can tell in advance." Speaking of a surprise air strike, he said that "after talking to others, it looked like we would have all of the difficulties of Pearl Harbor and not have finished the job."[55]

After a flurry of diplomatic communications, meetings with leaders in Congress, and the military rollout required by DEFCON 3, a heightened "defense readiness condition," President Kennedy broke the silence at 7 p.m. on Monday with a speech from the Oval Office broadcast on every major station. The Soviet Union was preparing "offensive missile sites" in Cuba to provide a "nuclear strike capability against the Western Hemisphere."[56]

These few days are an important chapter in the story of America and preventive force. The blockade, while minimally intrusive, was arguably such an act. Along the spectrum of uses of military force, however, it stood at one end. An armed attack, not the passive resistance of a blockade, was what Stimson had worried would cast "Americans as conquerors." The significance of this episode lies in what it did not become and why.

The persuasive hold the memory of Pearl Harbor had over the president and many of his advisers in reaching their decision is striking, particularly since the analogy was far from perfect. One exception was Acheson. On Thursday afternoon the former secretary of state had a few minutes with the president alone and told him he thought his brother's mention of Pearl Harbor was silly. In an article in *Esquire* in February 1969, with both of the Kennedys now dead, Acheson openly attacked Robert Kennedy's notion that a surprise air strike would have been a "Pearl Harbor in reverse." "This seemed to me," he went on, "to obfuscate rather than clarify thought by a thoroughly false and pejorative analogy. I said so, pointing out that at Pearl Harbor the Japanese without provocation or warning attacked our fleet thousands of miles from their shores. In the present situation the Soviet Union had installed ninety miles from our coast . . . offensive weapons that were capable of lethal injury to the United States." Although Acheson applauded the president's leadership, he scolded the brothers for the path they took, which he thought beset by moral confusion. That the crisis turned out as it did was attributable in large part to "plain dumb luck."[57]

Although at points Acheson's article sounds like the reflections of a grumpy old man and in some tension with his strong opposition to a preventive attack against the Soviet Union during the last years of the Truman administration, the differences he identifies are both correct and significant. Japan attacked Pearl Harbor in 1941 as part of a campaign of imperial expansion in Southeast Asia. The United States contemplated a surprise air strike on Cuba because the Soviets were secretly positioning nuclear missiles just off its southern shore—if not a significant strategic shift given the capacity of intercontinental ballistic missiles, at least a tremendous psychological shift. The one served the purpose of aggression; the other the purpose of self-defense. As President Kennedy declared, Khrushchev "initiated the danger. . . . He's the one that's playing at God, not us."[58]

Nevertheless, Kennedy and his advisers knew that an act of preventive force of the magnitude urged by the Joint Chiefs would risk being an act of aggression—the more so as the threat becomes more remote. The reason, expressed often in the comments above, is simple: faced with a potential threat, a state seeking to defend itself may well have, as McNamara often urged his colleagues to consider, alternatives short of lethal force. A surprise attack, however, would close any other door. As one of the participants recalled Robert Kennedy saying to the president and a few other advisers, "We could always blow the place up if necessary, but that might be unnecessary, and then we would then be in the position of having used too much force."

The likeness of a potential air strike on Cuba to Pearl Harbor, Robert Kennedy and others came to believe, was that it would fail to give the Soviet Union an opportunity to step back from the precipice it was edging toward. Such force, they worried, was not a last resort and therefore began to look something like the aggression of December 7.[59]

In retrospect, the Cuban missile crisis, and not 9/11, might have been the occasion for revising the norms governing the first use of force. The advent of nuclear weapons vastly changed the demands of defense from the days of cutlasses and cannons. An intercontinental missile fired from the Soviet Union might take fifteen minutes to reach the United States; a medium range ballistic missile fired from Cuba might take two or three. The challenge to Webster's Rule is obvious: if a state can strike first only when faced with an imminent threat, and if the time between when this point is reached and the act completed may be only a few minutes, with catastrophic results, then Webster's Rule might in effect be a demand to take the first, perhaps fatal blow. As President Kennedy said in his address to the nation on Monday, October 22, "We no longer live in a world where only the actual firing of weapons represents a sufficient challenge to a nation's security to constitute maximum peril. Nuclear weapons are so destructive and ballistic missiles are so swift, that any substantially increased possibility of their use or any sudden change in their deployment may well be regarded as a definite threat to peace."[60]

This change was not lost among the lawyers advising the president, as they discussed the legal basis for a quarantine. After deciding to institute a blockade, the president eventually agreed to go to the Organization of American States (OAS) for approval. The attorney general stated that in his opinion a blockade would not be legal absent approval from OAS. Secretary Rusk disagreed. Although the tape was not yet rolling, the minutes recall that Rusk "referred to the new situation created by modern weapons and he thought that rules of international law should not be taken as applying literally to a completely new situation." Despite the enormous changes brought by nuclear weapons, however, Webster's Rule held firm for at least two reasons. A preventive strike during the Cold War would almost certainly have included nuclear weapons, which by their nature are indiscriminate and would result in massive civilian casualties. Moreover, the emerging logic of deterrence led both sides to seek a "second strike" capacity, and, unless a first strike could eliminate all the means of retaliation, incentives pushed strongly against such action.[61]

Rather than serving as an occasion for revision, the Cuban missile crisis reinforced Webster's Rule and the growing consensus among the American people and its leaders that striking first is against the nation's traditions, at least under the circumstances encountered. This consensus was not without qualifications and contradictions. The firm stand taken during the third week of October 1962 followed a failed attempt by the CIA the previous year to plant Cuban exiles on the island in an effort to overthrow Castro. Although the invading forces were Cubans, and the Bay of Pigs invasion did not bring to bear the level of force an overt American invasion would, the event at least raised similar questions about what the nation's traditions might allow. And the president never ruled out that the United States might wage a surprise first strike in the future, under different circumstances—it appears later that Kennedy at least considered a first strike against China to prevent it from acquiring a nuclear capacity. Nonetheless, the decisions reached by the president and his advisers behind closed doors registered and reinforced a growing unease with striking first.[62]

America's use of preventive force to quell unrest (and sometimes to extend its borders) as a means of keeping Europe out of the Americas gradually became obsolete. Borders fixed. Colonialism antiquated. During the nation's first 165 years, it had never faced the urgent question of whether it should wage a preventive war directly against a potential threat. When the question arose in 1941 as the United States stood on the cusp of world leadership, Roosevelt discerned in America's past—perhaps more on the basis of principle than practice—that doing so would violate the nation's traditions. Pearl Harbor, the day of infamy, became the symbol of transgression. The widespread debate among policy makers and the public from 1945 until 1955 about a preventive strike against the Soviet Union confirmed Roosevelt's decision. And Pearl Harbor haunted the minds of Kennedy and many of his advisers when they finally decided against carrying out a surprise attack on Cuba. In the case of both Russia and Cuba, preventive force would have foreclosed other reasonable alternatives. As Eisenhower discerned in the Cold War context, a first strike absent some imminent threat was "against our traditions."

The question this narrative has not answered, however, is why? What was it about America—its history, its encounters with the world, and especially its principles—that led so many Americans to think striking first in these moments would leave them bearing the mark of Cain?

3

Just War at Home in America

THE MORAL QUALMS AMERICANS FELT about striking first—against Japan on the eve of Pearl Harbor, against the Soviet Union following the war, and against Cuba in 1962—reflected a shared intuition that, expedience aside, something about the national character placed the use of force under certain constraints. Most important, this intuition expressed the conviction that war should be a last resort. A preventive war at any of these moments, Americans and their leaders came to believe, would have crossed this moral line. It would have been un-American.

This conclusion reflected a long history of experience with the exercise of military force by the world's first modern republic and was an outworking of fundamental moral commitments long resident in American democracy, expressed in the Declaration of Independence, and frequently inscribed as principle if not always honored in practice. But the belief that war should be a last resort was not simply the achievement of American moral ingenuity. Rather, it was an inheritance of centuries of reflection on the morality of war that emerged long before a string of thirteen colonies clung to the Atlantic coast. Together these reflections made up the moral tradition on the just war which today provides the grammar for how Americans talk about war. Although not the native son, the tradition is comfortably at home in American thought and discourse. To understand why, and to understand what hold the tradition has upon Americans in their rethinking of the role of preventive force, one first needs to understand something about the tradition—where it came from and what it says.

74

A Just War Primer

Although moral accounts of war are many and nuanced, at a basic level the just war tradition rejects two alternatives. On the one hand, the tradition rejects pacifism, which holds that the use of armed force is morally illegitimate means. The roster of pacifists past and present is a varied list. Many Christians in the early church rejected war and violence, following Jesus' admonition in the Sermon on the Mount to turn the other cheek and love the enemy. The church leader Tertullian (155–222) scoffed at the idea of Christians serving in the Roman army: "In disarming Peter, [Jesus] unbelted every soldier." And after the Reformation various Protestant sects such as Quakers and Mennonites reclaimed this view. Between the two world wars a number of secular peace groups emerged, such as the War Resisters League. Whether on religious, ideological, or practical grounds, pacifists share the conviction that war is morally indefensible.[1]

On the other hand, the just war tradition rejects a number of views that loosely fall under the rubric of realism. These accounts range from the classical realism of Thucydides to a number of nuanced accounts emerging in the twentieth century, represented in the writings of Hans Morgenthau and others. Although these positions diverge in important ways, many share an underlying skepticism about the application of morality to the relations between states. In its strongest form, political realism rejects the idea that justice has anything to say about how states interact with one another, especially in war.[2]

The classic expression is the Melian Dialogue in Thucydides' *History of the Peloponnesian War,* recounting the ancient conflict between Athens and Sparta. Melos was a small island in the Cretan Sea. Although a Spartan colony, it had remained neutral throughout the conflict. Now sixteen years into their war with Sparta, the Athenians decided neutrality was not enough. Arriving with thirty vessels, they gave the Melian leaders a choice between submitting to the Athenian empire or facing certain death. The Athenians jeered at the Melians' suggestion that justice might govern their fate: "You know as well as we do that, when these matters are discussed by practical people, the standard of justice depends on the equality of power to compel and that in fact the strong do what they have the power to do and the weak accept what they have to accept." The Melians' appeal proved futile, they returned to their city, and the Athenians laid siege. In time, the city surrendered unconditionally to the Athenians, who slew the men and sold the women and children as slaves. As the Athenians had warned, "The strong do what they have the power to do."[3]

Rejecting both pacifism and realism, the just war tradition affirms the sometime responsibility of going to war but always under certain moral constraints governing when and how to fight. The tradition shares with realist views a sober assessment of human nature and the need to meet force with force. War is sometimes not only permissible; it is the moral obligation of responsible leadership. But the tradition holds that the requirements of justice place limits on the occasion and conduct of war.

For the tradition, the demands of justice do not merely arise from the social contract, governing relations within a political community yet silent beyond the city walls. Rather, they transcend political boundaries. In other words, and as the historical narrative in part II will examine more closely, the just war tradition is committed to an international theory of justice. I need not resolve the deep underpinnings of this theory. For much of its history the tradition was indebted to natural law as a means to explain why moral norms bound the sovereign in his dealings with other people. For my purposes, it is enough that the tradition as it exists today in America represents at least an ad hoc agreement around a set of practical norms limiting the occasion and conduct of war, even though persons will often not share a thick description of why those norms are binding.[4]

This tradition represents an accretion of moral wisdom over centuries of reflection and experience. Informed by religious and secular sources, the tradition took root in numerous cultural and political contexts. And the raw materials for the tradition were not only the ruminations of scholars, but also the practice of statecraft and military command. Although a historical account of the tradition as a whole is beyond the scope of this book, a brief sketch will provide helpful context.[5]

The idea of a just war appeared early in numerous classical writings. Plato, Aristotle, and Cicero all mention it. Some ancient sources refer to the practice of a select group of Roman priestly officials known as *fetials* who performed various rituals whereby the early Romans would declare a war just. And more important, Roman legal concepts like that of injury, necessity, proportionality, and the *jus gentium* (law of nations) laid the groundwork for ideas later incorporated into the tradition.[6]

As a distinct framework, however, with an identifiable set of core commitments conveyed across time, the moral tradition on the just war first emerged in the context of Christianity. Shaped by the Christian scriptures, early church fathers such as Eusebius, Chrysostom, Jerome, and Ambrose all contributed to the nascent idea of a just war. But the tradition found its most important early statement in the writings of Ambrose's unsuspecting convert, Augustine. Rejecting the pacifism of the early church, Augustine developed a larger account of why war might sometimes be just and discussed when the emperor and his legions might justifiably wield the sword.[7]

In the Middle Ages the tradition continued to evolve in the writings of canon lawyers, scholastic theologians, the emerging code of chivalry, and the customary practices of sovereigns. Gratian's *Decretum,* a compilation of canon law completed around 1140, became the sourcebook for the tradition. He devoted a section of the work to discussing issues of war and punishment, and his decision to include a broad selection of Augustinian texts solidified the saint's stamp on the tradition. Thomas Aquinas, a thirteenth-century theologian, offered a concise summary of the tradition to that point in time that drew on Gratian's work. In scholastic fashion, Aquinas asks "whether it is always sinful to wage war." He answers, "In order for a war to be just, three things are necessary. First, the authority of the sovereign by whose command the war is to be waged. . . . Secondly, a just cause is required, namely that those who are attacked should be attacked because they deserve it on account of some fault. . . . Thirdly, it is necessary that the belligerents should have a right intention, so that they intend the advancement of good, or the avoidance of evil." Although these requirements were all present in Augustine's writings, this formulation governing the decision of when a sovereign can go to war became the benchmark over time.[8]

In the early modern period, Spanish neo-Thomists drew on the work of Aquinas and applied the tradition to the changing political landscape in Europe and the wars waged by colonists in the New World. Soon scholars and diplomats in search of a law binding on all persons that could mediate religious conflicts and govern relations within the new system of nation-states looked to the moral tradition, while also reshaping it. Grotius's *On the Law of War and Peace* was the most important early work, followed later by the writings of Samuel Pufendorf, Emmerich de Vattel, and others. And though the tradition waned during the nineteenth and early twentieth centuries, it shaped the development of international humanitarian law in the nineteenth century and later the restrictions on the resort to force, enshrined in the UN Charter. As we will see, the tradition also left a profound mark on Webster's Rule.[9]

Although the Latin terms did not attach until the twentieth century, the tradition makes an initial distinction between the *jus ad bellum* (law to war), which governs the decision to use force, and the *jus in bello* (law in war), which governs how force is used. The jus ad bellum emerged very early and some mention of each criterion is discernible in the writings of Augustine. The jus in bello, however, took shape primarily in the Middle Ages. Pinpointing the precise moment when the criteria known today appeared in whole is difficult, but certainly by the early modern period the key norms were in place. These marks of a justified war would continue to evolve, applied to new technologies, new methods of warfare, and changing political arrangements—as well as reflecting shifting cultural and moral sensibilities —but the tradition had achieved its basic form.[10]

As to the jus ad bellum the tradition holds that the decision to use force must satisfy several requirements, the first three of which appear in Aquinas's threefold formulation. The person authorizing the resort to force must have sovereign authority. This criterion rules out wars among private individuals, who can resolve their disputes through the appropriate government channels. Only the sovereign, the person over whom no one has authority, can authorize the use of armed force. And that person can authorize force only where there is just cause. The tradition often distinguished two aspects of just cause: that which precipitates the use of force and the aim, or end, in using force. The former required some injury. As Augustine said, "To wage war against neighbours, and to go on from there against others crushing and subjugating peoples who have done no harm, out of the mere desire to rule: what else is this to be called than great robbery?" The latter concerned the purpose for using force, and the tradition recognized three: self-defense, punishment, and restitution of goods taken. Furthermore, a just war requires right intention. In other words, the just cause for using force must in fact be the motivation for so doing. In his classic statement of the threefold formulation, Aquinas quotes Augustine: "The passion for inflicting harm, the cruel thirst for vengeance, an unpacific and relentless spirit, the fever of revolt, the lust of power, and such like things, all these are rightly condemned in war." Stated positively, right intention requires the sovereign and the soldier to wage war with the aim of achieving peace, a recurrent theme in Augustine and a requirement that some accounts list as a separate criterion.[11]

In addition to these three requirements in the classic formulation, the tradition recognized three other marks for a just war that typically took on a prudential role in moral decision making. First, the sovereign should have a reasonable hope of success. A contemplated use of force may otherwise satisfy the seven marks of a just war but be wholly futile. Second, the sovereign should demonstrate a proportionality of ends, which is to say, the overall use of force must be proportionate to the ends sought. Finally, the tradition stood for the principle that led America on repeated occasions in the middle of the twentieth century to reject a preventive attack: war should be a last resort. The sovereign should exhaust all reasonable alternatives before using armed force. Writing to Boniface, a Roman general charged with protecting imperial Africa from barbarians, Augustine warned, "Your will ought to hold fast to peace, with war as the result of necessity, that God may free you from the necessity and preserve you in peace. Peace is not sought for the purpose of stirring up war, but war is waged for the purpose of securing peace. . . . Therefore, let it be necessity, not choice, that kills your warring enemy." As we saw in chapter 1, Webster's Rule interpreted the requirement of last resort to mean a state could strike first only when faced with an imminent attack. Only then would the use of force be necessary.[12]

Furthermore, the jus in bello includes two criteria, developed within the tradition and well established in international humanitarian law today: discrimination and proportionality of means. Discrimination is sometimes called noncombatant immunity and requires the avoidance of direct, intentional harm to noncombatants. Writers in the moral tradition often produced lists indicating the types of persons soldiers should not target, such as clergy, merchants, farmers, women, and the aged, sick, and disabled.

Likewise, proportionality of means requires a state to avoid uses of force that cause gratuitous or otherwise unnecessary harm.

Just War as American Grammar

Few Americans could list these marks or even know a moral tradition on the just war exists, yet the tradition provides the grammar for how the vast majority of Americans discuss, debate, and make decisions about war. Some traditions shape our beliefs and practice through catechesis: every good Presbyterian, for example, knows from the cradle that "man's chief end is to glorify God, and to enjoy Him forever." More often, however, people find themselves immersed in a world already formed by traditions of which they may never be aware. Theorizing those traditions and understanding their historical path is a task that comes later, if at all. The moral tradition on the just war is of this kind: latent in American culture, shaping our intuitions and explaining our experiences. Although both realism and pacifism have followings, the American consensus today is that war and morality are not separated by an impassable divide, either because the moral order would never permit war (pacifism) or because the moral order does not reach the question (realism, or realpolitik). Rather, the use of force is sometimes justified, although always within constraints as to when and how.

When Eisenhower concluded that a preventive war against the Soviet Union absent an imminent threat would be "against our traditions," he invoked American commitments deeply shaped by the just war tradition—in particular the moral claim that war must be a last resort. The foundational document of Cold War security policy, NSC 68, states the connection more clearly than any other statement during the Cold War: "A surprise attack upon the Soviet Union . . . would be repugnant to many Americans. . . . [T]he shock of responsibility for a surprise attack would be morally corrosive. Many would doubt that it was a 'just war' and that all reasonable possibilities for a peaceful settlement had been explored in good faith." A preventive war in this context, Americans came to believe, would not be a last resort. That Americans felt compelled to exhaust all reasonable alternatives before using force testified to a legacy tracing back to Augustine.[13]

As we will see in part II, the moral tradition reached its nadir in the nineteenth century. Although various movements drawing on just war ideas of discrimination and proportionality produced important treaties limiting the conduct of war, the right of states to wage war at will was unquestioned. Coinciding with attempts after World War I to limit or even outlaw war, several writers began to reclaim the moral tradition. Among them was James Brown Scott, a scholar of international law and solicitor for the State Department, who with support from the Carnegie Endowment for International Peace directed the publication of all the major works in the moral tradition beginning with Francisco de Vitoria. The most important developments came in the wake of World War II and the adoption of the UN Charter with its restrictions on recourse to force. Although the Charter's limits on war did not perfectly map the moral tradition, the new framework reflected it in important ways.

Since that time the dominance of just war thinking has only strengthened. John Courtney Murray's publication of "Remarks on the Moral Problem of War" (1959) invigorated renewed attention in the academy. Murray was a prominent public intellectual and Catholic theologian whose progressive views on the relationship between church and state landed him on the cover of *Time* magazine a few weeks after Kennedy won the presidential election in 1960. Although Murray did not pursue the task in his essay, he set the agenda for the intellectual work in the coming decades by noting a need to rethink the tradition in the context of the Cold War. In the 1960s Paul Ramsey, a Protestant theologian and public intellectual who voiced qualified support for the war in Vietnam, published two books that vigorously pursued the agenda Murray set forth. Scholars trained in theological sources continue to be at the forefront of just war scholarship.[14]

Persons working outside of theological circles also took up the tradition. Michael Walzer's *Just and Unjust Wars* (1977) today is standard fare for any college course discussing the ethics of war. Walzer's approach in writing the book, he explained, was "to account for the ways in which men and women . . . argue about war, and to expound the terms we commonly use." The justifications and judgments Americans make regarding war, Walzer concluded, reveal "a comprehensive view of war as a human activity and a more or less systematic doctrine." Walzer's work is a contemporary classic and more than any other book in the past half century has contributed to the ascendancy of just war theory as an object of scholarship and a living tradition shaping public discussion. Reflecting on the influence of his book in an article entitled "The Triumph of the Just War Theory," Walzer correctly described the tradition as moving out of "religious departments, theological seminaries, and a few Catholic universities" into the mainstream of public discourse.[15]

Indications that the moral tradition provides the grammar for how Americans think about the use of force today are ubiquitous. Concepts like last resort, proportionality, and noncombatant immunity structure the way we think about war, from weighty discussions in the Roosevelt Room to water fountain conversations on the job. The most important debates on the exercise of American military power are not between persons who disagree about whether or not the nation needs just cause; they arise between persons who dispute whether the conditions of that moment give rise to it.

Nowhere has the tradition taken deeper root than in the military. Classes on the subject are commonplace at the military academies, where the tradition provides the primary framework for ethical reflection on war. And outside the academies soldiers learn the rules of international humanitarian law, many of which formed and developed within the tradition. Beyond the military, the moral tradition pervades the language of presidents and protestors alike. Former president Clinton echoed the tradition in arguing that armed intervention in Kosovo was a "last resort." President George W. Bush invoked just war language in making the case for military action against Afghanistan, saying repeatedly that the United States had "just cause" to respond to the terrorist attacks of 9/11. Protestors who carry signs reading, "No blood for oil!" appeal to the tradition, as well—in particular the requirement that a state using force have right intention. In the months surrounding the decision to invade Iraq in 2003, myriad books and articles in all the major news sources drew on the tradition to make the case for or against the invasion.[16]

The prevalence of just war norms in American culture and elsewhere does not, of course, mean there is widespread agreement on the use of force in particular cases. Witness the debate that raged between, on the one side, Michael Novak and George Weigel, who explicitly employed the tradition in support of the Iraq War in 2003, and, on the other side, Rowan Williams, the

archbishop of Canterbury, and former president Jimmy Carter, who invoked
it in opposition. Moral norms, however, are not like mathematic equations
that yield a certain result. That the debate leading up to the invasion of Iraq
reflected a shared moral framework—the grammar of the debate—is striking. The historic moments at which Americans have achieved near consensus on whether to wage war are rare—December 7, 1941, and the days
after 9/11 are the only ones in recent memory. But that Americans appeal to
a shared tradition for deciding when to fight suggests that the resources for
responding to new challenges, including the challenge of when the nation
might strike first, are greater than one might imagine. Any new response
would have to satisfy the underlying norms governing the use of force embedded in the tradition.[17]

To understand the triumph of just war tradition in America and to understand the role the tradition must play in achieving legitimacy for any
framework that allows for preventive force, one must probe further. Why
has the moral tradition so readily found a home in America? Although the
tradition translates in many languages, its firm hold on American thought
and discourse is not happenstance but owes something to the nation's
unique national character. In brief, at the center of both the moral tradition
and America's national identity lies a commitment to the idea that the
claims of justice extend to all persons as moral equals—including the
enemy—which makes the moral tradition a fitting account of when and
how Americans should use force. To explain this affinity I first turn to Augustine and his larger narrative about humans and the world they inhabit,
a narrative in which the idea of a just war took root and the main contours
of which the tradition never left behind.

War in Augustine's Moral Universe

Augustine's life spanned the end of the fourth and the beginning of the
fifth centuries. The waning of the Roman empire in the West was part of a
larger shift from antiquity to the Middle Ages, and Augustine stood at its
crux. His inner journey to Christianity, recounted in his *Confessions,* and his
eventual appointment as a bishop in the North African town of Hippo are
well known. In view of the gradual toleration of Christianity and its eventual

elevation to the official religion of the empire in the first half of the fourth century, Augustine faced the colossal task of repositioning Christianity in the new context. Although recent scholars have challenged the generalization of Christianity as a purely pacifist religion in its first few centuries, the move from persecuted sect to ascendant imperial religion nonetheless challenged Christian thought, especially regarding the use of force. Augustine's writings provide a limited case for war, departing from early pacifism, but also giving a fundamentally different account than the essentially realist notions of the Greeks and Romans.[18]

Augustine's discussions of war as a moral issue are scattered, but references to the subject appear throughout his writings. In response to a request from Flavius Marcellinus, a high official at the court of Emperor Honorius, Augustine wrote *City of God* in part as a defense against the claim that Christianity was responsible for the sack of Rome in 410 by Alaric and the Visigoths. This work makes frequent reference to civil wars and takes up moral questions about war and empire. And Augustine drew his last breath with war at his doorstep, Hippo besieged by Vandals who swept across North Africa from the west.

Standing behind Augustine's understanding of the just war and the tradition he forcefully shaped is a larger narrative about self and society. Although Augustine offers this account in expressly theological terms, evoking Christian doctrines of creation, sin, and redemption, the themes he describes appear in some form throughout the history of Western thought, in both theological and secular versions. Three themes in particular are important, starting with Augustine's belief that humans have an endemic capacity for injustice. The biblical narratives of creation and fall shape Augustine's anthropology. The created state was one of perfect justice, which Augustine understands as a proper ordering in which everything receives its due. The self was rightly ordered in relation to itself, others, and God as the self's highest good. Peace, not war, is the primal condition. But Adam's decision to find his ultimate good in something other than God resulted in pervasive and constitutional disordering—or injustice—within the self. Although Augustine employs a wide range of images to describe this fundamental disordering, one he often invokes is the image of war.[19]

This disordering within the self spills out into conflict between persons, fueled by an insatiable "lust for domination" whereby the self wants to rule over others. Augustine observes with a tone of tragic irony that humans, created from one person as a symbol of their inherent sociality, now exist in a state of pervasive strife: "Even the beasts, devoid of rational will . . . would live in greater security and peace with their own kind than men would, whose race had been produced from one individual for the very purpose of commending concord. For not even lions or dragons have ever waged such wars among themselves as men have." Even where humans achieve a modicum of peace, the threat of conflict is always present. Fueled by the lust for domination, war is, for Augustine, the ultimate expression of the human capacity for injustice.[20]

Closely related to this theme is Augustine's understanding that political community is a remedial good in an unjust world. The most basic human good in the fallen world Augustine describes is a certain minimal order, what he calls an "earthly peace." Although only a faint image of the final rest to come, earthly peace is a measure of order possible in this life. It includes a relative absence of conflict and the attainment of certain basic goods: "God . . . has given to men certain good things appropriate to this life. These are: temporal peace in proportion to the short span of a mortal life, consisting in bodily health and soundness, and the society of one's own kind; and all things necessary for the preservation and recovery of this peace. These latter include those things which are appropriate and accessible to our senses, such as light, speech, breathable air, drinkable water, and whatever the body requires to feed, clothe, shelter, heal or adorn it." The threat or use of coercive force, and not a transformation of the self, secures this minimal order. The temporal law "employs fear as an instrument of coercion, and bends to its own ends the minds of the unhappy people to rule whom it is adapted. So long as they fear to lose these earthly goods they observe in using them a certain moderation suited to maintain in being a city such as can be composed of such men."[21]

The principal means of securing this order is the political community, the commonwealth. Humans are social beings who need each other to survive and flourish. This remains true for Augustine despite the widespread disorder in the world. While the political community is not part of the created order, it is part of God's providential order after the Fall. In a world where conflict rages in the self and often spills over into conflict between persons, the political community and its laws are necessary to preserve a measure of order for the attainment of basic human goods.[22]

Finally, lying behind Augustine's just war understanding is his conviction that the claims of justice reach beyond the city walls. Discussions of just war theory often view the tradition in isolation, as something of an intellectual orphan. In particular, most treatments fail to tie the tradition to a more basic understanding of justice. They mine the tradition for what it has to say about the morality of warfare in a particular case. But rarely do they examine the tradition for what it might tell us about justice, and more specifically what it might tell us about international justice, the area of inquiry addressing justice claims between and beyond states. We should not be surprised, however, to discover that the just war tradition embodies an account of international justice and that the tradition is but one application of this understanding. Behind its well-worn criteria, the tradition tells us something not only about the when and how of using force, but also something about why. At a deep level it tells us why we might fight in this case and not that case, and why we might wield this weapon but not that one. Taking this further step to look behind the tradition and ask what it tells us about justice is important for understanding why the tradition is at home in America.[23]

In no sense does Augustine spell out a theory of justice. His writings are discursive letters, sermons, narrative, and topical essays addressing the issues of the day and written to congregations, bishops, widows, nuns, and political rulers. Augustine is not a systematic thinker. Nonetheless, his understanding of the just war ties to an account of justice scattered piecemeal throughout his writings. Its broad lines underpin the tradition today. This account recognizes a moral order extending beyond the political community and including obligations to other persons merely on the basis of their shared humanity. The moral universe is structured such that persons find themselves subject to the demands of justice prior to the formation of the political community or an agreement among political communities. In so holding, the tradition would reject the claim heralded by the Athenian generals to the citizens of Melos, picked up by Niccolò Machiavelli, and later trumpeted by Thomas Hobbes—a story I turn to in part II—that justice has nothing to say about the relations between one political community and another.

Behind Augustine's conviction that the claims of justice reach beyond the city walls is an understanding that is as much an account of love as it is an account of justice. For Augustine, the two are inseparable. Humans are the kind of beings that love; it is how they relate to God, themselves, others, and every other created thing. While humans make choices about whom and what to love, they do not choose whether to love. This theme pervades Augustine's thought, including his account of justice. As we will see, justice in the self and society is realized only to the extent one rightly loves. Understanding this account is necessary to understanding Augustine's early affirmation of the moral equality of persons.

Augustine, as noted, begins with the classic definition of justice as a proper ordering in which everything receives its due. A person lives justly insofar as she loves properly: "He lives in justice. . . . who has an ordinate love: he neither loves what should not be loved nor fails to love what should be loved." Invoking Jesus' summary of the moral law in the Gospels as the twin love commandments, Augustine says a person loves justly when she loves God and loves her neighbor. Reinterpreting the classic quartet of virtue —temperance, prudence, fortitude, and justice—Augustine describes each as a form of love. Justice, he explains, is that virtue "by which we give each person his due, 'owing no man anything,' but loving all men." As Augustine read the scriptures, God created humans to love God as their highest good and, in so doing, also to love their neighbor. In this love a person renders what each is due in the created order.[24]

The Fall disrupted this state of perfect justice, however. With the disordering of love, the injustice which first took root in the self infects society. For this reason, Augustine rejects Cicero's definition of the commonwealth as a "multitude united in fellowship by common agreement as to what is right and by a community of interest." In a world of disordered loves, where injustice reigns in the fallen self, no political community could ever satisfy this definition. Only in the City of God, the assembly of Christians who now reflect a faint image of the perfect justice to come in the next life, can justice define a people: "In that City, both the individual just man and the community and people of the just live by faith, which works by love: by that love with which a man loves God as God ought to be loved, and his neighbour as himself."[25]

Loving the neighbor includes both positive and negative duties. Augustine quotes the apostle Paul who writes in Romans 13:10 that "love does no harm to its neighbor" and says a person can fail to love his neighbor "either by injuring him or by not helping him when in his power." Moreover, this love reaches body and soul: refraining from injury and helping to provide the basics of life, while also bringing the neighbor to direct his love toward God.[26]

Most important, Augustine understands the command to love the neighbor as a command to love every person. Recounting the story of the Good Samaritan, he concludes, "Every man is to be thought of as a neighbor." Recognizing that limitations of space and time will mean a person acts in love toward those who are near, he nonetheless starts with the claim that "all men are to be loved equally." He excoriates the Priscillianists, who interpreted the scripture to permit lying to foreigners, and insists that neighborly love is blind to political boundaries. Pressing this account of universal love to its outer fringes is Jesus' injunction to love even the enemy: "The claims of friendship . . . are not to be confined within too narrow range, for it embraces all to whom love and kindly affection are due . . . ; yea, it even extends to our enemies, for whom also we are commanded to pray. There is accordingly no one in the whole human family to whom kindly affection is not due by reason of the bond of a common humanity."[27]

Standing behind Augustine's universalism is an affirmation of the moral equality of persons. He describes a natural sociability on the basis of shared humanity. Augustine makes this point on repeated occasions by emphasizing that, unlike other animals, God formed the human race from one person. "God therefore created only one single man . . . that, by this means, the unity of society and the bond of concord might be commended to him forcefully, mankind being bound together not only by similarity of nature, but by the affection of kinship." From an original unity comes equality. Having created a community of equals, "[God] did not intend that His rational creature, made in His own image, should have lordship over any but irrational creatures: not man over man, but man over the beasts." The appearance of political communities organized by ruler and ruled came only after the Fall.

The clashing of swords fueled by an unbridled lust for domination is the ultimate expression of pride, which "hates a fellowship of equality under God, and wishes to impose its own dominion upon its equals, in place of God's rule." Starting with the classical formulation of justice as rendering to each his due, Augustine's account affirmed what Plato's and Aristotle's could not, committed as they were to a natural human hierarchy: a fundamental moral equality among persons, by which any person is the neighbor due the Christian's love.[28]

Although Augustine never drew the connection himself, his understanding of just war was an application of this account of justice to the nations. His recognition of endemic injustice and his affirmation of political community and its role in providing minimal security explains why war is sometimes necessary; his account of love for the neighbor explains why it is always subject to certain limits. The criteria for a just war, then, identify when soldier or sovereign can use armed force to preserve the minimal order necessary in a fallen world while still loving the neighbor. Woven into the fabric of the tradition from the beginning is an account of justice that extends beyond the city walls, recognizing a moral obligation to every person qua person, as bearers of God's image and equal in God's sight.[29]

On this ground, the tradition rejects the divide between domestic and international politics expressed by the Athenians at Melos. The occasion and conduct of war are always subject to limits. In this moral order, the demands of justice do not originate within political community, but are constitutive of creation and place a claim on human acts. Loving the neighbor is the fitting response to the kinds of beings God created, descending from the one man Adam to remind humankind of that "bond of concord." For Augustine, war is always a tragic reality and a sign of a disordered world. As his description of the relationship between love and justice suggests, however, the Christian soldier or sovereign can love his neighbor in waging a just war: protecting innocent third parties and correcting those who inflict wrongful harm.[30]

Just War as an "Expression of the American Mind"

More than any other reason, the just war tradition came to triumph in America because the moral tradition and the national creed share a cardinal conviction: the moral equality of persons. This core conviction that led Augustine to limit the occasion for war was taken up in the Enlightenment, reimagined, secularized in varying degrees, and employed to construct a nation. For the first time in the history of the modern world, a nation defined itself not by blood and soil; not by a common ancestry, culture, history, or ethnic identity; but by a shared commitment to an idea: the idea that all persons enter the world on the same moral plane and bear rights not derived from the state. From this starting point the revolutionaries founded a nation on a belief that before had only been the subject of intellectual banter and provocative script, rejecting the assumptions of natural or divine hierarchy that had structured political life for most of recorded history. Universal rights among equals—not divine right or natural superiority—was the seminal idea that gave birth to America. The story of the just war tradition in America is part of a larger story about a nation coming to terms with who it claimed to be.

Familiarity with this founding ideal makes it easy for Americans to miss how radical an idea it was in the late eighteenth century. Although the British subjects along the Atlantic seaboard enjoyed more freedom than anyone else in the world at that time, colonial America was a society of embedded hierarchies. Status and rank had more to do with the family into which you were born—and, if you were black, the color of your skin—than anything else. In many ways, society reflected the feudal systems of medieval Europe more than the liberal republics that would soon emerge in the New World. Past revolutions in the mother country had produced a chastened monarch, and the British boasted of their liberties, but the colonists, like their families in England, were still subjects of a king. Church pews were allotted by social rank. Harvard and Yale were exclusive clubs for the sons of gentlemen. Rights in land depended on kinship. Distinguished families controlled much of business and politics. Women were the property of their husband or father. And many white immigrants lived in indentured servitude as the cost of passage across the Atlantic. Most telling, and most notorious, nearly half a million blacks lived as hereditary slaves. In the middle of the seventeenth century nothing united the colonists to question or criticize these inequalities—certainly not as inconsistent with what it meant to be the subject of a king.[31]

The Revolution of 1776 was more than anything else a rejection of this hierarchy and an embrace of the idea that persons are moral equals—even if the implications of this idea were not altogether clear. As Gordon Wood has stated, "Equality was . . . the most radical and most powerful ideological force let loose in the Revolution. Its appeal was far more potent than any of the revolutionaries realized. Once invoked, the idea of equality could not be stopped, and it tore through American society and culture with awesome power. . . . Within decades . . . the United States became the most egalitarian nation in the history of the world." The most powerful statement of equality as a founding ideal was Thomas Jefferson's now-celebrated words in the Preamble to the Declaration of Independence: "We hold these truths to be self-evident, that all men are created equal, that they are endowed by their Creator with certain unalienable Rights, that among these are Life, Liberty and the pursuit of Happiness."[32]

Jefferson did not, with the strike of a pen, ignite in the nation an ardor for equality. Rather, he reflected what was already taking root across the colonies. As he commented several decades later, the purpose of the declaration had not been "to find out new principles, or new arguments, never before thought of, not merely to say things which had never been said before; but to place before mankind the common sense of the subject. . . . Neither aiming at originality of principle or sentiment . . . it was intended to be an expression of the American mind." Between April and July 1776, at least ninety local governments issued declarations of independence, many presaging Jefferson's ode to equality of July 4. Not an afterthought, equality was the engine of revolution.[33]

At the same time, the meaning of Jefferson's creedal affirmation—its importance as the nation's founding document and its implications for the nation's practice—evolved over time. At first the declaration was lauded principally as a statement of independence, not as a declaration of individual rights. As Jefferson later observed, "When forced . . . to resort to arms for redress, an appeal to the tribunal of the world was deemed proper for our justification. This was the object of the Declaration of Independence." It was foremost a revolutionary manifesto, listing grievances against the king and claiming independence. Especially important was the legal standing that followed in the wake of the declaration: a new, independent state, capable of forming alliances and receiving foreign aid, especially from France, which the Americans needed to sever their ties with the Crown. At the same time, the document would steel patriotic fervor for revolution and provide the impetus at home the new republic would need to gain independence as something more than ink on parchment. By and large, the framers affirmed the moral equality of persons for a limited end—political independence. The affirmation of equality meant that political authority was not the bestowal of God or birth. Few revolutionaries recognized the implications that later generations would read into this affirmation. The "self-evident" claim that "all men are created equal" was not the focus of the declaration and did not carry the meaning we celebrate today.[34]

That the founding generation read the declaration differently from the way we do explains in some measure its genesis within a nation of slaveholders, one of whom was the very man who wrote the declaration's lofty affirmation of universal rights. Even then, however, the now-glaring inconsistency did not go unremarked. Patrick Henry, a slaveholder who opposed abolition on practical and federalist grounds, queried whether "it [is] not amazing that at a time when the rights of humanity are defined and understood with precision, in a country, above all others, fond of liberty, that in such a country we find men . . . adopting a principle as repugnant to humanity as it is inconsistent with the Bible, and destructive to liberty?"[35]

In the decade following the end of the Revolution, nothing about the fading memory of the declaration—its task of independence now accomplished —suggested the place it would hold as a defining statement of national identity. Although the story of its resurrection is told elsewhere, starting in the 1790s among the Jeffersonian Republicans and then across partisan lines after the War of 1812, the declaration and especially its preamble emerged as a quintessential statement of the American creed. Marking this transformation was the completion of John Trumbull's celebrated painting of 1818 *The Declaration of Independence,* a twelve-by-eighteen-foot canvas displayed in the rotunda of the Capitol. Jefferson, who was only thirty-three years old when he drafted the declaration, had become a national icon in his later years. The path to Monticello was well trod by pilgrims seeking an audience with the patriot hero, until his death on the fiftieth anniversary of the declaration, July 4, 1826 (Jefferson's corevolutionary John Adams died the same day).[36]

As the Declaration of Independence took center stage in the memory of the nation's founding drama and attention gravitated more and more to the preamble and its affirmation of individual rights among persons created equal, starting in the 1820s one cause after another enlisted the document as a call for America to be true to itself. Workers, farmers, women all invoked Jefferson's words. In 1848, the Women's Rights Convention at Seneca Falls made the outrageous call for women's suffrage and issued a Declaration of Sentiments, written by Elizabeth Cady Stanton: "We hold these truths to be self-evident: that all men and women are created equal; that they are endowed by their Creator with certain inalienable rights; that among these are life, liberty, and the pursuit of happiness." Opponents of slavery lifted up the declaration as a mirror to the nation's hypocrisy. The radical abolitionist William Lloyd Garrison published a letter in the *Boston Courier* for July 9, 1829, decrying the annual readings of the declaration on the Fourth of July as "unmeaning declamations in praise of liberty and equality" and "hypocritical cant about the inalienable rights of man." In his argument in 1841 before the Supreme Court in the case of the *Amistad,* former president John Quincy Adams made his final appeal by gesturing toward a copy of the declaration hanging from a courtroom pillar, calling the justices to consider its higher law. Frederick Douglass pressed the cruel irony before a crowd in Rochester, New York, on July 5, 1852, in an oration entitled "What to the Slave is the Fourth of July?" And more than anyone else, Abraham Lincoln solidified the declaration's affirmation of equality as the foundation of America, a nation "dedicated to the proposition that all men are created equal." In affirming a fundamental equality of persons, the founders "set up a standard maxim for free men which should be familiar to all, and revered by all; constantly looked to, and constantly labored for, and even though never perfectly attained, constantly approximated and thereby constantly spreading and deepening its influence." The declaration had become a moral benchmark for the nation, even though its original signers may have never imagined the power Jefferson's words would unleash.[37]

In the very act of defining the particular—a new nation no longer under scepter and crown—the founders had invoked the universal. The idea which gave birth to the American nation declared all people moral equals, prior to any political attachments and simply on the basis of a shared humanity. And so it was inevitable that as Americans discussed, debated, and fractured over the domestic implications of this claim, at some point the nation would face its international implications as well. No encounter with the outside world would press this question more acutely than the prospect of war. What does a people founded on the idea of equality owe other peoples—their moral equals, "endowed by their Creator with certain unalienable Rights"—before raising the sword?

The occasion for considering this question came early, in the republic's dealings with Indians as an exploding American population hungered for land. The person to raise the question most forcefully was Henry Knox. A young Boston bookseller, Knox earned a lifetime of respect from General George Washington when, against all odds and in the middle of winter, he led his men as they slogged three hundred miles with fifty-nine cannon in tow from Fort Ticonderoga in upstate New York to the outskirts of Boston. The artillery played a decisive role in causing the Crown's retreat. When Washington became president, he appointed Knox his first secretary of war. One of Knox's primary responsibilities was to guide the nation's policy toward the Indians, most of whom had sided with the British during the War for Independence. As Knox would later write, he firmly believed "the independent nations and tribes of Indians ought to be considered as foreign nations, not as the subjects of any particular states." After the war but before Knox took office, U.S. policy toward the Indians had been to show no mercy and force them to yield their land. Indian resistance, the specter of war for a new nation ill-equipped to respond, and—as Knox would press—the moral misgivings about the policy, all worked to undermine it.[38]

In a report of June 15, 1789, transmitted to Congress by President Washington, Knox charted a new course. The Indians had a right to the land they possessed that "cannot be taken from them unless by their free consent, or by the right of conquest in case of a just war. To dispossess them on any other principle, would be a gross violation of the fundamental laws of nature." The United States must purchase the land. Most important, he rejected the use of force to seize Indian lands. Under such a policy, "an inquiry would arise, whether, under the existing circumstances of affairs, the

United States have a clear right, consistently with the principles of justice and the laws of nature, to proceed to the destruction or expulsion of the savages." He went on to say, "It is presumable that a nation solicitous of establishing its character on the broad basis of justice, would not only hesitate at, but reject every proposition to benefit itself, by the injury of any neighboring community, however contemptible and weak it might be, either with respect to its manners or power." From the start, the nation had to reckon with the implications of its creed, not only at home but abroad as well.[39]

I will not narrate the transmission and evolution of just war tradition in America, nor do I press a claim about the nation's fidelity to it. Rather, my claim is simply that from the beginning there was a deep affinity between the moral tradition and the national creed in their shared affirmation of a fundamental moral equality among all persons, possessing a worth not bestowed by the state but held on the basis of shared humanity. As we will see, a commitment to the moral equality of persons has not always produced a normative account of relations between states that places limits on the use of force. In many ways the font of contemporary liberal thought, Immanuel Kant possessed an illiberal view of the relation between states, at least in his nonideal theory. Nonetheless, considerable tension arises in such accounts that affirm the prepolitical moral equality of persons but hold a normative account of the relation between states as an all-out state of war. It is not surprising that the questions Knox asked echo today in a nation that still embraces its creed.

As other scholars have recognized and as the debate in American society over the use of preventive force suggests, the underlying concerns Knox expressed in 1789 have become particularly acute in recent decades. John Gaddis describes how "the line between what was allowed overseas and what was permitted at home disappeared altogether" as the Cold War progressed. Leslie Gelb makes a similar observation: "Something quite important has happened in American foreign policymaking with little notice or digestion of its meaning. Morality, values, ethics, universal principles—the whole panoply of ideals in international affairs that were once almost the exclusive domain of preachers and scholars—have taken root in the hearts, or at least the minds, of the American foreign policy community." Justice has a place at the table.[40]

The changes Gaddis and Gelb describe are closely related to what Walzer has termed the triumph of the just war tradition in America. I have no stake in when this shift occurred—if shift is even the right word to describe what happened. But this triumph is not surprising. The moral tradition and the national creed share fundamental commitments that in time made the tradition a fitting aspiration for when and how America would use force.

The American consensus in the last half of the twentieth century that preventive war is "against our traditions," at least under the circumstances then encountered, was a reflection of the hold the moral tradition has on the American people. The nation's affirmation of the moral equality of all persons render every exercise of American military force a question not merely of expedience, but of ethics as well. Principle, not merely prudence, is at work. Knox recognized early on this dimension of America's place in the world, and no president can ignore it today. The moral tradition and the criteria it specifies for when force is justified tell us the moral questions we must ask: do we have just cause? is this a last resort?, and so on. If the just war tradition is at home in America and bears a deep affinity to the nation's moral core, achieving legitimacy for any expanded notion of preventive force will have to satisfy the moral tradition. Can it?

PART TWO

TRADITION

4

Early Modern Rivals

THE THREAT OF GLOBAL TERRORISM IS new, but moral reflection on the question of striking first is not. Beginning in the sixteenth century a distinct conversation on the use of anticipatory force emerged within the just war tradition. Although recognizing its perils, the moral tradition came to accept a limited right to strike first.

In the last chapter I explored how the just war tradition has a certain hold on Americans: it is a fitting account of the legitimacy and limits of war for a nation dedicated to the proposition that all are created equal. That is not to say the tradition as it looked at any one point in time binds us. Sensibilities change, and we can point to new circumstances that modify or perhaps even undermine the rules, even if we continue to affirm underlying principles in some measure. But we cannot ignore the moral tradition. Moreover, as we will see, the tradition profoundly shaped Webster's Rule. By understanding the larger moral framework of which the imminence rule was a part, we are a step closer to finding a principled way forward: a path that preserves underlying moral commitments that the United States and others have affirmed in recognizing Webster's Rule since at least the end of World War II.

What has the moral tradition said about anticipatory force? I focus here on key moments—a short story, where I might have written a novel. And I limit my attention to the ideas that emerged, although they developed in tandem with geopolitical movements and events I can only mention. I also

99

give attention to a consistent, countervailing voice that developed alongside the moral tradition. This rival tradition on the use of anticipatory force—what I will refer to as the just fear tradition—had roots in political realism and granted broad permission to strike first. Attention to the just fear tradition is important because the moral tradition on the just war evolved in direct conversation with it. In some moments, the lines even blurred. Moreover, once the moral outcast, the rival tradition would achieve increasing ascendancy and by the nineteenth century would become the accepted theory explaining the modern system of sovereign states and the role of war within that system.[1]

Vitoria's Doubt

Although the basic framework of the moral tradition on the just war was formed in the Middle Ages, not until the early modern period did proponents of the tradition give sustained attention to the issue of anticipatory force. Specifically, they extended the tradition in two ways. First, they developed various tests to determine when just cause, understood as an injury, arises absent an actual attack. Second, they refined the principle of necessity, a separate and subsequent requirement of exhausting reasonable alternatives that took on special importance in this context. Together, these norms carved out a limited space for anticipatory force.

Fleeting references to the use of anticipatory force appeared early in the tradition. In his treatise *On Free Will,* Augustine makes reference to "the law that allows any man or woman to slay, if he can, any one who comes with intent to ravish, *even before the crime has been committed.*" In *City of God,* he denounced Rome's decision to wage the Third Punic War against the Carthaginians, who, he concluded, did not pose a sufficiently present threat. He praises Scipio Nasica, a Roman statesman who opposed going to war merely on the fear of a revived Carthage. And a gloss on Gratian's *Decretum* declared, "If it is directed at persons, then force may be resisted before it strikes."[2]

A distinct conversation, however, began in sixteenth-century Spain among a few theologians. Their thinking about war was shaped, more than anything else, by a troubled conscience over Spanish dealings in the New World:

namely, the conquest and enslavement of Indians in the Americas. These theologians sparked a revival of interest in the thought of Thomas Aquinas known as neo-Thomism, and their retrieval of Aquinas ensured the transmission of just war tradition into the modern era. Among them was Francisco de Vitoria (ca. 1485–1546), a monk who published nothing during his lifetime but lived at the vanguard of this intellectual movement. Vitoria's ideas proved enormously influential.[3]

Vitoria entered the Dominican order in 1504 and studied at the University of Paris, where he stayed from 1509 to 1523. His mentor was Pierre Crockaert (1450–1514), a scholastic theologian at the university. Although Crockaert lectured early on from Peter Lombard's *Sentences,* the traditional university text of the time, he eventually broke from convention and began teaching from Aquinas's *Summa Theologica,* which for the past two centuries had been attacked in part for its assimilation of Aristotle's ideas into Christian theology. With the aid of Vitoria, Crockaert published a commentary on the last part of the *Summa.* When Vitoria returned to Spain he was a committed Thomist and eventually took a prestigious chair of theology at the University of Salamanca.

Vitoria delivered yearly lectures on Aquinas's *Summa* and discourses on various issues of the day, the most pressing of which was the Spanish wars in the Americas. After learning about the massacre at Cajamarca, Peru, in which Spanish conquistadors under Francisco Pizarro killed thousands of Inca Indians, Vitoria wrote to his spiritual master, "As for the case of Peru, I must tell you, after a lifetime of studies and long experience, that no business shocks me or embarrasses me more than the corrupt profits and affairs of the Indies. Their very mention freezes the blood in my veins." Although Vitoria did not take up the question of anticipatory force while directly addressing the Spanish conquest, the conquest provided the practical context for everything Vitoria said on the subject.[4]

The Crown had justified its policies in the New World on the basis of the "Bulls of Donation," a decree Pope Alexander VI issued in 1493 granting to Ferdinand and Isabella possession of lands they might discover in the Atlantic that were not already inhabited by Christians. In his discourse *On the American Indians,* delivered in 1539 and continued a few months later in *On the Law of War,* Vitoria reaffirmed his rejection of the papal claim to temporal authority upon which the Crown's justification rested. He then proceeded to refute one by one the other arguments that circulated in defense of Spain's actions: the Indians were sinners, they were non-Christians, they were mad, their cultural inferiority made them slaves by nature, and other rationales. Although Vitoria countenanced the possibility of a just war against the Indians—for example, to save innocent persons from death by human sacrifice—he did not conclude that the Crown had waged such a war. Vitoria recognized practical problems with a Spanish withdrawal at this time, but the clear implication of his discourse was that Spain's policies in the Americas rested on very shaky legal and moral grounds.[5]

Vitoria crafted his account of a just war on a moral theory that, along its main lines, bears the clear marks of Aquinas. He develops many of his ideas, in fact, through commentary on the *Summa*. Although Aquinas's moral theory differs from Augustine's in important ways—and Vitoria does not simply parrot Aquinas—mapping these departures is not necessary here. At the center of the Thomistic account is the notion of a moral universe governed by laws that flow, at least in part, from God's reason. An eternal law structures the universe, giving it order and harmony. This law directs everything in the cosmos, including humans, toward some end. That portion of the eternal law accessible to humans, normative for action, and leading them to their moral end is the natural law. Rooted in God's reason, natural law is unchanging and comprehensible, imprinted on the human mind. The precepts of the law are revealed in natural human inclinations toward a good. These include self-preservation, an inclination shared with all substances; procreation, an inclination shared with all animals; and sociability and a desire for divine truth, the rational inclination unique to humans and pointing them toward living with others and knowing God. Natural law follows from these three basic inclinations. Human laws are valid insofar as they are derived from or not in conflict with the natural law. Human actions in the sphere of the political are never outside this moral order.[6]

The commonwealth is part of this order. Humans did not always live in political communities, but associations emerged to provide for human needs and aid persons in the pursuit of their moral ends: "Since, therefore, human partnerships arose for the purpose of helping to bear each other's burdens, amongst all these partnerships a civil partnership is the one which most aptly fulfils men's needs. It follows that the city is . . . the most natural community, the one which is most conformable to nature." The commonwealth can lawfully use force against another person or political community, but only in the case of some injury. Citing Augustine and Aquinas, Vitoria concludes, "The sole and only just cause for waging war is when harm has been inflicted. . . . We may not use the sword against those who have not harmed us; to kill the innocent is prohibited by natural law." But where there is sufficient injury and the other criteria of just war doctrine are satisfied, a commonwealth can and sometimes must use force.[7]

When Vitoria raised the question of anticipatory force, it was not obvious what he would conclude. The perduring requirement in the tradition that just cause always requires some injury might well be taken to rule it out altogether. But Vitoria carefully employs just war norms to posit a limited case for using force first. From this point forward, all the figures in the moral tradition take up the issue and turn to Vitoria as their starting point. His primary statement appears in his commentary on Aquinas's *Summa* II.II.64.7, "whether it is lawful to kill someone in self-defence." In typical neoscholastic fashion and commenting on the *Summa*, Vitoria summarizes Aquinas's answer to the particular issue and then addresses one or more so-called doubts raised by the passage. These doubts are associated with particular individuals who have criticized Aquinas or sometimes are questions Vitoria himself raises. After stating the doubt, he anticipates possible answers before reaching his own.[8]

In the course of commenting on Aquinas's treatment of self-defense, Vitoria asks, "If the Doctor's conclusion is true, i.e., that it is lawful to kill an attacking enemy, would it be lawful to *anticipate* him and seek to intercept and kill him?" The root word consistently used in the text for anticipatory force is *praevenio*, which means "to come before," "prevent," or "anticipate." He then gives this example: "If I were a poor man, and did not have the wherewithal to hire guards and allies, and my enemy were a noble or rich man, and I know that he is recruiting guards and allies to kill me, then the question is whether it is lawful for me to preemptively kill him, 'to kill him before he kills me.'" In other words, can a person use force first if circumstances are such that failure to do so would deny the individual an effective defense?[9]

This doubt primarily concerns the tradition's requirement of just cause. Recall that for Augustine, just cause has two related aspects: the precipitating event (an injury) and the legitimate end or aim in using force (restitution of goods taken, punishment, or self-defense). The doubt Vitoria raises is perplexing because it satisfies one aspect of just cause but seemingly not the other. In other words, a person in the situation Vitoria describes acts toward the legitimate end of self-defense—in the example a failure to respond at some point prior to the attack would otherwise effectively preclude an effective defense—but the precipitating event, that is, some sufficient injury in the form of an actual physical attack, has not yet occurred. Because the injury conceptually precedes and determines the legitimate end, the situation described is especially problematic. At the same time, the lawfulness of using force toward the end of self-defense is a basic and unquestioned precept of natural law. While Augustine and Ambrose had forbidden Christians to kill in self-defense, medieval jurists and theologians, including Aquinas, had rejected this view. As Vitoria concluded, "By natural law it was always lawful, among all nations, 'to repel force with force.' But I may not be able to defend myself in any other way than by killing my attacker."[10]

Responding to this dilemma, Vitoria carves out a limited space for the use of anticipatory force with two moves. His first move is to consider when just cause might arise absent an actual attack. He does this by rethinking the concept of injury as the precipitating event. The tradition had described this concept in its most present sense: in the case of physical attack as an actual harm—a wound already inflicted or a blow being struck. Because Vitoria recognizes in the hypothetical a case in which a person would be harmed with no effective means to defend himself, he considers the nuances of the concept of injury. To strike first in this scenario "is not to attack, but rather it is to defend oneself. Indeed, the other is attacking when he is preparing himself to kill him." Later writers will refer to an "incomplete injury," but Vitoria's response already implies this notion. Among the two aspects of just cause, the precipitating event is conceptually prior to the legitimate end insofar as the injury gives rise to the end. Nonetheless, here Vitoria looks to the end of self-defense to shape his concept of injury.[11]

Accepting that an injury can arise prior to an actual attack, Vitoria goes on to describe a standard for when this situation might occur. Extending the example he mentions earlier, Vitoria says a person would be justified in using force if, "supposing that he has journeyed to another city, he knows with scientific certitude that his enemy will seek him and kill him." This standard requires what I will call certain intent: the potential victim knows that the plotting assailant intends to do him lethal harm. Moreover, this standard would also seem to require some knowledge that the enemy has sufficient means to carry out his intent. Although the standard is vague, later writers in the tradition will build upon it to establish a concrete list of tests the potential victim must satisfy before striking first.[12]

Vitoria's second move in constructing a limited space for the use of preemptive force is to employ the principle of necessity. He conceives of necessity in terms of last resort, a requirement that the potential victim exhaust all reasonable alternatives prior to using force. The man Vitoria describes has "no other way" to defend himself. In developing his answer, he explains, "If the man has some [other] means to defend his life, such as flight to another city where, without a great loss of his property, he would be safe from his enemy, he should do that and not preemptively strike his enemy. For so to strike him would *not be a means necessary to defend himself* 'within the bounds of blameless defense,' since he could defend his life in another way." He repeats this admonition several times in the course of his concise treatment of the issue. Although this principle of necessity has special importance in the context of anticipatory force, it is also a more general principle Vitoria states elsewhere. For example, in discussing the use of force against Indians in the Americas who might violate rights given the Spanish by natural law (for example, the right to trade with the native inhabitants), Vitoria considers several alternatives the Spanish must pursue before armed force becomes a last resort. Having created a limited space for anticipatory force, Vitoria worries aloud that such a right might open Pandora's box, giving "a great excuse to men everywhere to kill other men." Therefore he cautions, "It certainly is dangerous to speak so. . . . Thus it is necessary to speak with moderation and caution lest scandals arise, and therefore, this should in nowise be preached."[13]

While Vitoria develops this account of anticipatory force in terms of individual self-defense, it seems he meant it to apply to the commonwealth as well. A marginal gloss on Vitoria's commentary, states, "It is lawful for the emperor for the defense of the republic to get a start on war, if he knows that another hostile king is conspiring against his kingdom. Therefore, in the same way, it is lawful for me to get a start on my enemy." The analogy here works in the opposite direction: from the political community to the individual. At least one other passage suggests this gloss may represent Vitoria's own thinking. In *On the Law of War,* a continuation of his lecture about the situation in the Americas, Vitoria alludes to the possibility of using force first in some cases. Answering the question whether a Christian can wage war, Vitoria states in his final proof for the affirmative that many "good men" "have not only protected their homes and property with defensive war, but also punished the injuries committed *or even planned* against them by their enemies." Whether or not the same standard applies in the case of states, Vitoria does not clearly answer, and the standard in both passages is vague. The marginal gloss seems to equate the two acts. But Vitoria often grants more freedom to states than to individuals acting in self-defense because of structural differences between the two and because more is at stake in the political community.[14]

Vitoria extends the just war tradition to the question of anticipatory force. Although later proponents of the tradition rework the moral theory lying behind it and explore the nuances of the standard Vitoria develops, from this point forward his account becomes the benchmark for what the tradition has to say about the issue.

The Just Fear Rival

At the same time Vitoria and other neo-Thomists were extending the just war tradition to address issues of conquest in the New World, the Lutheran heresy, and the question of striking first, a rival tradition holding a permissive account of war was taking root. Like the just war tradition, this account extends back into classical times. Its flourishing among humanist writers in Renaissance Europe drew from a revival of interest in the writings of Tacitus, a Roman historian often associated with a prudential politics. The term *raison d'état* (or, among Italian humanists, *ragion di stato*) appeared in the middle of the sixteenth century. By the time of the publication of Giovanni Botero's *The Reason of State* (1589), it was a widely discussed conception of statecraft. Speaking of his travels to the courts of European rulers, Botero remarks, "I have been greatly astonished to find Reason of State a constant subject of discussion and to hear the opinions of Machiavelli and . . . Tacitus frequently quoted." Among the Italian humanists, the doctrine primarily developed as a practical discourse on statecraft rather than carefully crafted theory. The task of devising a theory fell to Hobbes, who provided the rival tradition with a theoretical foundation that would have influence into the present.[15]

The most important representative of this account of war in the early modern period is Niccolò Machiavelli (1469–1527). No account can overlook him, the tradition's most notorious proponent (with Hobbes registering a close second) and the person who put the tradition's claims in their starkest form. Although never using the term *reason of state,* he came to personify its most potent expression. Machiavelli served in the government of the Florentine republic from 1498 until 1512. When the government collapsed and the exiled Medici family regained its position of power, Florence took on the character of most northern Italian city-states at that time, governed by a single, strong ruler. Having lost his position in government, Machiavelli wrote *The Prince* in 1513, hoping to gain approval of the new ruler and a position of influence. In writing *The Prince,* Machiavelli joined a long tradition of advice books going back to at least the thirteenth century and meant to impart worldly wisdom to the ruler. At the same time, the work was a repudiation of the kind of advice given by previous humanist writers. Earlier humanists had often written for the citizens of the republic and championed the virtues necessary to sustain liberty. Since most of the early republics had fallen to strong rulers, Machiavelli was not the first to address the prince rather than the citizenry. The book was unique, however, in rejecting the medley of classical and Christian virtues his predecessors had commended to the noble ruler.[16]

Machiavelli does not hedge his starting premise: "Many have imagined republics and principalities that have never been seen or known to exist. However, how men live is so different from how they should live that a ruler who does not do what is generally done, but persists in doing what ought to be done, will undermine his power rather than maintain it. . . . Therefore, a ruler who wishes to maintain his power must be prepared to act immorally when this becomes necessary." Supporting this premise is a deeply pessimistic view of human nature: "For this may be said of men generally: they are ungrateful, fickle, feigners and dissemblers, avoiders of danger, eager for gain." Pursuing the traditional virtues, Machiavelli argues, will only sap the sovereign's strength. But he does not outright reject them. The prince will want to retain an appearance of these virtues when possible: "One must be sufficiently prudent to know how to avoid becoming notorious for those vices that would destroy one's power. . . . Yet one should not be troubled about becoming notorious for those vices without which it is difficult to preserve one's power."[17]

Machiavelli joins to this prudential politics broad permission—even commendation—to use force prior to being attacked: "Wise rulers . . . have to deal not only with existing troubles, but with troubles that are likely to develop, and have to use every means to overcome them. For if the first signs of troubles are perceived, it is easy to find a solution; but if one lets trouble develop, the medicine will be too late." He praises the Romans, who knew that "wars cannot really be avoided but are merely postponed" and therefore elected to start them at a time and place of their choosing.[18]

Although Machiavelli does not directly target the just war tradition, *The Prince* is a clear repudiation of it. He confesses that his "advice would not be sound if all men were upright," but because they are treacherous the prince has no other choice. His conclusions are brazenly prudential: rather than constructing a new morality, the impression is left that the ruler often operates outside of morality.[19]

As the writings of Alberico Gentili (1552–1608) show, even those who employed the language and forms of the just war tradition sometimes reached similar conclusions. Born on the Italian peninsula, Gentili trained for law at the University of Perugia, where he immersed himself in humanist sources and methods. His family's Protestantism, however, necessitated a hasty escape in 1581 and he eventually settled in England. Gentili became Regius Professor of Civil Law at Oxford, a chair he kept for almost twenty years. His most important work was *On the Law of War*, published in 1588.

Throughout this work, Gentili employs the basic concepts of the just war tradition as they were described in his day. He subscribes to natural law as the basis for international norms: "We hold the firm belief that questions of war ought to be settled in accordance with the law of nations, which is the law of nature." This law of nature is a "portion of the divine law," implanted within all rational beings. Although sometimes dim, obscured by human weakness, it is nonetheless accessible to those who faithfully seek it. Rightly discerning this law is crucial, as it defines the basis of just relations in the international realm.[20]

Gentili also follows the just war tradition in identifying the circumstances under which a state can justly go to war. Like the theologians before him, he raises the central question of "whether wars can be just" and places his own thought in the company of Augustine and his heirs. War always requires just cause: "It is brutal to proceed to murder and devastation when one has suffered no injury." He cites Augustine in support and chides the barbarian in Tacitus's *Annals* who proclaims that "might makes right." The principle of necessity understood as last resort appears throughout the text. And he proposes the political community should first seek to settle its disputes through an arbiter before using armed force.[21]

Yet in two ways Gentili shows himself more the heir of Machiavelli than Augustine. First, he rejects the long-standing belief within the just war tradition that a war cannot finally be just on both sides. In *On the Indians,* Vitoria had said that a party to the conflict might fight out of "invincible ignorance," but finally justice fell only on one side. Vitoria and others extended this logic to rule out wars for the sake of empire, since in such wars one side would fight a just war to extend its territory and the other side would fight a just war of defense. Gentili gestures toward a "purest and truest form of justice," perhaps in the mind of God, but concludes, "We aim at justice as it appears from man's standpoint." In terms of human justice, he concludes that in nearly all wars both sides fight justly. The practical effect of this move is to deny justice a role in limiting the occasion and conduct of war.[22]

Second, and most important for my purposes, Gentili adopts a broadly permissive account of anticipatory force. He raises the issue in a chapter entitled "Defense on the Grounds of Expediency." He explains: "I call it a defence dictated by expediency, when we make war through fear that we may ourselves be attacked. No one is more quickly laid low than one who has no fear, and a sense of security is the most common cause of disaster. . . . Therefore . . . those who desire to live without danger ought to meet impending evils and anticipate them." Gentili cites numerous authorities in support of his position. Noticeably absent are any sources from the moral tradition on the just war. Rather he turns almost exclusively to classical sources. He presents his permissive account as common sense, citing several proverbs: "'Meet a disease half-way', 'check it at the start, otherwise remedies are prepared too late.' 'Neglected fires always spread,'" and so on.[23]

The standard Gentili offers is broadly permissive: the attacking state must have a "just fear." In the case of individual self-defense, he states, "Now a just fear is defined as the fear of a greater evil, a fear which might properly be felt even by a man of great courage." This standard, however, is too stringent for the political community. Rather, he says that the state can justly use force "even when it may happen that no damage is done; even though there is no great and clear cause for fear, and even if there really is no danger, but only a legitimate cause for fear."[24]

Gentili describes this allowance as a necessary tool for maintaining a "balance of power" within Europe. "Since there is more than one justifiable cause for fear, and no general rule can be laid down with regard to the matter, we will merely say this . . . namely, that we should oppose powerful and ambitious chiefs." The modern origin of the balance of power concept traces to the city-states of Renaissance Italy, and Gentili is one of the earliest theorists to apply the concept to the emerging European state system. He praises the policies of Lorenzo de' Medici, who sought to align the other city-states against the threatening power of Venice, and calls for the same action in his day against the ascendant Hapsburg dynasty in Spain. He concludes the chapter with a sweeping allowance for states to strike first: "A defence is just which anticipates dangers that are already meditated and prepared, and also those which are not meditated, but are probable and possible."[25]

Although Gentili invokes the language and forms of the just war tradition, he departs from it in significant ways. He does not deny a just moral order from a divine perspective, but such is of no use in governing relations among states. The practical effect of his position is to shelter from moral scrutiny the decisions sovereign rulers make about going to war. In a candid moment, Gentili signals his debt to Machiavelli. Acknowledging Machiavelli's now-widespread notoriety, Gentili concludes, "If I give a just estimate of his purpose in writing, and if I choose to reinforce his words by a sounder interpretation, I do not see why I can not free from such charges the reputation of this man who has now passed away. . . . There is no doubt that Machiavelli is a man who deserves our commiseration in the highest degree."[26]

Gentili almost certainly shared his ideas on anticipation with Francis Bacon (1561–1626), his contemporary and friend. In Bacon's discourse *Considerations Touching a War with Spain* (1624), he urged England to make war with Spain, which was growing in power. He invoked the same standard, saying, "Wars preventive upon just fears are true defensives," and urged such a war to maintain a balance of power in Europe. Bacon openly attacked the neo-Thomists as "fitter to guide penknives than swords." The object of his attack was the just war tradition's insistence that every use of force follow a sufficient injury: "A just fear is justified for a cause of an invasive war, though the same fear proceed not from the fault of the foreign state to be assailed."[27]

By the close of the sixteenth century, two rival traditions with opposing views on the legitimacy of anticipatory force were firmly in place. Vitoria and his heirs ensured the transmission of just war tradition into the modern period. At the same time, Machiavelli, Gentili, and others espoused a broadly permissive account, one allowing for preventive force on the mere basis of fear. As Gentili's invocation of just war language suggests, moreover, the two traditions would not proceed untouched by each other. Hugo Grotius is perhaps the best example of the intertwining of the rival views: he extends Vitoria's account of anticipatory force but at the same time unwittingly prepares the path Hobbes would tread.

5

Anticipation in a State of Nature

THE RIVALRY BETWEEN THE TWO TRADITIONS continued into the seventeenth century in the writings of Hugo Grotius and Thomas Hobbes. Both likened states to individuals living outside the bounds of civil government, in what Hobbes would call a "state of nature." Starting with the crude test Vitoria offered, Grotius crafted a nuanced, multifactor standard for when a state can strike first. At the same time, he grounded his understanding of force and its limits on a moral theory that only shakily supported the account of justice that the moral tradition had always required. The lines between the two traditions were not always tidy. Hobbes exploited this weakness to conclude that striking first out of fear is not only the permissible, but the rational response of states not bound to an international Leviathan. His ideas would prove remarkably enduring, appearing in some form even today.

Grotius and the Domestic (Dis)Analogy

Hugo Grotius (1583–1645) was a native of the Netherlands. A child prodigy, he entered the University of Leyden at the age of eleven and received a humanist education there, studying philology, history, theology, and law. He went on to earn a doctorate of law at the University of Orleans, France. His religious convictions were Protestant and perhaps closest to Dutch Arminianism, and he was a strong advocate of tolerance for religious minorities. While serving in public office, he was accused of treason by his political enemies and locked up in Loevestein Castle under life sentence. After two years in confinement, however, he escaped to France in a book chest, aided by his wife and a house servant. Grotius devoted his first three years in Paris to writing *On the Law of War and Peace,* which he published in 1625. He left France for a few years but eventually returned to Paris as ambassador to Sweden. This office placed Grotius in a critical position to negotiate an agreement by which France entered the final stage of the Thirty Years War as an ally of Sweden. He held this position until his death in 1645: having survived a shipwreck on the Baltic Sea, he succumbed to exhaustion a few days later. The Peace of Westphalia, which ended the war and established the modern state system, was only three years away.

In offering his account of anticipatory force, Grotius enters the conversation sparked by Vitoria. Grotius was well versed in the writings of the neo-Thomists, especially those of Vitoria, whom he often references. In *On the Law of War and Peace* and an earlier work, *On the Indies,* he cites Vitoria 126 times. Moreover, Grotius develops his account as an express rejection of the just fear tradition. Citing Gentili in a marginal note, he concludes, "Quite untenable is the position, which has been maintained by some, that according to the law of nations it is right to take up arms in order to weaken a growing power which, if it becomes too great, may be a source of danger."[1]

As in his treatment of war generally, Grotius approaches the subject of anticipatory force by first examining the rules governing individuals and then considering those governing states. This approach is often referred to as the domestic analogy and rests on the assumption that the relationship between individuals within a domestic political system bears some resemblance to the relationship between states within an international order. But as Grotius demonstrates, some of the most important claims about when states can strike first arise when pressing the differences between the domestic and international spheres.[2]

Starting with individuals under a common power, Grotius lays down this general rule governing anticipatory force: "War in defence of life is permissible only when the danger is immediate and certain, not when it is merely assumed." He further explains, "The danger, again, must be immediate and imminent in point of time. I admit, to be sure, that if the assailant seizes weapons in such a way that his intent to kill is manifest the crime can be forestalled." Like Vitoria, Grotius thinks of an injury as beginning earlier than the actual blow. When he extends this discussion to states, he refers to "a wrong action commenced but not yet carried through." Both Vitoria and Grotius describe such a wrong by looking to qualities objectively rooted in the nature of the threat, not to the subjective state of the threatened individual.[3]

Following Vitoria, Grotius includes in his standard both certainty of intent and sufficient means. The assailant here "seizes weapons" capable of inflicting a lethal blow, an action which makes clear an "intent to kill." Added to the list, however, is a requirement that the threat be imminent. As I discussed in chapter 1, this requirement concerns the temporal proximity of the attack. The meaning of *imminent* has some flexibility, and a footnote Grotius includes referencing an incident in Thucydides' *History of the Peloponnesian War* suggests he may have a somewhat broader meaning for the term than Webster's "necessity of self-defense, instant, overwhelming, leaving no choice of means, and no moment for deliberation." But this debate goes on within certain limits.[4]

Grotius defines these limits by contrasting a justified first strike with cases in which the threat is not imminent: "Further, if a man is not planning an immediate attack, but it has been ascertained that he has formed a plot, or is preparing an ambuscade, or that he is putting poison in our way, or that he is making ready a false accusation and false evidence, and is corrupting the judicial procedure, I maintain that he cannot lawfully be killed, either if the danger can in any other way be avoided, or if it is not altogether certain that the danger cannot be otherwise avoided. Generally, in fact, the delay that will intervene affords opportunity to apply many remedies, to take advantage of many accidental occurrences." I will return to this important passage in part III but note for now that the enemy has engaged in some kind of active preparation to commit the act but has not yet executed the plan such that the threat is imminent.[5]

The difference between the two scenarios is one of necessity, or what the tradition sometimes referred to as last resort. As we have seen, in addition to certainty of intent and sufficient means, Vitoria added necessity as a requirement for striking first. The victim must have "no other way" to defend himself. Grotius agrees: "If an attack by violence is made on one's person, endangering life, *and no other way of escape is open,* under such circumstances [private] war is permissible, even though it involve the slaying of the assailant." But Grotius emphasizes that in almost all cases striking the first blow is necessary only in the case of an imminent attack. His mention of "theologians . . . who would extend their indulgence somewhat further" is perhaps in part a gesture toward Vitoria, who did not limit last resort to cases in which the threat is imminent. Absent an imminent threat, Grotius is confident that individuals generally have other means to avoid the impending harm. The most obvious reason is that persons have recourse to civil government.[6]

The requirement of imminence as a prerequisite for anticipatory force in the context of individual self-defense was not Grotius's achievement. Roman law permitted an individual to respond to an armed attack *in continenti,* that is, immediately or without delay. A forceful response to an attack after some time had elapsed, *ex intervallo,* was unlawful. These rules are illustrated in the following passage from the *Digest,* part of the *Corpus Iuris Civilis,* a compendium of Roman law assembled for Emperor Justinian in the sixth century: "Therefore, we can repel by the use of arms anyone who comes armed, but this must be done immediately, and not after some time has elapsed [*non ex intervallo*]; if we remember that not only resistance can be offered to forcible ejection, but also that he who has been ejected can himself expel the intruder, if he does so at once [*ex continenti*], and not after any time has passed."[7]

This requirement that a person use force *in continenti* describes the character of the defensive response, whereas Grotius and Webster use the term *imminence* to describe the threatened attack. Most often this requirement ruled out uses of force that come too late after the blow is struck, drawing a line between self-defense and vengeance. Debates persisted as to how long was too long, but the focus was typically on the character of the defensive response. In its most basic sense, however, the concept concerned the amount of time between the attack and the response. Just as a purportedly defensive response might come too late relative to the original blow, a use of force in anticipation of a coming attack might also come too early. Some uses of the term seem to have employed *in continenti* in this context.

With the rediscovery of Roman law in the eleventh century, jurists commenting on the *Corpus Iuris Civilis* transmitted this requirement into the Middle Ages. For example, the requirement of immediacy appears in a gloss on Gratian's *Decretum:* "If it is directed at persons, then force may be resisted before it strikes. But certain people have contended that no one ought to resist force before it strikes; yet it is permitted to kill an ambusher and anyone who tries to kill you. . . . If, however, someone returns violence, this should be done with the assumption that it is for defense, rather than for revenge . . . ; otherwise, if the attacker does not intend to strike once more and the other person still returns force, this should be seen as revenge rather than resistance to force. And this is what I understand when it is said that force may be resisted 'on the spot' [*in continenti*]."[8]

Vitoria invokes this concept as well. His discussion of anticipatory force in his commentary on Aquinas never mentioned a requirement of imminence or even addressed the temporal proximity of an attack, although his requirement of last resort might often demand the attack be imminent. But he does mention the requirement of *in continenti* elsewhere in his writings. In *On the Law of War,* continuing his discourse on Spanish dealings with the American Indians, Vitoria describes individual self-defense as "private war." He concludes, "Self-defence must be a response to immediate danger, made in the heat of the moment or *incontinent* as the lawyers say. Once the immediate necessity of defence has passed, there is no longer any license for war." Although possibly in tension with his account of anticipatory self-defense in his commentary on Aquinas, where Vitoria did not require imminence, the context of this passage suggests Vitoria is focused on the amount of time that can elapse *after* an attack; he is not here considering the use of anticipatory force. When Grotius required an imminent threat he was drawing on this lengthy heritage.[9]

Grotius next moves to a discussion of states. While drawing parallels between the two contexts, he gives allowance for appropriate variances: "What has been said by us up to this point, concerning the right to defend oneself and one's possessions, applies chiefly, of course, to private war; yet it may be made applicable also to public war, if the differences in conditions be taken into account." The differences Grotius has in mind are two. First, an individual retains her right of self-defense only as long as she lacks protection from civil government. Where this protection is available and effective, the right lapses. States, however, bear final responsibility for their own defense. Second, the individual's right to use force extends only to self-defense. Lacking higher authority, however, states have a right to use force not only for this purpose, but also for two other ends recognized by the tradition since Augustine: restitution and punishment.[10]

Grotius takes these differences into account when he turns to the issue of anticipatory force. As in the case of individuals, he requires both certainty of intent and sufficient means to effect the intended attack. In addition, he requires some active preparation on the part of the person intending to carry out the attack. The enemy's intention must be "revealed by some fact," by "external acts"—the enemy must have "done [something] to bring [his intention] about." In other words, not only must the enemy have intended the attack, he must have "planned and initiated" it as well. Recall that Grotius rejects active preparation as a sufficient criterion in the context of individual self-defense, and in so doing illustrated what the criterion might mean. He describes a potential assailant who has "formed a plot, or is preparing an ambuscade, or . . . is putting poison in our way, or . . . is making ready a false accusation and false evidence, and is corrupting the judicial procedure." Last, Grotius demands that the coming harm be of sufficient magnitude: "Crimes that have only been begun are . . . not to be punished by armed force, unless the matter is serious, and has reached a point where a certain damage has already followed from such action, even if it is not yet that which was aimed at; or at least great danger has ensued."[11]

Strikingly absent from the list is any mention of imminence. Grotius in fact expressly rejects this requirement in the context of states. After saying his discussion of individual self-defense will shed light on the rules governing states "if the differences in conditions be taken into account," Grotius immediately points to anticipatory force to illustrate these differences: "For [states] it is permissible to forestall an act of violence which is not immediate, but which is seen to be threatening from a distance . . . by inflicting punishment for a wrong action commenced but not yet carried through."[12]

As we saw earlier, Grotius understands imminence as a more particularized requirement of last resort in the context of individual self-defense: generally, the use of anticipatory force by a person under a functioning civil government is only a last resort when the threat is imminent. And while Vitoria did not require imminence, he did require necessity. Not only does Grotius free states from an imminence requirement, he is silent on whether states (not individuals) using force must do so only as a last resort. This absence of necessity is peculiar given the early trajectory of the tradition but perhaps follows Grotius's anomalous decision to classify anticipatory force as a form of punishment rather than self-defense. As a matter of prudence he thinks states should often refrain from exercising this right, but he does not place a requirement of necessity on the use of force to punish. Later writers in the tradition would always subject the use of anticipatory force to a requirement of necessity. Moreover, the tradition would affirm the conclusion of Vitoria and Grotius that states are not bound by the imminence requirement in deciding whether to strike first.[13]

Although Grotius does not invoke necessity when addressing punishment, he insists that force for the purpose of self-defense must be a last resort and on this basis rejects the now-widespread notion that fear is a sufficient reason to strike first. He makes the point succinctly: "Fear with respect to a neighbouring power is not a sufficient cause. For in order that a self-defence may be lawful it must be necessary." The just fear tradition rests on misguided notions about security and how states interact:. "When a gladiator is equipped for fighting, the alternatives offered by combat are these, either to kill, if he shall have made the first decisive stroke, or to fall, if he shall have failed. But the life of men generally is not hedged about by a necessity so unfair and so relentless that you are obliged to strike the first blow, and may suffer if you shall have failed to be first to strike." And he aims his sight at Gentili when he concludes, "That the possibility of being attacked confers the right to attack is abhorrent to every principle of equity. Human life exists under such conditions that complete security is never guaranteed to us."[14]

As Grotius was grappling with the circumstances under which the lonely traveler or the menaced state could strike the first blow, he was also revising the moral theory undergirding his account of force and its limits. The moral tradition on the just war has always required some account of justice beyond the city walls: a basis for saying that persons qua persons are moral equals and that the claims of justice lay some limits on how I treat the person who lives across the border from me. While attuned to this need,

Grotius faced new intellectual and political challenges that threatened the classic natural law theory which in some form had carried the tradition since Augustine. Grotius is often taken to mark the beginning of a distinctly modern theory of natural law.[15]

To understand the shift he represents, one needs to understand at least two developments that confronted Grotius at the dawn of the seventeenth century. The first was the rise of skepticism, fueled by Reformation struggles over the means of religious knowledge and a retrieval of classical skeptic sources in the Renaissance. This reappearance of skepticism was enormously influential. Perhaps more than anything else it explains the obsession with epistemology that marked modern philosophy. Finding a foundation for knowledge was especially important for a defense of morality, against the skeptics who described persons as driven purely by self-interest. In his prolegomena to *On the Law of War and Peace,* Grotius takes the Greek skeptic Carneades to represent his main opponent: "Carneades . . . was able to muster no argument stronger than this, that, for reasons of expediency, men imposed upon themselves laws, which vary according to customs . . . ; moreover that there is no law of nature, because all creatures, men as well as animals, are impelled by nature toward ends advantageous to themselves; that, consequently, there is no justice." This skepticism threatened the case for an international theory of justice, upon which the tradition depended.[16]

Modern natural law theory develops with the burden of defeating the moral skeptic. Grotius and those who follow after him search for a single point of understanding that all humans can accept and from which other moral truths follow. They find this point in an account of human nature. Unlike the Thomistic account, however, which offered a deeply metaphysical understanding of the self and its ends, the modern theorists offer a minimal account of human nature, which they believe all persons share.

The second development was that religious conflict turned violent, resulting in confessional wars that divided Europe along religious and national lines. Grotius sought a concept of natural law as a set of unchanging and universal moral norms that all people could access, simply on account of their nature as rational beings. This achievement, he and others hoped, could mediate the conflicts in Europe. As a result, increasingly throughout the modern period natural law theory was lifted from a robust theological framework that accounted for the self and its ends and placed in a framework that relied on this minimal account of human nature.

Grotius applied his understanding of natural law to prescribe limits on the use of force. He outlines the main features of this account in his prolegomenas to *On the Indies* (1604) and *On the Law of War and Peace* (1625). The law of nature is "a dictate of right reason, which points out that an act, according as it is or is not in conformity with rational nature, has in it a quality of moral baseness or moral necessity, and that, in consequence, such an act is either forbidden or enjoined by the author of nature, God." Although Grotius does not use the term, he explores these laws by employing the idea of a state of nature, in conjunction with the domestic analogy. By considering what rules would govern conduct in a prepolitical condition, where individuals are not subject to a common power, he hopes to learn something about the same governing states, which also exist in a state of nature. This application of the domestic analogy becomes the central tool for thinking about the relations between states into the nineteenth century, and the rival traditions both employed it.[17]

Approaching his subject in this manner, Grotius remains ever aware of Carneades' challenge. As he understands them, the skeptics argued that nature impelled all persons to act in their own self-interested ends, threatening the possibility of justice between persons or between states. His strategy is to accept the antecedent of this claim but deny its consequent. In other words, persons do act from self-interest, but this conclusion does not preclude a just moral order.

His starting point is the "fundamental law" of nature: God has created all things to pursue their own interest, with the result that persons have a right above all else to self-preservation: "Every animal from the moment of its birth has regard for itself and is impelled to preserve itself, to have zealous consideration for its own condition and for those things which tend to preserve it. . . . [Hence] it is one's first duty to keep oneself in the condition which nature gave to him." This fundamental law has two consequences: "First, that It shall be permissible to defend [one's] life and to shun that which threatens to prove injurious; secondly, that It shall be permissible to acquire for oneself, and to retain, those things which are useful for it." These laws are "indisputable axioms," observable among humans and animals alike and acknowledged by the skeptics.[18]

Following this fundamental law of nature is what Grotius calls the "law of sociability." In *On the Indies,* he describes this law in terms of two negative duties: "Let no one inflict injury upon his fellow. [And] let no one seize possession of that which has been taken into the possession of another." Grotius finds this second law in both human instinct and reason. He describes sociability as a "trait," an "impelling desire for society" or a "social impulse" and one of "the affections shared in common with other creatures." At the same time he locates it in "the sovereign attribute of reason" and describes it as something worked out in "the power of discrimination." This law of nature is the basis both for a universal society, "the brotherhood of man," and for particular political communities: "Among the traits characteristic of man is an impelling desire for society, that is, for the social life—not of any and every sort, but peaceful, and organized according to the measure of his intelligence." The sometimes "mutual accord of nations" is a sign of this sociability in the international realm.[19]

For Grotius sociability is the basis for justice, which governs not only relations within a political community, but also relations between persons, and by extension between states as well: "Now, men agree most emphatically upon the proposition that it behoves us to have a care for others. . . . Here we have the starting-point of that justice, properly so called." As a product of both human reason and a natural impulse that God has implanted in all persons, this justice is prepolitical: it is not contingent upon the agreement of persons to form a society and the laws they pass. Moreover, this justice establishes only negative duties. Positive duties, or what Grotius calls "mutual aid," show up only in the civil state, in which persons have freely bound themselves to others.[20]

The law of sociability is Grotius's response to the skeptic, for whom might makes right. With it he rejects the claim that persons are driven only to seek their own good. His argument is twofold. He advances the empirical claim that humans do not just seek their own; that in practice people act in ways that are good for others. At the same time he argues that the skeptic's starting premise of self-interest leads to sociability.[21]

God willed this law of sociability because humans could not preserve themselves without it. He quotes Seneca: "You must needs live for others, if you would live for yourself." Earlier, Grotius had seemed to conclude that justice is rooted in the paramount impulse persons have to preserve their own beings. Immediately after introducing the law of self-preservation, Grotius states, "Consequently, Horace should not be censured for saying, in imitation of the Academics, that expediency might perhaps be called the mother of justice and equity. For all things in nature . . . are tenderly regardful of self, and seek their own happiness and security." The implication is that the skeptic's starting premise, carried through on its own, leads to justice. Humans need something like justice if they are going to hold on to property, produce goods, and have everything else one needs to survive and flourish. When self-preservation and sociability conflict, the former must win. Moreover, individuals and states are by right their own judges of what is necessary for self-preservation. For a later theorist like Hobbes the door was left open for a theory in which sociability and the justice claims it engenders limiting the use of force are swallowed up by self-preservation.[22]

On the basis of these two laws, Grotius moves to an account of the formation of the state and finally the relations between states. After a period of existing in a state of nature, persons formed political communities for security and to realize the benefits of cooperative efforts. The formation and continuation of the state are contingent upon the individual consent of those persons who enter into it. Although he does not use the language, the idea is that of a social contract. Within civil society, justice takes on a different shape, including not only negative but also positive duties to others. By entering civil society, individuals largely give up their right in the state of nature to be their own judge and enforce their own claims.[23]

States retain the same or similar rights that individuals had prior to the formation of the political community. This notion of states remaining in a state of nature is shared among all Grotius's heirs. Like individuals, states remain judges in their own cases, but they are not free from the bounds of justice. The law of nature, and particularly the law of sociability, is binding on all persons and, by extension, on all states, even in war. Accordingly, the central norm is negative and requires that one state not commit an injury against another and respect its rightful property claims.[24]

On this foundation of modern natural law theory, a significant reworking of its medieval ancestor, Grotius places the traditional just war criteria as restraints on the use of force. Grotius structures *On the Law of War and Peace* around the basic framework of just war doctrine. Book 1 deals with legitimate authority, book 2 with the just causes for war, and book 3 with just means for fighting a war. The unanswered question, however, is whether his account of justice can support the moral tradition's claims.

Hobbes and the Logic of Anticipation

Thomas Hobbes (1588–1679) is the single most important figure in the just fear tradition, offering a more sophisticated form of the international skepticism Grotius sought to refute. He provided a worked-out theory supporting a permissive account of striking first, drawing on the modern natural rights theory Grotius so forcefully dispersed into the intellectual air of the seventeenth century. For Hobbes, it is fair to say, persons—and, by extension, states—are compelled by both passion and reason to strike first. "Anticipation" is the practical and inevitable outcome of the state of nature. Despite being scorned as an atheist, relativist, and defender of absolutism by his contemporaries and later generations of scholars, Hobbes elaborated ideas about self and state that exerted enormous influence. As we will see, his notion of states standing in a condition of war will continue to resonate in the major international law treatises of the nineteenth century.[25]

Hobbes received a typical humanist education, taking his degree from Oxford in 1608. In the early years of his career, prior to publication of *On the Citizen* (1642) and *Leviathan* (1651), Hobbes had considerable contact with Bacon and perhaps Gentili as well. He likely heard Gentili lecture at Oxford, and he worked as an occasional assistant to Bacon. In addition, Hobbes's earliest works show sustained attention to the classical sources, including Tacitus, that were so influential on the *raison d'état* theory of statecraft that blossomed in the seventeenth century. Hobbes's first publication was a translation of Thucydides into English. And he was almost certainly familiar with the writings of Grotius.[26]

Hobbes's political commitments were with the Crown, and his works give a strong defense of monarchy. His first work on political theory, *The Elements of Law*, took up this task, which he continued in his later political writings during and shortly after the English Civil War. Unlike Grotius, Hobbes in his political writings focuses on civil rather than international concerns. Given that he was entwined in the events of his day, this comes as no surprise. Nonetheless, his thought has clear implications for the international realm, which he at times makes explicit.

Like Grotius, Hobbes develops his ideas by beginning with an account of the self. Borrowing the new science, Hobbes thinks of humans as clusters of atoms in space, constantly moving on the basis of desire and aversion. He employs this notion of constant desire at the center of life to reject explicitly Thomistic accounts of desire resting in some final good. The reason for this endless desire is a constant need to secure its future fulfillment: "Felicity is a continuall progresse of the desire, from one object to another; the attaining of the former, being still but the way to the later. The cause whereof is, That the object of mans desire, is not to enjoy once onley, and for one instant of time; but to assure for ever, the way of his future desire. And therefore the voluntary actions, and inclinations of all men, tend, not onley to the procuring, but also the assuring of a contented life." This insatiable thirst for security lies behind the fear that characterizes the state of nature, making it a state of war.[27]

Hobbes then takes up several kinds of desire, one of which is the desire for power: "In the first place, I put for a generall inclination of all mankind, a perpetuall and restlesse desire of Power after power, that ceaseth only in Death. And the cause of this, is not always that a man hopes for a more intensive delight, than he has already attained to; or that he cannot be content with a moderate power: but because he cannot assure the power and means to live well, which he hath present, without the acquisition of more. And from hence it is, that Kings, whose power is greatest, turn their endeavours to the assuring it at home by Lawes, or abroad by Wars." Power is the means to provide the security persons need to ensure fulfillment of their future desires. With this psychology in place, Hobbes set the stage for a drama of unceasing conflict.[28]

Prior to forming political communities, this self exists in a state of nature. Hobbes seems to be the first writer to assign this term to a concept already present in Grotius: the condition of persons living outside political community. The state of nature for both Grotius and Hobbes is not simply a heuristic device, but also a present reality. Hobbes often points to the unsettled parts of the Americas as an example of a present-day state of nature. And like Grotius, Hobbes places states in this condition: "But though there had never been any time, wherein particular men were in a condition of warre one against another; yet in all times, Kings, and Persons of Soveraigne authority, because of their Independency, are in continuall jealousies, and in the state and posture of Gladiators; having their weapons, and their eyes fixed on one another." His description of what an individual can rightfully do in a state of nature is by extension the same for the state, which is nothing but an "Artificiall Man." While Grotius rejected the image of the Gladiator, with its notion of "kill or be killed," to describe the commonwealth in an international state of nature, Hobbes embraces it.[29]

He also asserts that the fundamental right of persons in a state of nature is one of self-preservation. This right closely reflects his account of human desire:

> Amid so many dangers . . . we cannot be blamed for looking out for ourselves; we cannot will to do otherwise. For each man is drawn to desire that which is Good for him and to Avoid what is bad for him, and most of all the greatest of natural evils, which is death; this happens by a real necessity of nature as powerful as that by which a stone falls downward. It is not therefore absurd, nor reprehensible, nor contrary to right reason, if one makes every effort to defend his body and limbs from death and to preserve them. And what is not contrary to right reason, all agree is done justly and of Right. For precisely what is meant by the term Right is the liberty each man has of using his natural faculties in accordance with right reason. Therefore the first foundation of natural Right is that each man protect his life and limbs as much as he can.

This fundamental right follows in two steps. First, Hobbes claims that persons are compelled by an exceedingly strong force to seek their own individual good toward the end of self-preservation. Nature has implanted this desire in each person. Hobbes describes the operation of this desire in terms of a physical law of nature. It is a "real necessity." The result, as observed earlier, is something close to inevitable conflict. Second, Hobbes reasons that if nature has created this inescapable drive, then persons must have a natural right to act toward their self-preservation. The goal of self-preservation becomes the primary and most important end toward which persons are oriented.[30]

Although Grotius placed limits on this right of self-preservation, Hobbes boldly concludes the right is nearly unlimited. He follows Grotius in asserting that individuals are the first and final judges of whether an act follows from this right. Persons have a right to all things because "there is nothing [a person] can make use of, that may not be a help unto him, in preserving his life against his enemyes." This right extends not only to another's material goods, but even to his life: "In [a state of nature], every man has a Right to every thing; even to one anothers body."[31]

For Grotius, the right of self-preservation was constrained by his law of natural sociability. Hobbes accepts certain natural laws, but given his account of human psychology these laws have no meaning until a "common power" compels persons to keep their agreements: "For the Lawes of Nature (as Justice, Equity, Modesty, Mercy and (in summe) doing to others, as wee would be done to,) of themselves, without the terrour of some Power, to cause them to be observed, are contrary to our naturall Passions." In a state of nature persons have no moral commitments among persons qua persons, except perhaps to leave that condition. In practice, then, the fundamental right of self-preservation is the beginning and end of morality in the state of nature. No normative principle of sociability mitigates this absolute right. Grotius's move to derive sociability from self-preservation left the door open for Hobbes to find self-interest all the way down. Carneades, it seems, was alive and well.[32]

With these pieces in place, it comes as no surprise to learn that for Hobbes the state of nature is a state of war. He famously concludes, "Hereby it is manifest, that during the time men live without a common Power to keep them all in awe, they are in that condition which is called Warre; and such a warre, as is of every man, against every man." If not one of actual fighting, this state is marked by insecurity and a disposition to fight. The primary reason for this outcome is the "continuall feare" persons have toward one another: "The cause of men's fear of each other lies partly in their natural equality, partly in their willingness to hurt each other. Hence we cannot expect security from others or assure it to ourselves." This fear compels persons to leave the state of nature and enter into a social contract with others.[33]

Until that time, a rational person will protect himself through force, and especially by striking first. In perhaps the most telling passage for my purposes, Hobbes states, "And from this diffidence of one another, there is no way for any man to secure himselfe, so reasonable, as Anticipation; that is, by forces, or wiles, to master the persons of all men he can, so long, till he see no other power great enough to endanger him: And this is no more than his own conservation requireth, and is generally allowed." Hobbes is careful to point out that the will to strike first in anticipation of future harm is characteristic not only of the malevolent but also of the modest man: "Even if there were fewer evil men than good men, good, decent people would still be saddled with the constant need to watch, distrust, anticipate and get the better of others, and to protect themselves by all possible means." Nothing more characterizes persons in this state than fear of possible future attacks. He carefully defines fear as "any anticipation of future evil." Striking first is the rational response. As rational, it is also a right.[34]

In the state of nature, moreover, a man does not follow any of the careful tests laid down by Grotius but is willing to attack anybody who might now or in the future threaten him. This same permissive right to strike first characterizes states in their relationships to other states. Like individuals, the sovereign acts in his self-interest, namely, self-preservation, and has a natural right to attack anyone and everyone who might pose a threat. Although the route to this conclusion traverses a carefully worked out theory, largely absent in earlier writers, the practical conclusions about the use of anticipatory force are the same as for Machiavelli, Gentili, and Bacon. "Justified fear" is sufficient basis to strike first. More than anything else, the state of nature is a state in which actors scheme to strike first, as of right and reason.[35]

In this condition there is no justice: "To this warre of every man against every man, this also is consequent; that nothing can be Unjust. The notions of Right and Wrong, Justice and Injustice have there no place. Where there is no common Power, there is no Law: where no Law, no Injustice. Force, and Fraud, are in warre the two Cardinall virtues." Only under a "common power" does the fundamental right of self-preservation rationally permit consideration of claims coming from other persons: "Injustice actually there can be none, till the cause of such feare be taken away; which while men are in the naturall condition of Warre, cannot be done. Therefore before the names of Just, and Unjust can have place, there must be some coercive Power, to compel men equally to the performance of their Covenants." With no global Leviathan in sight, Hobbes concludes that justice cannot constrain the occasion or conduct of war.[36]

Grotius and Hobbes reach very different conclusions about the use of anticipatory force. Grotius significantly advances the standard offered by Vitoria while for Hobbes anticipation is the rational response in a state of nature. He offers an enduring foundation for the just fear tradition and in some ways a more consistent application of Grotius's starting point. For those who could not accept Hobbes's vision, the task was to rescue sociability as the basis for an account of international justice.

6

Evolution and Eclipse

FROM THE PUBLICATION OF *LEVIATHAN* in 1651 through the early twentieth century the story of the moral tradition is a narrative of both evolution and eclipse. Proponents of the tradition added further nuance to the standard for striking first. Hobbes remained an intellectual pariah that nearly every respectable philosopher felt compelled to denounce, but his notion of an international state of nature dominated by the singular right of self-preservation became an attractive account of the emerging order after Westphalia. Within this order, the dominant idea was that of a balance of power between the states of western Europe. While this concept has many meanings, during the eighteenth century it took on a prescriptive, largely Hobbesian sense: that states should liberally employ military force to prevent any one state from acquiring hegemony. Echoing a claim first sounded by Gentili, even mainstream intellectuals came to defend just fear as a legitimate ground for striking first to maintains this balance.[1]

Pufendorf's Rejoinder

Samuel Pufendorf (1632–94) took up Grotius's project and provided the earliest response to the "Hobbesian heresy." In particular, he searched for an alternative to Hobbes's state of war, with its nearly unlimited right to strike first. Pufendorf was born in Saxony, the son of a Lutheran pastor. He entered the University of Leipzig to study theology in 1650, just two years after

129

the Treaty of Westphalia brought a lasting end to the Thirty Years War. Westphalia was the single most important event shaping the political context in which he wrote. The war had spread across Europe, fueled by the hegemonic ambitions of the Hapsburg dynasty and religious conflict between Lutherans, Calvinists, and Catholics among the German principalities. The treaty prepared the way for Europe to develop into a collection of independent states, equal among themselves and sovereign in their internal affairs. Many hoped this arrangement would prevent another grasp at European dominance. Pufendorf's career included service for the Swedish and later the Prussian governments as well as many years as a professor of law. His two most important works for my purposes are *On the Law of Nature and Nations* (1672) and *On the Duty of Man and Citizen According to Natural Law* (1673), a compendium that circulated widely in European universities.[2]

Pufendorf speaks the language that was widespread in scholarly circles, namely, that of modern natural law. Like Grotius, Pufendorf seeks a law governing relations between states that transcends confessional and cultural differences. Humans have three means to discern their moral duty: reason (through natural law), civil law, and divine revelation. Pufendorf bluntly concludes that the *jus gentium*, or law of nations, is the natural law. His account follows the well-trod path and begins with a description of the self in a state of nature. In a passage that could have been peeled from the pages of *Leviathan*, Pufendorf writes, "Someone living in natural liberty does not depend on anyone else to rule his actions, but has the authority to do anything that is consistent with sound reason by his own judgment and at his own discretion. And owing to the inclination which a man shares with all living things, he must infallibly and by all means strive to preserve his body and life and to repel all that threatens to destroy them . . . and since in the natural state no one has a superior to whom he has subjected his will and judgment, everyone decides for himself whether the measures are apt to conduce to self-preservation or not." Self-preservation is a basic feature of human nature, and each person must be the final judge of her actions in a state of nature. This state is one of "war, fear, poverty, nastiness, solitude, barbarity, ignorance, savagery." Persons are compelled by reason and their natural inclinations to seek security in civil society, which they do through a social contract. In forming a commonwealth, the citizens are collectively one person in a state of nature. Finally, like Grotius and Hobbes, Pufendorf analogizes this condition of the self in a state of nature to the present condition of states: "Commonwealths and their officials may properly claim for themselves the distinction of being in a state of natural liberty."[3]

Pressed to refute Hobbes's claim that justice only follows the social contract, Pufendorf insists that God's will and not mere self-interest produces the obligating force of natural law. To discern this law Pufendorf looks to human nature. Like Hobbes, he adopts an empirical approach that observes the "nature, condition, and desires of man," and from these observations arrives at the fundamental law of nature. He agrees that all humans, like animals, seek their own preservation. This natural tendency signals a right to "secure and do everything that will lead to [self-] preservation," within the limits of natural law. At the same time, however, the fact of human dependency points to the "fundamental law of nature," which for Pufendorf is the duty of sociability Grotius had described: "It is quite clear that man is an animal extremely desirous of his own preservation, in himself exposed to want, unable to exist without the help of his fellow-creatures. . . . For such an animal to live and enjoy the good things that in this world attend his condition, it is necessary that he be sociable, that is, be willing to join himself with others like him, and conduct himself towards them in such a way that, far from having any cause to do him harm, they may feel that there is reason to preserve and increase his good fortune." From this fundamental law follow all the other laws of nature. Pufendorf departs from Grotius by concluding that sociability requires some measure of mutual aid. It is not sufficient merely to do no harm: "A man has not paid his debt to the sociable attitude if he has not thrust me from him by some deed of malevolence or ingratitude, but some benefit should be done me, so that I may be glad that there are also others of my nature to dwell on this earth." This duty, however, does not require one to incur any appreciable loss. Most important, this minimal morality governs in the state of nature: "By a sociable attitude we mean an attitude of each man towards every other man, by which each is understood to be bound to the other by kindness, peace, and love, and therefore by a mutual obligation."[4]

Pufendorf attempts to reclaim a minimal and universal justice between persons—and, by extension, between states—by presenting the law of sociability as harmonious with, but finally independent of, the right of self-preservation. At this point, Pufendorf surmised, Grotius cracked a door that Hobbes burst through. Pufendorf rejects Hobbes's conclusion that persons living outside the threat of a common power and eager for security live in a state of fear that prompts them, above all else, to "Anticipate" others who might threaten them now or in the future: "That equality of strength, which Hobbes proposes, is more likely to restrain the will to do harm than to urge it on. Surely no man in his senses wants to fight with a person as strong as he is, unless he is under some necessity." Experience, he says, suggests otherwise: "It is not proper to oppose a state of nature to a social life, since even those who live in a state of nature can, and should, and frequently do, lead a mutually social life." He points to the international state of nature as the best example: "It is contrary to the judgment of all nations to maintain that even those states which are joined by treaties and friendship are in a mutual state of war." Against the claim of incongruity, Pufendorf asserts that security demands sociability.[5]

Sociability is not only harmonious with the right of self-preservation, but also finally independent of it. Its origin lies in human nature: "Although by the wisdom of the Creator the natural law has been so adapted to the nature of man, that its observance is always connected with the profit and advantage of men . . . yet, in giving a reason for this fact, one does not refer to the advantage accruing therefrom, but to the common nature of all men. For instance, if a reason must be given why a man should not injure another, you do not say, because it is to his advantage, although it may, indeed, be most advantageous, but because the other person also is a man, that is, an animal related by nature, whom it is a crime to injure." While Grotius gave reason to believe that all moral principles derived from the right of self-preservation, Pufendorf firmly rejects this suggestion.[6]

With these rudiments of a theory of universal justice, Pufendorf develops his account of anticipatory force. For Hobbes, anticipation was the final prescription for persons in a state of nature. Perhaps for this reason, Pufendorf gives more attention to anticipatory force than to self-defense generally. The question about when an individual or a state could strike first had become a central test for determining what one person (or state) owed another qua person, outside the bounds of civil society.

Pufendorf's account follows the rough approach that had now emerged within the tradition. He extends the concept of injury to include some cases in which the actual attack has not yet occurred. In these cases of "incomplete injury" the "aggressor" is not the first one to use force, but the one first preparing to do harm. Rejecting fear as a sufficient reason, Pufendorf says generally that "cases of innocent defence commonly require a danger that is at hand, and, as it were, right upon one, and they do not allow a mere suspicion or uncertain fear to be sufficient cause for one person to attack another."[7]

Pufendorf adapts the domestic analogy, mining it as much for differences as for similarities. A person under civil government faces a more stringent standard than an individual living in a state of nature. Unlike the latter, "an equal license is by no means allowed those who live in states. . . . If I hear [that a person] is preparing to injure me, or if I find him making fierce threats, . . . he should be haled before our common sovereign, and made to give bond to keep peace." He lays down this general rule: "The beginning of the time at which a man may, without fear of punishment, kill another in self-defence, is when the aggressor, showing clearly his desire to take my life, and equipped with the capacity and the weapons for his purpose, has gotten into the position where he can in fact hurt me, the space being also reckoned as that which is necessary, if I wish to attack him rather than to be attacked by him." He describes a person faced with a charging assailant, sword in hand and intending to kill in a matter of seconds. The potential victim in this case, confronting "the imminence of so great a danger," can justly fire his gun: "If a man is being actually attacked by force, and is reduced to such extremities that he is unable to call the help of a magistrate or of other citizens, then he may, in order to ward off from himself the onslaught of his assailant, go to any lengths against him . . . because his own life cannot be snatched from its present peril without killing him." Pufendorf cites the key passage from the *Digest,* allowing a person to use force *in continenti.* So on the question of individual self-defense, Grotius and Pufendorf agree. Where the threat is imminent, a person need not receive the first and perhaps fatal blow.[8]

Lacking the protections individuals have in civil society, a person in the state of nature has more latitude to use force prior to an actual attack. As we will see, the criteria he adopts for individuals outside the bounds of civil society are nearly mirrored in what he says about states: "If I am to attack another under the name of my own self-defence, signs are required, forming a moral certainty, of his evil design upon me, and intention of harming me, so that, unless I anticipate him, I may expect to receive the first blow. . . . But even if a person shows the desire as well as the ability to work harm, still even this fact gives me no immediate reason to proceed against him, if he has not yet put his purpose into action against me." Clear intent, sufficient means, and active preparation are all necessary conditions for striking first. Moreover, like Grotius, he requires that anticipatory force be a measure of last resort. If the above criteria are met, a person can use force "provided there be no hope that, when he has been approached as a friend, he will put off his evil intention." Again, imminence, as a measure of temporal proximity of the attack, is not required.[9]

In a later chapter, Pufendorf applies nearly the same standard to states as he does to individuals living outside civil government. His treatment of the issue comes in the context of rejecting the just fear argument, which was steadily gaining ground: "Fear alone does not suffice as a just cause for war, unless it is established with moral and evident certitude that there is an intent to injure us. For an uncertain suspicion of peril can, of course, persuade you to surround yourself in advance with defences, but it cannot give you a right to be the first to force the other by violence to give a real guarantee, as it is called, not to offend. . . . For so long as a man has not injured me, and is not caught in open preparation to do so . . . it should be presumed that he will perform his duty in the future." As with individuals, a state's decision to strike first must be a last resort. Pufendorf rejects Grotius's decision to classify anticipatory force as a form of punishment and returns to Vitoria's treatment of it as a form of self-defense. After listing the just causes for war, one of which is defense, Pufendorf states, "Sometimes credit for defence stands with him who is the first to take up arms against another, if, for instance, . . . by a swift movement [a man] overcomes an enemy who is already bent upon attacking him, but is still engaged in his preparations."[10]

Vattel and the Waxing Eclipse

Although the rival traditions on the use of force remain discernible throughout the eighteenth century, the most remarkable development is the rise of the Hobbesian tradition nearly to eclipse the moral tradition on the just war. This development in many ways mirrored geopolitical developments that followed in the hundred years after Westphalia, particularly the coming of age of strong, sovereign states. Signaling this eclipse was Emmerich de Vattel (1714–67), the Swiss jurist and diplomat whose *Law of Nations* (1758) was translated into English, circulated broadly in Europe and America, and became the definitive text in the field for more than half a century.[11]

Vattel subscribes to the now-commonplace account of states as moral persons living in a state of nature and possessing the rights of natural liberty. These rights arise from duties that a state has both to itself and others. Vattel affirms that "the right of self-preservation carried with it the right to whatever is necessary for that purpose," insofar as the means are just. At the same time, he agrees with Pufendorf that the natural law lays down a separate principle of sociability that is finally harmonious with the right of self-preservation. His argument for a fundamental law of sociability is largely along Pufendorfian lines. Humans are dependent beings who need each other to live happily and improve their condition, which demands a measure of cooperation: "The general law of this society is that each member should assist the others in all their needs, as far as he can do so without neglecting his duties to himself." This law finds its most intensive application in civil society, but it governs all persons, even those in a state of nature, including states in their relationships with each other. Vattel describes a "universal society" as a "necessary result of man's nature," giving rise to certain minimal duties.[12]

In a chapter entitled "The Just Causes of War," Vattel repeats the general lines of the just war tradition regarding the decision to use force: "The right to use force, or to make war, is given to Nations only for their defense and for the maintenance of their rights. . . . We may say, therefore, in general, that the foundation or the cause of every just war is an injury, either already received or threatened." Even when a state has just cause for war because of some actual injury that has occurred, natural law forbids a state to resort to armed force before it has exhausted other reasonable alternatives, even when it uses force for the purpose of punishment or restoring goods taken.[13]

On the issue of anticipatory force, Vattel echoes the norms developed by Grotius and Pufendorf while also reflecting the European international order that had developed since Westphalia. His account appears in consideration of the now "celebrated question" of whether states can use force out of fear of a neighboring state that is growing in power. His starting point is the duty a state has to augment its military and economic power to defend itself. In a previous chapter Vattel had explained that "a state is powerful enough when it is able to . . . repel any attacks which may be made upon it. It can place itself in this happy situation either by keeping its own forces upon a level or above those of its neighbors, or by preventing the latter from acquiring a position of predominant power." He qualifies this seemingly broad duty states owe themselves by saying natural law prohibits a state from reaching this end by unjust means. Affirming the tradition, he concludes that, absent some injury, the use of force on the basis of fear alone is prohibited: "Since war is only permissible in order to redress an injury received, or to protect ourselves from an injury with which we are threatened, it is a sacred rule of the Law of Nations that the aggrandizement of a state can not alone and of itself give any one the right to take up arms to resist it."[14]

Both sufficient means and clear intent appear in Vattel's standard for anticipatory force: "Power alone does not constitute a threat of injury; the will to injure must accompany the power." Vattel, however, is much more liberal in his measure of intent than any of his predecessors within the tradition. A state can discern intent from a variety of factors, all of which are open to broad interpretation: "As soon as a State has given evidence of injustice, greed, pride, ambition, or a desire of domineering over its neighbors, it becomes an object of suspicion which they must guard against." In addition, the potential aggressor must "betray . . . his plans by preparations or other advances," suggesting the requirement of active preparation. All use of force is subject to a requirement of last resort, but, like Pufendorf and Grotius, Vattel does not require that the threat be imminent. Last, his standard requires states to take into account the magnitude and probability of the harm: "One is justified in forestalling a danger in direct ratio to the degree of probability attending it, and to the seriousness of the evil with which one is threatened. If the evil in question be endurable, if the loss be of small account, prompt action need not be taken; there is no great danger in delaying measures of self-protection until we are certain that there is actual danger of the evil." Both measures were present in the tradition historically, though only Grotius had applied the measure of magnitude to the standard governing anticipatory force.[15]

Although Vattel adds a consideration of probability to the evolving standard for anticipatory force, his attempt to reconcile the moral tradition with the ascendant theory that states have a right to use preventive force to maintain a balance of power threatens to undermine the just war constraints on striking first. For example, he later concludes, "There is perhaps no case in which a State has received a notable increase of power without giving other States just grounds of complaint. Let all Nations be on their guard to check such a State, and they will have nothing to fear from it."[16]

Even more important for the future of the just war tradition is the limits Vattel places on the tradition's scope of applicability. Both Grotius and Pufendorf had recognized a body of rules outside natural law that arose from state practice. Grotius, for example, recognized the *jus gentium* as a law of custom emerging from the practice of states. But his hope for shared norms that would limit the use of force and reach across confessional and cultural lines looked entirely to natural law, to which he devoted the vast portion of his seminal work. Pufendorf, moreover, recognized the presence of various customs regarding war but refused to ascribe to them the term *law of nations,* which he instead simply identified with natural law.

Following the lead of Christian Wolff, a prominent eighteenth-century German philosopher, Vattel makes a distinction between the norms governing a just war and the practical law governing states: "Let us . . . leave to the conscience of sovereigns the observance of the natural and necessary law in all its strictness; and indeed it is never lawful for them to depart from it. But as regards the external operation of that law in human society, we must necessarily have recourse to certain rules of more certain and easy application, and this in the interest of the safety and welfare of the great society of the human race. These rules are those of the voluntary Law of Nations." He ascribes this necessary law of nations to the inner forum of the conscience, while the more permissive voluntary law of nations structures international society. Many earlier, pre-Westphalian accounts of sovereignty would have never countenanced this distinction: adhering to natural law was constitutive of sovereignty; otherwise the ruler was a tyrant whose legitimate hold on power came into question. In the eighteenth century the moral responsibility of the sovereign to the common good is stripped away, and sovereignty is defined in terms of legal authority within a territory. Vattel accommodates this shift.[17]

The just war restraints are all part of this "necessary law of nations" and apply only to the sovereign's moral sense. The voluntary law of nations, however, assumes both sides to the conflict have just cause: "Regular war, as regards its effects, must be accounted just on both sides." This law is completely silent as to the justice of going to war in the first place. In practice, this distinction brings Vattel much closer to Hobbes than Vattel's lengthy discussion of just war norms might suggest.[18]

Vattel gives several reasons for this move, the most important of which is an outworking of the idea that states are free moral persons living in a state of nature: "It belongs to every free and sovereign State to decide in its own conscience what its duties require of it, and what it may or may not do with justice. If others undertake to judge of its conduct, they encroach upon its liberty and infringe upon its most valuable rights." At the heart of Vattel's distinction between the necessary and voluntary law of nations is the notion of the state as a free person living in a state of nature and bearing a fundamental right of self-preservation. Proponents of the just war tradition had resisted an unfettered right of freedom by employing varying ideas about a separate principle—most often called sociability and having roots in Augustine—that placed states in a moral order limited by the constraints of justice. The absolute freedom implied by this narrative of states existing as moral selves in a state of nature and the universal justice which the just war tradition assumed, however, were never finally commensurable. The heirs of Tacitus always threatened to eclipse the heirs of Augustine. In Vattel, this eclipse is underway.[19]

Rousseau, Kant, and the Ascendancy of Hobbes

Like Vattel, the two most important political philosophers of the eighteenth century, Jean-Jacques Rousseau (1712–78) and Immanuel Kant (1724–1804), followed Hobbes in surprising ways. Rousseau's most important political writings, *The Discourses* and *The Social Contract*, were published, respectively, just a few years before and after the publication of Vattel's The *Law of Nations* in 1758. Although Rousseau does not directly engage Vattel, these writings show him to be well acquainted with Grotius, Hobbes, and Pufendorf. And despite his sustained effort to set himself against Hobbes, the degree to which Rousseau adopts a Hobbesian position on the use of force is striking. He rejects Hobbes's identification of a state of war with the state of nature. Admitting that his state of nature is purely heuristic, Rousseau says that humans originally lived peaceful, solitary, self-sufficient lives, easily fulfilling their true needs. Only in their sociable interactions with others did corruption follow. This distinction in place, Rousseau nonetheless largely accepts Hobbes's description of a state of war and the rights states possess to use force. For man in a natural state, "his first law is to attend to his own preservation, his first cares are those he owes himself, and . . . he is the sole judge of the means proper to preserve himself." Prior to the social contract, man has "an unlimited right to everything that tempts him and he can reach."[20]

This state of war follows inevitably and leads persons to secure themselves through striking first: "The constitution of this universe does not allow for all the sentient beings that make it up to concur all at once in their mutual happiness[;] but since one sentient being's well-being makes for the other's evil, each, by the law of nature, gives preference to itself. . . . Finally, once things have reached a point where a being endowed with reason is convinced that his preservation is inconsistent not only with another's well-being but with his very existence, he takes up arms against the other's life and tries to destroy him as eagerly as he tries to preserve himself, and for the same reason."[21]

Rousseau analogizes the individual to the state, which becomes a "moral self" through the social contract and which exists in a (corrupted) state of nature with other states. With an emphasis not seen before, Rousseau asserts that the social contract allows individuals to escape one state of war only to enter another that is even more menacing: "The Bodies Politic thus remaining in the state of Nature among themselves soon experienced the inconveniences that had forced individuals to leave it, and this state became even more fatal among these great Bodies than it had previously been among the individuals who made them up. From it arose the National Wars,

Battles, murders, reprisals that make Nature tremble and that shock reason. . . . More murders were committed in a single day's fighting . . . than had been committed in the state of nature for centuries together over the entire face of the earth." As in the case of individuals, Rousseau attributes an inevitability to this outcome. States are limitless in their desire for more, whereas individuals can acquire only so much. And while persons are prone to rest, a state survives by movement and expansion. Rousseau is finally cynical about the possibility of escaping this state of war among nations.[22]

Rousseau explicitly rejects the claim that persons or nations existing in a state of nature have moral obligations one to another, summed up by the just war tradition in the idea of sociability and presented most powerfully for Rousseau by Pufendorf: "It is not a matter of teaching me what justice is; it is a matter of showing me what interest I have in being just. . . . Where is the man who can thus separate from himself and, if care for one's self-preservation is the first precept of nature, can he be forced thus to consider the species in general in order to impose on himself duties whose connection with his own constitution he completely fails to see." In one moment, Rousseau directly criticizes the just war tradition, with its roots in Christianity: "Let us restore to the Philosopher the examination of a question which the Theologian has never dealt with except to the prejudice of mankind." Like Hobbes, Rousseau denies the possibility of justice claims outside the social contract. Acting justly is possible only in political society because it is only under the social contract that self-interest unites with a respect for the rights of others, or the common good. Outside civil society, interest and justice clash.[23]

Writing a generation later, Immanuel Kant accepts Rousseau's conclusion that human corruption is realized in society. The outcome of this corruption is a state of war between individuals that finally spills over into a state of war between nations. Unlike Rousseau, however, Kant sets his account of human corruption within a teleological framework, as part of the means nature uses to progress toward a just order between individuals and among states. This progression is gradual and almost always indiscernible in any given lifetime. Nonetheless the natural antagonism that exists between individuals and states propels humanity toward a just order.[24]

Kant often refers to this natural antagonism as "unsocial sociability": "that is, [the human] tendency to come together in society, coupled, however, with a continual resistance which constantly threatens to break this society up." Both propensities are rooted in human nature. On the one hand, persons are compelled to live in society, for their preservation and also their perfection. Only with the cooperation of others can a person achieve security and develop her natural capacities. On the other hand, persons are compelled to live as individuals, since they want to order their existence in accordance with their own ideas. The result is resistance and conflict between persons and finally between the political societies they form. This conflict is the engine of enlightenment. In striving for power and status among each other, humans develop their natural abilities and move from barbarism to civilization.[25]

The conflict that exists among nations is one means nature uses to lead states toward a just international order. Like Rousseau, Kant believes the present condition, in which individuals but not states have left the state of nature, is worst of all. Unlike Rousseau, however, Kant is optimistic. The condition of fear and actual hostilities between states will eventually lead states to enter voluntarily a federation governed by law and supported by a credible sanction: "Wars, tense and unremitting military preparations, and the resultant distress which every state must eventually feel within itself, even in the midst of peace—these are the means by which nature drives nations to make initially imperfect attempts, but finally, after many devastations . . . to take the step which reason could have suggested to them . . . of abandoning a lawless state of savagery and entering a federation of peoples in which every state, even the smallest, could expect to derive its security." Even wars of aggrandizement are a part of this movement. The changes, however, are gradual, and Kant is clear that war plays a necessary role: "So long as human culture remains at its present stage, war is therefore an indispensable means of advancing it further; and only when culture has reached its full development—and only God knows when that will be—will perpetual peace become possible and of benefit to us." The result is a complex normative account of war in the present, in which Kant obliges states finally to leave this state of war but sanctions a permissive account of the use of preventive force under the present conditions and into the foreseeable future.[26]

Although Kant's vision of perpetual peace is celebrated as a liberal vision of international justice—and Kant stands at the font of liberalism more generally—his account of war under present conditions is remarkably Hobbesian and often overlooked. In an important footnote in *Religion within the Boundaries of Mere Reason,* he says, "Hobbes's statement, *status hominum naturalis est bellum omnium in omnes,* has no other fault apart from this: it should say, *est status belli . . . etc.* For, even though one may not concede that actual *hostilities* are the rule between human beings who do not stand under external and public laws, their condition . . . is nonetheless one in which each of them wants to be himself the judge of what is his right vis-à-vis others, without however either having any security from others with respect to this right or offering them any: and this is a condition of war, wherein every man must be constantly armed against everybody else."[27]

In the state of war and absent the assurance of equal restraint that a federation of states would create, power, not justice, is the rule. While states in this condition have rights, they are only "provisional," since there is no means to adjudicate and enforce them. Hence, this state of war is "devoid of justice." Each state follows its own judgment. Assessments of whether or not a state goes to war justly are ruled out: "War is, after all, only the regrettable expedient for asserting one's right by force in a state of nature (where there is no court that could judge with rightful force); in it neither of the two parties can be declared an unjust enemy (since that already presupposes a judicial decision), but instead the outcome of the war . . . decides on whose side the right is." He famously chides Grotius, Pufendorf, and Vattel as "only sorry comforters." Justice demands an external lawgiving and a credible sanction to enforce it, both of which come only with the social contract.[28]

Kant holds that states are compelled by reason to leave this condition of war and enter a federation of states. By failing to exit the state of nature, each state commits a wrong against another and thereby gives occasion for war: "It is usually assumed that one may not behave with hostility toward another unless he has actively wronged me; and that is also quite correct if both are in a condition of being under civil laws. For by having entered into such a condition one affords the other the requisite assurance (by means of a superior having power over both).—But a human being (or a nation) in a mere state of nature denies me this assurance and already wrongs me just by being near me in this condition, even if not actively (*facto*) yet by the lawlessness of his condition (*statu iniusto*), by which he constantly threatens me; and I can coerce him either to enter with me into a condition of being under civil laws or to leave my neighborhood."[29]

The consequence is a broadly permissive account of anticipatory force, in line with Hobbes. This constant wrong that states commit against each other merely by refusing to leave the state of nature is sufficient grounds to strike first: "It is not necessary to wait for actual hostility; one is authorized to use coercion against someone who already, by his nature, threatens him with coercion." As with Gentili and Hobbes, a mere increase in power is enough to justify the use of preventive force: "In addition to active violations . . . [the state] may be threatened. This includes another state's being the first to undertake preparations, upon which is based the right of prevention (*ius praeventionis*), or even just the menacing increase in another state's power (by its acquisition of territory). . . . This is a wrong to the lesser power merely by the condition of the superior power, before any deed on its part, and in the state of nature an attack by the lesser power is indeed legitimate. Accordingly, this is also the basis of the right to a balance of power among all states that are contiguous and could act on one another." Despite Kant's optimism that a just international order can exist among states, he largely accepts Hobbes's description of the present as a state of war in which states can rightfully strike first on the mere basis of fear.[30]

Clausewitz and Hall at Peak Eclipse

The nineteenth century witnessed the solidification of the Hobbesian idea that states possess a nearly unfettered right to wage war, especially preventive wars. Carl von Clausewitz (1780–1831), a Prussian soldier who experienced the wars of the French Revolution and the Napoleonic wars and wrote the monumental work on military theory, *On War,* admonished generations of military strategists to take the offensive in a preventive war rather than wait until a point in time when conditions may be less favorable: "Supposing that a minor state is in conflict with a much more powerful one and expects its position to grow weaker every year. If war is unavoidable, should it not make the most of its opportunities before its position gets still worse? In short, it should attack."[31]

Clausewitz's advice was the calculation of a shrewd strategist, but it also reflected the consensus within the emerging field of international law. Representative is the widely read *Treatise on International Law* (1880) by Edward Hall (1835–94). Hall reflected the shift toward positivist accounts of law, a significant departure from the natural law theory that earlier held sway. He makes a methodological commitment to distinguish law and morality. While the two spheres may often overlap, morality is not a necessary precondition for legal validity. An account of the moral norms governing the use of force says little about what counts as law. In contrast, earlier sources, represented by Grotius's *On the Law of War and Peace,* had looked to a moral order inscribed in nature to discern the law governing states.[32]

For positivists like Hall, international law obtains its validity only through the consent of states. The measure of consent and the source of binding legal norms is state practice. The task of the international legal scholar is one of interpreting the acts of states on different issues of international importance: "The rules by which nations are governed are unexpressed. The evidence of their existence and of their contents must therefore be sought in national acts—in other words, in such international usage as can be looked upon as authoritative." This commitment to positivism reflected not only a growing skepticism that natural law existed, but also a robust view of state sovereignty that granted states virtually unlimited rights. Even if there was an architectonic morality, it was not binding as law. International law treatises in the nineteenth century were nearly unanimous in their adoption of a largely Hobbesian account of an international state of nature and a robust right of self-preservation, giving states wide latitude in deciding whether to use force.[33]

Hall agrees that states are independent moral persons: "It is postulated of those independent states which are dealt with by international law that they have a moral nature identical with that of individuals, and that with respect to one another they are in the same relation as that in which individuals stand to each other who are subject to law. They are collective persons, and as such they have rights and are under obligations." States have at least two basic rights: the right of independence and the right of self-preservation.

He defines the right of independence as "a right possessed by a state to exercise its will without interference on the part of foreign states in all matters and upon all occasions with reference to which it acts as an independent community." Likened to the individual moral agent in the state of nature, states have a right to conduct their internal affairs as they see fit, absent the intervention of other states.[34]

In tension with the right of independence, however, is the related right of self-preservation: "Since states exist, and are independent beings . . . they have the right to do whatever is necessary for the purpose of continuing and developing their existence, of giving effect to and preserving their independence." When the right of independence clashes with the right of self-preservation, Hall is clear that self-preservation prevails: "In the last resort almost the whole of the duties of states are subordinated to the right of self-preservation. Where law affords inadequate protection to the individual he must be permitted, if his existence is in question, to protect himself by whatever means necessary."[35]

Hall represents a sweepingly broad account of self-preservation. This right justifies the use of force not only in the case of an actual or imminent attack, but also in the case of a mere threat: "If a country offers an indirect menace through a threatening disposition of its military force . . . if at the same time its armaments are brought up to a pitch evidently in excess of the requirements of self-defense, so that it would be in a position to give effect to its intentions . . . the state or states which find themselves threatened may demand securities . . . and if reasonable satisfaction be not given they may protect themselves by force of arms." States may use preventive force early on to avoid going to war later. Any attempt to offset the balance of power between the major powers is legitimate grounds for preventive war.[36]

As independent moral persons with no higher authority, states are the first and last judge of their decisions to use force. Hall recognizes a principle of necessity or last resort limiting the use of force, but states must make these decisions for themselves and are accountable to no one. Even if there were a decision maker that could arbitrate between states, there is no effective way to sanction states that might violate the decision. Hall concludes, "International law has consequently no alternative but to accept war, independently of the justice of its origin, as a relation which the parties to it may set up if they choose, and to busy itself only in regulating the effects of the relation." As legal scholars of the day had widely concluded, the distinctions between offensive and defensive, just and unjust wars are the province of morality and have nothing to say to law: "Such matters as these are supremely important; but they belong to morality and theology, and are as much out of place in a treatise on International Law as would be a discussion on the ethics of marriage in a book on the law of personal status."[37]

While both Pufendorf and Vattel advanced the just war tradition's account of anticipatory force, in Vattel the eclipse of the moral tradition evidenced by accommodation to the ascendant notion that states should use preventive force to maintain a balance of power—and on the mere basis of fear—was already underway. Moreover, the two most prominent political philosophers of the eighteenth century, Rousseau and Kant, openly embraced a Hobbesian account of the relations between states, granting broad permission to strike first. Especially for Kant, the consequence was a strained alliance between a liberal theory of domestic justice and an illiberal, realist account of the present relation between states. While nearly every philosopher of importance took great care to deny the "pernicious" ideas of Hobbes, it is remarkable how close many of them remained in their embrace of "Anticipation." A tradition marked early on by intellectual outcasts such as Machiavelli and Hobbes was now mainstream.

I concluded part I by asking whether the moral tradition on the just war, bearing a deep affinity to America's moral identity, might support the case for an expanded right to use force first. This account of the sustained conversation within the just war tradition on the use of anticipatory force provides the raw materials for reaching an answer in part III. More precisely, the question is this: Does the moral tradition provide grounds for accepting a limited role for preventive force, without opening the door to using force on the mere basis of fear?

PART THREE

REVISION

7

Behind Webster's Rule

Despite the waxing of a hobbesian worldview, the eclipse of the moral tradition was never total. As we saw earlier, the tradition was on the rise throughout the twentieth century in America—an ascent so remarkable one can fairly conclude the moral tradition today provides the grammar for how most Americans talk about war. After World War II and with the efforts to regulate the recourse to force, Webster's Rule took on a new role as a broad limit on the use of anticipatory force. This rule grants singular importance to the presence of an imminent threat. In Webster's words: "It will be for that Government to show a necessity of self-defence, instant, overwhelming, leaving no choice of means, and no moment for deliberation." As chapter 1 concluded, however, a categorical prohibition against using force absent an imminent threat can no longer provide states the security they require. With the fall of the Twin Towers came the ability to imagine that using force against a less-than-imminent threat might be a last resort to prevent a coming attack of unacceptable harm. The challenges this new security environment poses are daunting, but the moral tradition on the just war and the narrative from Vitoria to Vattel suggests a way forward. To begin, one needs to consider the moral tradition's understanding of imminence and Webster's departure from it.

Imminence in Context

The thread I followed in part II offers a perspective on imminence otherwise lost if one starts with Webster, as most commentators do. From Vitoria onward the tradition consistently made two affirmations. First, it affirmed that the imminence criterion applied only as a general rule to individuals living under the protections of a functioning civil government. Vitoria never mentioned imminence in discussing the question of whether justice would ever permit a man to strike the first blow. His requirement that the man know "with scientific certitude" that the aggressor will in fact attack implied only the requirements of certainty of intent and sufficient means. And, consistent with the tradition, he insisted anticipatory force always be a measure of last resort. Grotius retrieved the Roman law concept of *in continenti,* transmitted through the medieval jurists, as a measure of the temporal proximity of the attack. Speaking of the individual in society, he states, "War in defence of life is permissible only when the danger is immediate and certain, not when it is merely assumed. The danger, again, must be immediate and imminent in point of time. . . . [I]f the assailant seizes weapons in such a way that his intent to kill is manifest the crime can be forestalled." The mere drawing up of plans and other preparations for an attack are insufficient; the attacker must initiate the actual movement that will result in the victim's harm. Turning to the state, however, Grotius makes a crucial qualification. Here, the domestic disanalogy is all-important: "What has been said by us up to this point . . . applies chiefly, of course, to private war; yet it may be made applicable also to public war, *if the differences in conditions be taken into account.*" He is explicit that a state need not wait until the attack is imminent. Rather, a state can "forestall an act of violence which is not immediate."[1]

Pufendorf affirms this concept. Considering a person who lives under a functioning government, he describes an attacker charging with weapon drawn. In addition to the clear intent to harm and the means to do so, the aggressor must also be near in space and time, having begun the action that will result in the victim's harm. In other words, the threat must be imminent. The standards he describes for states and for individuals outside the protections of political community have much in common. Here, the criteria of certain intent, sufficient means, active preparation, and last resort are all included, but imminence is noticeably absent.[2]

This insistence that individuals under a functioning civil government can strike first only when faced with an imminent threat was reflected in the common law. The English jurist William Blackstone (1723–80) defined the common law of his day in his *Commentaries on the Laws of England,* which was enormously influential in the new republic. Blackstone treats the subject of anticipatory self-defense in his chapter "Of Homicide": "The self-defence, which we are now speaking of, is that whereby a man may protect himself from an assault. . . . This right of natural defence does not imply a right of attacking: for, instead of attacking one another of injuries past or impending, men need only have recourse to the proper tribunals of justice. They cannot therefore legally exercise this right of preventive defence, but in sudden and violent cases when certain and immediate suffering would be the consequence of waiting for the assistance of the law. Wherefore to excuse homicide by the plea of self-defence, it must appear that the slayer had no other possible (or, at least, probable) means of escaping from his assailant." Although Blackstone does not use the term *imminence,* the standard is the same.[3]

Blackstone's rationale is the same as that found in Grotius and Pufendorf: individuals within a state whose lives are threatened usually "have recourse to the proper tribunals of justice." Therefore, a "preventive" attack against an "impending" threat is typically ruled out; in these cases a civil remedy is available. Rather, the threat must be "certain and immediate." Although Blackstone's subject is English common law, he agrees with the moral tradition's affirmation that the same standard does not govern between independent states, which lack recourse to a higher authority and for which more is at stake.[4]

Today nearly all states demand imminence or something like it in their laws governing self-defense. Wisconsin's provision is typical: a person may use potentially lethal force in self-defense if the person "reasonably believes such force is necessary to prevent imminent death or great bodily harm." This area of doctrine has received frequent attention from both legislators and scholars—particularly concerning the duty, if any, to retreat and the demand for imminence in the case of battered women. Nonetheless, an imminence requirement remains widely in place.[5]

In addition, the moral tradition made a second affirmation: that where the imminence criterion does generally apply, it serves as a proxy only for the more fundamental requirement of necessity. With the exception of Grotius, who conceptualized anticipatory force by states as a form of punishment rather than self-defense, the tradition consistently held that such force is legitimate only when necessary. The individual or state must exhaust all reasonable alternatives short of using force, which is always a last resort. Where the tradition also required the presence of an imminent threat, it employed this criterion as a more concrete, measurable indicator of when armed force was necessary.[6]

Grotius's account of individual self-defense is most telling. Although he requires an imminent threat as a general constraint, he does so with a qualification: "If a man is not planning an immediate attack . . . I maintain that he cannot lawfully be killed, *either if* the danger can in any other way be avoided, or *if* it is not altogether certain that the danger cannot be otherwise avoided. Generally, in fact, the delay that will intervene affords opportunity to apply many remedies, to take advantage of many accidental occurrences." Although the general rule requires an imminent threat, he hedges this demand by hinting that in the rare case where necessity is satisfied and imminence is not, the individual may use force. The suggestion is that necessity is the underlying moral imperative.[7]

Pufendorf's writings reflect the same close relationship. He explicitly defines imminence in terms of necessity. Speaking of the individual in society, Pufendorf writes, "It seems possible to lay down the general rule that the beginning of the time at which a man may, without fear of punishment, kill another in self-defence, is when the aggressor, showing clearly his desire to take my life, and equipped with the capacity and the weapons for his purpose, has gotten into the position where he can in fact hurt me, the space being also reckoned *as that which is necessary,* if I wish to attack him rather than to be attacked by him." In other words, an imminent attack is an attack so near in space and time that the potential victim has no alternative but to attack first if she is not to take the first blow. In the case of individual self-defense, then, imminence functions as a proxy for necessity. By not requiring an imminent threat for states or individuals outside civil society but still demanding that force be a last resort, Pufendorf implicitly acknowledges that in some cases a state may have no reasonable alternative short of using force to defend itself against a less than imminent threat. Again, necessity bears the moral weight.[8]

Even Webster's Rule follows similar lines. The first half—"a necessity of self-defence, instant, overwhelming, leaving no choice of means, and no moment for deliberation"—expressly defines necessity in terms of imminence. Using force is necessary because the threat is "instant," so near in time that the target has "no choice of means" to defend itself. It can prevent the coming harm only by being the first to use force. Interpreted outside the larger tradition of which it is a part, however, it is difficult to discern in Webster's language the nuanced relationship between these two requirements as they developed in the tradition. Webster suggests near identity, with no reason to think necessity the more fundamental moral measure.[9]

The requirement of imminence, then, functions as a proxy for necessity: force is necessary when a coming attack is so near in space and time that the potential victim lacks any other means to escape. Under most circumstances, this use of imminence as a translator for necessity is sound: the further a potential attack is removed in time, the greater chance "many accidental occurrences" might allow a person to secure herself short of using potentially lethal force, thereby rendering such force unnecessary. This relationship between imminence and necessity, however, is not perfect. On the one hand, it is not difficult to imagine cases in which a threat is imminent but the use of force is not necessary. For example, in the case of individuals a person might easily flee, which is why the common law recognized a duty of retreat. More important for my purposes, not only might a person confront an imminent threat in which the use of force is not necessary, but the opposite might occur. The moral tradition conceives of the possibility that for states the use of defensive force might be a last resort against a not-yet-imminent threat. Therefore the tradition refused to place imminence as a general demand on states, even though the requirement of necessity on its own may often—and perhaps nearly always—require that the threat be imminent.

Even in the domestic context the tradition's demand for imminence, reflected in the law today, does not altogether foreclose the use of force absent an imminent threat. In other words, even the contemporary law of self-defense in the United States does not equate necessity and imminence. Anticipatory force might be necessary at some time before a threat becomes imminent, but the tradition and state law leave the exercise of such power in the hands of government, not the individual. The imminence criterion creates a division of labor between the government and the individual in the domestic context. Again, necessity, not imminence, bears the moral weight. Imminence plays a functional role of identifying which agent has the authority to act but does not reach the deeper moral question of when lethal force is just.

In sum, although the moral tradition recognized that the demand of last resort may in most, or even nearly all, cases require an imminent threat, it never placed imminence as an absolute condition on states using anticipatory force in self-defense. The moral tradition countenanced that under a narrow range of circumstances a state might use not only preemptive but also preventive force. The often-heard claim that the just war tradition categorically condemns preventive force may reflect the moral intuitions of some who identify with the tradition today, but it runs counter to the tradition's consistent affirmations in the past.[10]

Webster's Departure

Webster's Rule, crafted in the crucible of diplomacy and retrieved more than a century later by the architects of the new international order after World War II, reversed the moral tradition's unwavering insistence that states are not subject to the imminence demand. Webster never acknowledged his departure and, more important, neither have most commentators today who routinely start with Webster and look no further. The question for Webster, then, is why? Webster's correspondence and other sources related to the *Caroline* affair shed little light, but another maritime controversy Webster argued two decades earlier gives some insight: the case of the *Marianna Flora*.

Although little known today, this case touched on some of the most pressing matters of the 1820s, including the quest to stamp out piracy and the slave trade. Webster's involvement traces to the founding of the American Colonization Society in 1816. The organization formed to resettle freed slaves in Africa, premised on the belief they could never peacefully integrate in white America. It was an uneasy marriage of progressive northerners who in varying degrees opposed slavery and southern slaveholders and defenders of slavery who feared a growing population of emancipated blacks would threaten the institution upon which their way of life depended. This alliance would eventually contribute to the organization's undoing, aided by the withering attacks of Garrison and other abolitionists beginning in the 1830s who painted the society as a slaveholder's scheme to perpetuate slavery. In its early years, however, the society boasted a litany of eminent Americans. Present at the founding meeting in Washington, D.C., were President James Monroe; Justice of the Supreme Court Bushrod Washington, nephew of the nation's first president; Francis Scott Key, whose verse later became the national anthem; the future president Andrew Jackson; Webster; and the convener of the group, then-Congressman Henry Clay.[11]

While the society was raising funds to support its cause, several developments in Congress shaped the organization's early course. When the Framers adopted the Constitution they included a clause prohibiting Congress from banning the importation of slaves before 1808. Driven by movements at home and abroad, Congress passed the Act of 1807, which went into effect on January 1 the next year and banned trading in slaves. Not until 1819, however, did Congress give the president means to enforce the ban. The later law authorized the president to use the nation's naval forces to interdict vessels used for "piratical aggression" and the transportation of slaves, appropriated funds, and provided that slaves captured in passage would be returned to Africa. A year later Congress spoke further on the issue, expanding the definition of piracy to include slave traders, thereby making them candidates for the death penalty.[12]

President Monroe ordered the construction of five ships in exercise of his new powers. One was the *U.S.S. Alligator,* built at Charlestown Navy Yard in Boston in 1820. White oak sheathed with copper planked the hull, and ten to twelve cast-iron cannons lined the deck. The *Alligator* embarked on its maiden voyage in spring of 1821, bound for the west coast of Africa under the command of Lieutenant Robert Stockton (1795–1866), whose grandfather was a signer of the Declaration of Independence. Stockton's career took him from the navy to the U.S. Senate and then to private business as president of the Delaware & Raritan Canal. But he made his most lasting marks at sea. In 1820 the colonization society had launched an expedition to form an outpost of former slaves on an island off the coast of Sierra Leone, but the mission proved fatal as nearly all quickly succumbed to disease. Eager to try again, prominent members enlisted Stockton's aid. Among the lieutenant's passengers was Eli Ayres, an agent for the society tasked with founding a new colony. With Stockton taking the lead in sometimes hostile negotiations (some accounts have him dictating terms through the barrel of a pistol), the mission purchased a tract of land on the coast. This region was more hospitable, and the colony grew. In 1847 it would declare independence and become the Republic of Liberia.[13]

After returning to Boston for a brief stay, Stockton and his crew again set sail for the west African coast in pursuit of pirates and slave traders. In the middle of the Atlantic and far from any shore, the *Alligator* spotted a ship some nine miles distant on the morning of November 5, 1821. Stockton sent up signals to determine its status, but no response ensued. The ship, later identified as the *Marianna Flora,* then lowered some or all of its sails and, according to Stockton's account, hoisted a blue pendant to half mast, indicating distress. Stockton set course for the ship to provide assistance. As the *Alligator* approached, however, the unidentified vessel, which had a longer range than Stockton's ship, began firing. At once Stockton hoisted the American flag, but the volleys continued. The *Alligator* remained unscathed and once within range returned fire. Faced with the prospect of battle with the more heavily armed American vessel and perhaps seeing Stockton's military garb, the other ship raced a Portuguese flag skyward and the firing ceased on both sides.[14]

Stockton ordered the ship's captain, an elderly man named De Britto, to board the *Alligator* and explain his actions. De Britto showed his logbooks, which revealed the *Marianna Flora* was carrying sugar, cotton, hides, tobacco, and other goods from Brazil en route to Lisbon. The Portuguese captain explained that he was afraid the *Alligator* was a privateer only feigning to be an American military ship—a not uncommon ruse. Nonetheless, Stockton ordered the crew bound and sent the vessel on a seven-week journey through icy waters to Boston so the courts could decide whether the prisoners were guilty of piracy.

After reviewing the criminal charges, a federal judge in Boston ruled the prisoners did not commit acts of piracy; rather, each side mistakenly believed the other was pirates intent on doing harm, shrouding their true character under deceptive colors. The owners of the *Marianna Flora,* however, had also filed a claim for damages against Lieutenant Stockton, claiming he had wrongfully bound the ship's crew and sent them to Boston when the facts at sea revealed the mutual mistake. Finding Stockton's actions unreasonable under the circumstances, the court awarded damages against him. The circuit court reversed.[15]

Representing Stockton before the Supreme Court was the U.S. attorney for Massachusetts, George Blake, and Daniel Webster. Webster was friends with the Stockton family and by that time a well-established advocate before the high court. Blake and Webster had enjoyed a long friendship, including frequent excursions to hunt and fish. Dividing the time with Webster, Blake argued that Stockton rightfully captured the *Marianna Flora* because he acted under authority of the law passed by Congress in 1819 giving the president power to pursue and apprehend persons committing "piratical aggression."[16]

Blake then proceeded to argue that not only the antipiracy statute justified Stockton's actions, but "the more general grounds of natural and public law" did as well. In returning fire, the *Alligator* acted under the universal precepts of self-defense. Moreover, the *Marianna Flora* initiated fire without justification. Blake acknowledged the genuine possibility that Captain De Britto may have mistaken the *Alligator* for a pirate ship, but even so the decision to attack at the time he did was not justified. To support this argument Blake looked to writings on the subject of anticipatory force.[17]

He began by describing the two ships as being in a "state of nature . . . upon the ocean, and waging war with each other." All the theorists examined in part II would not hesitate to agree. At their moment of intersection neither ship had the protections of a civil government, and both represented nations who stood in a permanent and international state of nature. Having made this observation, however, Blake began by looking to the standard governing individuals under a functioning government: "The analogies of the municipal law may assist to illustrate this branch of the inquiry. . . . By the rules of the common law, the rights of the party assailed are confined within very narrow limits. The danger must be manifest, impending, and almost unavoidable." The requirement here is imminence. Blake did not hesitate to conclude the *Marianna Flora* was not faced with imminent attack when it loosed its guns.[18]

Having made this point, Blake then recognized that according to well-recognized treatises a less stringent standard governed the actions of the Portuguese captain: "But the writers on natural law may, perhaps, on this occasion, be more properly cited." He turns to both Grotius and Pufendorf, quoting Pufendorf's standard for individuals in a state of nature (which, as we have seen, parallels the requirement for states): "Before I can actually assault another under colour of my own defence, I must have tokens and arguments amounting to a moral certainty that he entertains a grudge against me, and has a full design of doing me mischief, so that, unless I prevent him, I shall immediately feel his stroke. Among these tokens and signs giving me a right to make a violent assault upon another man, I must by no means reckon his bare superiority to me in strength and power."[19]

The use of the word "immediately" in this translation may suggest the imminence requirement, but several considerations require one to conclude otherwise. Blake clearly recognizes that the standard under the natural law is different and less stringent, contrasting the requirements of the "municipal law" with that of "the writers on natural law." Moreover, the passage from Pufendorf's *Law of Nature and Nations* that Blake quotes, read in its original context, unmistakably refers to a more lenient standard governing in a state of nature that does not limit anticipatory force to cases of imminent attack. The mention in the passage of the need to establish the enemy's certain intent to do harm would be eclipsed if Pufendorf were really requiring an imminent threat. The requirement of some active preparation in the paragraph that follows suggests the same.[20]

Blake is confident the *Marianna Flora* did not satisfy even this more permissive standard. None of Stockton's actions provided adequate assurance of his intent to harm. In making this argument, Blake accepted what the moral tradition had consistently affirmed: that states and individuals living in a state of nature, beyond the protections of a superior or functioning civil government, may use force absent an imminent threat when other criteria are satisfied. Although it was Blake who pressed this claim, no doubt he did so in agreement with Webster, who was by that time fully acquainted with the writings of the moral tradition and the lead attorney before the Court. In an early autobiographical fragment, Webster mentions several books he read in 1804 while training as an apprentice in a Boston law office, and included on the list are Vattel and Pufendorf.[21]

This earlier episode shows that Webster was both well versed in the moral tradition and, through his cocounsel, pressed the very nuance I have traced in the evolution of the tradition: that states are not categorically subject to the imminence requirement. Why, then, did Webster apply such a stringent imminence test in his letter to Henry Fox in 1841, under circumstances that in many ways paralleled those of the *Marianna Flora*? One can only surmise, but at least two explanations make some sense. Webster was a lawyer, and in the *Caroline* affair his client was the United States. He sought to make the strongest case he could on behalf of his client, even if it required a creative departure from his sources. In the volleys with Britain, the United States was well served by an especially strict standard for striking first. Moreover, when Webster wrote his letter to his British counterpart he was not making any sweeping generalizations about when states could resort to anticipatory force. As we saw earlier, states in the nineteenth century did not consider themselves bound by rules governing when a state could resort to arms. Webster's case was particular and involved the use of force under a bilateral neutrality agreement between the United States and Canada. It was only in the wake of World War II, Webster's letter having collected dust for more than a century, that the architects of international law, eager to place stringent limits on the use of force after two global conflicts and rejecting the Hobbesian picture of the world, found in Webster's language historical support for a narrow rule. They employed it in a way that meant saying much more than Webster could have ever said in his day.

This account of the moral tradition from which Webster both drew and departed points toward a morally principled case for rethinking Webster's Rule as it has been applied in the past several decades. The tradition consistently affirmed that states are not bound by the imminence requirement and that where it does apply, it serves only as a proxy for the fundamental moral principle that the use of armed force must be a last resort. In a clash between necessity and imminence—where using force is a last resort against a not-yet-imminent threat—the moral tradition gives reason to think necessity should govern. While Webster's Rule as it was appropriated under the UN Charter system was an attempt to limit the overall use of force, it was from its inception a notable departure from the moral tradition.

The imminence requirement served the international system well in the years after World War II, but the new threat of global terrorism has altered circumstances in such a way that unbending allegiance to that rule is no longer possible. The narrative in part II should break any hold Webster's Rule might have simply on grounds of historical inertia: for centuries thoughtful moralists, theologians, diplomats, and statesmen were willing to conclude that an absolute allegiance to an imminence requirement among states was asking too much, even while taking seriously the task of limiting the use of force among states and developing a nuanced standard toward that end. An imminent threat of sufficient magnitude will almost always make the use of force necessary if a state is to defend itself, but in the absence of an imminent threat such force might still be necessary—and just, as well. If one can imagine rare but real scenarios in which Webster's Rule may have to yield, what norms should take its place?

8

Beyond Webster's Rule

IN CHAPTER 1 I CONCLUDED THAT THE NEW threat of global terrorism does not require merely a refocusing of energies; it demands a rethinking of the rules. Against an enemy that lacks a sense of measured risk, seeks to effect maximum devastation, has or may soon have the means to do so, and easily evades detection, an unyielding commitment to Webster's Rule may bind us to take the first and perhaps fatal blow. At the same time, we must ensure revision does not violate America's moral identity—that what we are willing to do in the name of security does not fundamentally compromise who we claim to be. The Bush Doctrine left many Americans with a sense—ranging from a worry to a conviction—that the nation was somehow betraying itself. If the need for preventive force is plausible, what are the marks of just prevention?

To this question the moral tradition has much to say. Already we have seen that the tradition never placed an absolute imminence requirement on states. At the same time, the tradition does not speak to every aspect of the challenge we confront. Because the moral tradition evolved as a set of substantive norms, centuries before the UN Charter framework was in place, the tradition has less to say about the procedural norms that should govern preventive force. Although I begin with a few thoughts on procedure to signal where the debate may go, my focus lies where the tradition has the most to offer: developing substantive criteria governing the decision to strike first.

A Word on Procedure

Procedural norms focus not on the character of the threat or the response to it, but on the institutional path for reaching a decision. Under the prevailing interpretation of the Charter prior to 9/11, states decide whether to use preemptive force against an imminent threat, but only the Security Council can sanction preventive force. Webster's Rule is a substantive norm that identifies when the threat of attack is so near in space and time that the target state can justifiably preempt the harm. The requirement that a state considering the use of preventive force bring the matter before the Security Council for decision is a procedural norm. At present, no recognized substantive norms guide the Security Council's decision.

Any mix of procedural and substantive constraints on the use of preemptive or preventive force reflects a judgment about costs and benefits. The benefits of some procedural constraints on the use of preventive force follows rationales commonly discussed in legal theory. In an ideal world it is possible to imagine a system of only substantive norms. Parties to a dispute know the laws and all the relevant facts, the rules give guidance to the particular circumstances shaping the dispute, and the parties apply the rules to the situation at hand and in good faith comply with the determined outcome. The world we inhabit, however, looks very different from this ideal world. In any given situation we lack perfect knowledge of the laws and facts. Even assuming good faith and a capacity for objectivity, we will often not know everything we need to know. Furthermore, the law is written with some level of abstraction and is not sufficiently tailored to the specific circumstances at hand. A new rule needs to specify the law, as an interpretation of an ambiguous word or phrase or perhaps a balancing of factors to determine an outcome. And, last, we must assume parties to a conflict always enter this decision-making process beset by partiality. We construe rules and facts in a way that serves our interests. Procedural norms attempt to address each of these deficiencies. In the Anglo-American legal system devices such as discovery, cross-examination, and the jury are all procedural means to address these failures with the goal of reaching a correct result, while taking into account the costs of doing so.[1]

Each of these problems touches decisions regarding preventive force as well. Substantive norms governing such force will demand certain information about facts on the ground. Webster's Rule, for example, requires information about the movement of enemy forces so that a state can judge when an attack falls within the spectrum of actions posing an imminent threat. Any substantive norm will require high levels of intelligence about the intent and actions of the enemy. Information may not be forthcoming, however, or the intelligence available may be incomplete and carry varying degrees of reliability. Moreover, reaching a decision about preventive action will always require a specification of the substantive norm to a certain set of facts. Reasonable parties may disagree about whether circumstances satisfy a certain condition. And when states make these judgments on their own the problem of partiality will arise. The temptation will be for states to amplify risk to themselves and discount the costs of error imposed on others.

Requiring some multilateral organization to approve the use of preventive force is a procedural rule that attempts to address the problems of imperfect knowledge, indeterminate norms, and partiality. Bringing a threat to a multilateral organization may facilitate intelligence sharing and allow for more certainty. But, more important, such authorization provides a means of legitimization. By insisting that states make their case before the Security Council, the Charter regime seeks to limit the use of preventive force and spread responsibility for such decisions among several actors—those states that approved the action, and more generally every state that recognizes the United Nations' regime governing the use of force.

As the present willingness to rethink the Charter's restrictions on the use of preventive force suggests, however, the benefits of any procedural constraint must be weighed against the costs imposed. Although dynamics within the Security Council have shifted to some degree since the end of the Cold War, global politics continue to bear on how nations exercise their voting power—and, in the case of the five permanent members, their veto power. Describing this dynamic as a a system of checks and balances evokes a cherished concept in American democracy but rests on an analogy that cannot finally bear the weight. Lawmakers who oppose the president's agenda become politically accountable for their actions within a democratic system. If France or China blocks authorization to use preventive force on the basis of economic interests, they may bear little or no cost if the anticipated threat is realized. Moreover, in some cases the mere fact of bringing the threat before the Security Council could trigger an attack. Or the time involved in so doing could jeopardize the opportunity for an effective defense during a narrow window of opportunity to address the threat.[2]

In any legal regime one needs to ask whether the norms governing certain actions place too high an obstacle to reach outcomes that may be necessary under certain circumstances. The current de jure requirement that states attain Security Council approval before using preventive force tilts the balance strongly against such action. Nonetheless, given the scenarios in which security might demand otherwise, states have strong incentives to act even though the system might forbid action, either because the Security Council has denied the request or because the act of bringing the request would imperil an effective defense.

As we saw in chapter 2, events earlier in the twentieth century brought into question the balance between the costs and benefits of a system that gave the Security Council a monopoly over the use of preventive force. But 9/11 and the Iraq War of 2003 led to a new willingness to rethink the rules. Since then several states have signaled a readiness to recognize a narrow range of preventive actions against terrorists, absent Security Council approval. While a loosening of the Charter's restriction of preventive force to only those actions authorized by the Security Council is underway, the extent of revision is not yet clear.[3]

The present willingness to reconsider the limits on preventive force under the Charter should not mean a rejection of that framework, but rather a reinterpretation of it through the mechanism of customary law. Most legal systems sanction certain actions otherwise forbidden but subsequently deemed justified as necessary measures of self-defense. As Paul Robinson explains in his treatise *Criminal Law Defenses*, "The harm caused by the justified behavior remains a legally recognized harm that is to be avoided whenever possible. Under the special justifying circumstances, however, that harm is outweighed by the need to avoid an even greater harm or to further a greater societal interest." As Robinson explains, justification defenses have the same internal structure: a set of triggering conditions that permit a necessary and proportional response.[4]

This formula should be familiar: it is the same requirement Webster argued the British did not satisfy when they attacked the *Caroline*. Recall Webster's language: "It will be for that Government to show a necessity of self-defence, instant, overwhelming, leaving no choice of means, and no moment for deliberation." Furthermore, "the act, justified by the necessity of self-defence, must be limited by that necessity, and kept clearly within it." The first requirement is necessity; the second, proportionality; and the triggering condition is an imminent threat.[5]

Article 51 of the UN Charter is an exception to the otherwise broad ban on the "threat or use of force" in Article 2(4). Recall that under the exception, states retain "the inherent right of individual or collective self-defence if an armed attack occurs." In this framework, Webster's Rule represents a widely recognized defense bearing the status of international customary law. A state that employs preventive force absent Security Council approval, however, might still make the case under the general formula of self-defense that its actions were necessary and proportional given the emergency it confronted. Given enough exceptions and over time the contours of a widely recognized rule may emerge. That is to say, customary law may evolve to grant the same status to a narrow norm governing preventive force that states came to recognize in the last half of the twentieth century for preemptive force under Webster's Rule.[6]

Although states adapting to the new balance between security and restraint have already begun the process of revision, proposals that would radically revise the procedural constraints on preventive force at this point in time are misguided. These revisions should come incrementally and be limited and narrowly tailored to what experience demands. For example, while states may recognize a more liberal allowance for preventive force under Article 2(4) against terrorists operating in territory beyond state control, the case for the same against other states is far less compelling (see below).

Toward a Substantive Standard

Where the moral tradition has the most to offer is in the substantive norms governing the use of preventive force. As the secretary-general's High-level Panel on Threats, Challenges, and Change recognized, the international community lacks criteria that spell out when a first strike is permissible. Whether the decision maker is the Security Council, some multi-lateral organization, or individual states, agreement on a set of substantive norms governing preventive force is an urgent task. Procedural constraints alone are not enough; we need a jurisprudence of just prevention.[7]

Substantive norms are important for several reasons. A recognized framework will facilitate shared expectations about when preventive force is permitted. Of course all norms carry some measure of indeterminateness, but in the absence of such a framework states may have widely divergent views. Achieving agreement on strict and narrow limits will enhance security. The alternative is that states will craft the norms in the heat of decision making, with incentives aligned to make them overinclusive. Last, while procedural norms can lend legitimacy, they do not alone speak to the morality of any particular use of preventive force. Toward that end, a substantive account of just prevention is needed.

Before identifying what circumstances might justify a first strike absent an imminent threat, one needs to consider whether the norms should take the form of a rule or a standard. This common distinction in legal theory is based on the degree to which each constrains the person applying them. A rule is more restrictive. It includes a triggering condition and a consequence. Once the rule and the facts are clear, the consequence follows as a matter of course. Speeding laws are a good example: when the radar clocks your car going eighty-seven mph in a seventy mph zone, the officer quickly concludes you broke the law—she may decide not to enforce the law against you, but that is a different question from whether you broke the law. Standards are less constraining and give more discretion to the person applying them. Rather than identifying a triggering condition and a consequence, a standard will often provide one or more indeterminate considerations which the decision maker must apply to the circumstances at hand. The idea in the common law of torts that a person is negligent when she fails to do what a reasonable person would do under the given circumstances is an example of a standard.

The trade-offs between rules and standards are several. One concerns predictability. A rule allows the rule maker greater ability to ensure certain results because the norm is marked by a higher level of determinateness, giving the person who applies it less discretion. A standard offers less predictability and gives the person applying it greater leeway. When policy makers want to ensure certain actions do not happen, for example, they will often regulate behavior through a rule rather than a standard. A related trade-off concerns enforceability. Rules are often easy to enforce, standards less so because of the possibility of reasonable disagreement about whether the standard was satisfied in a given situation. And a final trade-off concerns versatility. A rule by virtue of its simplicity often excludes relevant circumstances that might otherwise make the action lawful. The man who exceeds the speed limit as he rushes to the hospital with a passenger moments from death breaks the law, but it is not difficult to imagine a law that makes an exception in such circumstances. A standard takes more factors into account, giving greater flexibility in light of circumstances that might arise. On the other hand, for this same reason a standard might invite some actions that should not occur.

Webster's demand for a "necessity of self-defence, instant, overwhelming, leaving no choice of means, and no moment for deliberation" is a rule. Once the triggering condition—namely, the presence of an imminent threat —is met, the consequence—namely, the right to use anticipatory force—follows. But rules and standards come in hard and soft forms, and the contemporary imminence rule is a soft rule. Whether a threat is imminent admits of some debate, and reasonable persons may disagree. Speed limits, on the other hand, are hard rules defined by bright lines.[8]

Although both types of norm come with some limitations, the norm governing preventive force should be a standard rather than a rule. In particular, we need a hard standard that provides specific criteria for determining the rare moments when force might be necessary absent an imminent threat. Webster's Rule is attractive for its simplicity, but in drawing a line at imminence it eclipses a whole range of considerations that may be relevant to whether a state needs to use force in self-defense where the threat is not yet imminent. The drawback of a standard is greater discretion in determining whether to use preventive force. But favoring a standard recognizes that the costs of inaction are likely greater.

Toward this end, the moral tradition on the just war has much to offer, having developed such a standard over centuries of thoughtful reflection. The emergence of imminence as the predominant criterion in assessing anticipatory actions had the effect of obscuring other points of moral assessment developed within the tradition. These other criteria were, to some degree, preconditions of an imminent threat: where the threat was imminent, there was no pressing reason to consider them. The standard I will describe includes the now-recognizable criteria that developed within the tradition: certainty of intent, sufficient means, active preparation, magnitude of harm, probability of harm, proportionality (of ends), and, most important, necessity (or last resort). The first five criteria look to the nature of the threat (threat-assessment criteria); the last two look to the nature of the response (response-assessment criteria). What these criteria might mean today is an open question. Although I will not answer all the questions that arise, I will sketch the main lines of a standard.

Certainty of intent

Vitoria required certainty of intent, and everyone following him in the tradition did so as well. This requirement marked a sharp divide between the just war tradition and its just fear rival. Mere power—sufficient means—could never in itself justify a first strike. This criterion, however, raises several questions. For example, what is the object of intent that the state considering the use of anticipatory force must discern? Intent to do what? Of course, under the Charter system the use of force toward the end of self-defense is only legitimate against an "armed attack." Although most commentators conclude that under customary law any armed attack is sufficient to warrant a defensive use of force, in the case of preventive action the target state should also know something about the magnitude of harm, which I will examine shortly.

This requirement also raises the question as to how specific one's knowledge of the aggressor's intent must be. Is it sufficient to possess knowledge of only a general will to attack? Must this knowledge concern a highly specific threat of attack, including some knowledge of the time, place, or method (or all three) of the anticipated harm? Although these details will often bolster the case for preventive force—and in some cases may be necessary to fulfill other criteria, such as magnitude of harm—requiring them could raise the bar too high. An actual attack always carries an address. It is inscribed in space and time. It is not knowledge of this particular address, however, that warrants the use of defensive force once the attack is in progress, but rather the mere fact of an armed attack. Specific intelligence as to the time, place, and method may often be very difficult to ascertain, as the events leading up to 9/11 show. More important, even if these details are known, they do not make the anticipated action more or less an armed attack, against which states have a right not to take the first blow. Knowledge of another's intent to attack the state is all this criterion requires, since it is the mere act that justifies a defensive response. Requiring knowledge of time, place, and method of an attack might distinguish lofty claims of intent from those actively pursued, but this demand would ask too much of this first criterion. Rather, the separate requirement of active preparation weeds out mere aspirational claims.

Furthermore, what does it mean that a state must be certain of the aggressor's intent? Conjecture alone is insufficient; rather, the state must have evidence conveying a strong assurance that the potential aggressor intends to attack. Certainty in the tradition has never meant the most exacting demand this term might convey. Grotius makes this point by drawing on Aristotle's distinction between the certainty required in mathematics and the same in morals. Obviously, the fact that anticipatory force by definition always takes place at some point prior to an actual attack rules out an account of certainty that precludes the possibility of future contingencies.[9]

Finally, what are the means for registering intent? Actual testimony is one form. In some cases this evidence is available through intercepted communications, other forms of intelligence gathering, and even public statements. Actions, however, can also register intent. Detailed satellite images of persons in terrorist training camps undertaking exercises that have no purpose other than wanton destruction or a past record of terrorist attacks could all support the case for intent.

In a small number of cases, the possession or near possession of certain weapons of mass destruction (WMD) by terrorists would immediately satisfy this requirement. Strong evidence that a cell possesses a nuclear bomb or a highly lethal chemical or biological agent would establish intent, since such weapons have no legitimate purpose in the hands of a nonstate actor. At least one purpose in requiring clear intent is the tradition's concern to distinguish less threatening accumulations of power, such as a strengthening economy, from those directed toward an actual armed attack. Where the means of power have no benign use, such as a terrorist's possession of WMD, possession betrays intent.

Sufficient means

The moral tradition predicated anticipatory force on a showing that the potential aggressor had the means to carry out the intended attack. A threat of harm absent the actual means to effect it would not justify a first strike. The events of September 11, however, altered the sense of what counts as sufficient means. Conventional arms and WMD are always sufficient. Civilian aircraft employed in the service of terror, however, carried out the destruction of 9/11. One forward-looking lesson of that day is to consider unsuspecting means as possible vehicles for an attack. Inevitably, the enlarged imagination of contemporary terrorists has the effect of lowering the standard for what counts.

Although actual possession will always satisfy this criterion, in some cases the near proximity of attaining the means would suffice as well. The answer will depend on a full assessment of the situation, taking into account all the criteria. For example, if the aggressor's intent is clear, the probability of attaining the means is high, the potential harm that would result is severe, and a narrow window of opportunity to forestall the harm makes it likely that acting now would be an act of last resort, then circumstances may justify some anticipatory military action.

Active preparation

A further requirement is evidence of active preparation on the part of the aggressor to carry out the intended attack, but not necessarily the action that initiates the actual attack. Active preparation is activity short of that which marks an imminent attack. In some cases this assessment will take place in the course of discerning certain intent. Especially where WMD are involved, the mere attainment of the means to carry out the attack will satisfy the requirement of active preparation. But where nonconventional means are used, such as was the case in 9/11, assurance of the enemy's intent alone would not justify anticipatory force absent knowledge of some active preparation underway.

Returning to the discussion of certainty of intent, the effect of requiring knowledge of the aggressor's intent to conduct an armed attack, and not necessarily the time, place, and method of attack, is that states considering the use of anticipatory force need not know every detail about how preparations fit into a planned attack. It is sufficient that certain activities are taking place in preparation for terrorist attacks. For example, knowledge of a terrorist training camp could satisfy this criterion, even if the particulars of the trainees' missions are not fully known. In the case of 9/11, for example, several terrorists that conducted the operation did not know their assigned mission until the very end.

Magnitude of harm

A revised standard must also look to the magnitude of harm that would result from an armed attack. An assessment of this kind is generally thought not to apply in cases of an actual armed attack under customary international law. Rather, the "inherent right of self-defense" applies in the case of any armed attack (though states are limited in their response by the customary law requirement of proportionality). Again, however, the differences between using defensive force against an actual attack and using it as an anticipatory action justify a more stringent standard. The possibility of interpretive misjudgment and intervening circumstances to prevent or forestall an attack push in the direction of raising the barriers.[10]

As mentioned earlier, sometimes this assessment will require a measure of knowledge about the time, place, and method of the coming attack. In other cases, however, states considering the use of anticipatory force can reach reliable judgments about the magnitude of harm by having knowledge of both the means possessed by the terrorist group and its intentions and possibly its record of past terrorist activities. A state need not know that a foreign terrorist cell present in the target state plans to release nerve gas at this place and at this time; it is sufficient to know the cell possesses the potent agent and is seeking opportunity to use it.

The weight to attribute to the magnitude of harm will depend on other assessments. There is no single level of harm, the exceeding of which warrants the use of anticipatory force. Some forms of attack, such as the detonation of a large dirty bomb in a dense urban area, the release of a highly lethal pathogen, or the blowing up of a chlorine tank, quickly satisfy this criterion. Forms of attack such as these that hold the potential for widespread destruction may tip the balance in favor of allowing anticipatory force, even when other measures under this standard are not as strong.

Probability of harm

The use of preventive force must also depend on the probability of the anticipated attack. In addition to serving as a proxy for necessity, imminence also measured the probability of the harm: an imminent attack was highly probable, likely coming in a matter of moments. In the case of preventive force, a determination of the probability of an attack is still very important even though measures other than imminence are needed. In reaching judgments about probability, several factors are relevant. Announced threats, a past record of aggression, and the ideology of the state or terrorist organization will inform this judgment. Other criteria already mentioned are applicable as well. For instance, the availability of sufficient means to carry out the attack as well as the level of preparation for the attack will play some role.

Proportionality

Unlike the five threat-assessment criteria, the last two criteria, necessity and proportionality, assess the potential response. Customary international law recognizes both norms as limits on any use of force. Moreover, they composed the two prongs of Webster's Rule and are deeply rooted in the moral tradition. The uncertainty that marks any use of preventive force elevates the importance of both considerations above what is required in the case of response to an actual armed attack.

The demand for proportionality, sometimes called proportionality of ends, measures the proposed use of force against the legitimate end for using force, namely, self-defense. It might be that the end of a particular anticipatory action, judged overall, is disproportional to what self-defense requires. Using Webster's language, "The act, justified, by the necessity of self-defense, must be limited by that necessity, and kept clearly within it." Proportionality, then, asks whether this particular proposed use of preventive force is necessary for the end of self-defense. The types of action a state might take as an act of anticipatory self-defense spread across a spectrum ranging from a military blockade to a single surgical strike to a full invasion. In each instance, the proposed use of force must be proportional to the perceived threat. This judgment has weighed heavily in assessments of the Iraq War of 2003, as critics have questioned whether invasion with the goal of regime change—at the far end of the spectrum of anticipatory force—was a proportional response necessary for the defense of the United States and its coalition partners.[11]

Last resort

Finally, and perhaps most important, just preventive force is always a last resort: the state considering such action must first exhaust all reasonable alternatives. The moral tradition discussed this assessment long before it ever turned to the question of striking first, although it was not one of the core marks of a just war included in Aquinas's formulation. Starting with Vitoria the tradition elevated the importance of last resort in the context of anticipatory force. No longer did it serve a mere prudential role. As Vitoria stated, a man can strike first only if it is "a means necessary to defend himself." That the tradition would place special emphasis on necessity in the context of anticipatory force is not surprising, given the unavoidable possibility an anticipated threat may not occur. So the requirement of last resort bears a heavy burden.[12]

Taken to its extreme, this demand might preclude all but the most imminent of attacks: only at the last moment before the blow arrives can a person say that using force is a last resort. This reading, however, would simply equate necessity with imminence, but, as we have seen, the moral tradition rejected this reading. At some point other alternatives become unreasonable insofar as pursuing them would seriously jeopardize achieving the legitimate end of self-defense. An alternative that might obviate the need to use force is not necessarily a reasonable alternative, especially taking into account the magnitude of the harm.

Nonetheless, anticipatory force may not be a last resort until the threat is imminent. The kinds of threats America confronted after World War II have not disappeared. In most, perhaps nearly all, cases imminence will continue to be the triggering circumstance and only rarely will necessity arise when imminence does not. But categorically conditioning a first strike on an imminent attack is misguided. Faced with an overwhelming threat to their security, states will not wait until this point is reached to defend themselves.

Reasonable alternatives to preventive force may include strategies of deterrence, denial, and engagement. Deterrent strategies involve the creation of disincentives to threatening behavior. This strategy matured in the Cold War as one of the principal means employed by the two superpowers to achieve security in the context of nuclear armament. The effectiveness of deterrence, however, transcends that conflict. Even rogue regimes are eager to maintain their control on power and will often respond to deterrent strategies meant to prevent the use of WMD or transfer of the same to terrorists, especially as technologies capable of tracing nuclear weapons to their source advance. At the same time, for reasons examined in chapter 1, deterrence may have little value against terrorists who have no defined territory and are willing to die on behalf of their cause.[13]

Denial strategies will also have a continuing and important role to play. The regime of nuclear inspections under the International Atomic Energy Agency is one example and has proved an important restraint on nuclear proliferation. Strengthened border controls and better inspection regimes for containers arriving in the United States are just two of the myriad means to deny malevolent actors the ability to inflict harm. Finally, strategies of engaging potentially harmful state actors have also proved to have some value. The United States helped end the Libyan quest for nuclear arms through this strategy, which included both sanctions and incentives for compliance. Again, both strategies have limits when applied to terrorists, who are either not subject to the various inspection regimes, may easily evade them, or may have evil ends that engagement will not curtail.

Together these seven criteria form a standard for deciding when anticipatory force is permissible, looking both to the character of the threat and the shape of the intended response. Applying this standard is not a science but an exercise of practical reason. The assessments are several, and the weight to be accorded each point differs with circumstances. The failure to satisfy any one requirement will mean the state has not made its case for preventive action. The just fear tradition sanctioned preventive force in those cases in which one state had the means to threaten another, even if the state failed to demonstrate any intent to harm. The moral tradition on the just war, however, rejected the claim that sufficient means was enough to justify anticipatory force (in the case of states). Nonetheless, a strong showing in one area can make up for a weak showing in another. This standard lacks the simplicity of Webster's Rule, but the severity and complexity of today's threats demand a more nuanced framework for making these difficult judgments. Applying a shared standard will not guarantee shared conclusions, but having a common framework will facilitate reasoned debate on the decisive issues.

Cases

A few cases illuminate how such a standard might balance the twin goals of security and restraint. I offer not a thorough assessment, but some comments focusing on what the substantive standard might reveal.

The Iraq War of 2003. Any framework recognizing an expanded place for anticipatory force will have to assess the Iraq War of 2003, insofar as it was justified as a preventive war. The Bush administration provided several arguments in support of the invasion. Elie Wiesel, a survivor of Auschwitz and winner of the Nobel Peace Prize, visited President Bush a few weeks before missiles fell on Baghdad and told him intervention was a moral imperative given the atrocities Saddam had committed. Various voices within the administration hinted at this argument as well. When war did come, the president expressly justified the invasion on resolutions dating back to the First Gulf War and culminating in Security Council Resolution 1441 (2002), demanding Iraq comply with its disarmament obligations. At the same time, the president also cast the war as an act of preventive force. The Bush Doctrine emerged in the lead-up to the war in Iraq. The claim was that Saddam Hussein both possessed and sought to acquire more WMD and that he was able and willing to supply terrorists who might harm the United States, its citizens, and its interests. Whether the administration formally relied on it or not, prevention was a primary rationale. The exemplar of the Bush Doctrine became a war at the far end of the spectrum of anticipatory force: a full invasion with the stated goal of regime change.[14]

Setting aside the humanitarian and violated resolution rationales, one might ask, was the invasion justified solely as an act of preventive force? The Bush administration argued that Hussein would transfer WMD to terrorists, who would then harm the United States. Several top officials searched feverishly for a way to connect Iraq and al Qaeda. Although various claims were floated to the public, none were substantiated. The strongest case for intent was based on Hussein's abysmal track record. While actions can be a proxy for intent and the claim was certainly plausible, it lacked support based on present actions.

Questions of intent aside, attention has focused on the question of whether Iraq had sufficient means, namely, whether it possessed or was close to possessing WMD. The administration claimed Hussein had biological weapons and mobile production facilities, had stored and was continuing to produce chemical weapons, and had reconstituted the country's nuclear weapons program. The release in 2003 of portions of the National Intelligence Estimate *Iraq's Continuing Program for Weapons of Mass Destruction* (2002) made the charge public. After more than a year of investigation by the Iraq Survey Group (ISG), a fact-finding team formed by the coalition governments after the invasion, the ISG issued a report concluding that "Saddam wanted to recreate Iraq's WMD capability" and that the regime possessed and was seeking to produce missiles that exceeded the 150km range allowed under Security Council Resolution 687. On the central claims concerning WMD, however, the report found no credible evidence:

1. Nuclear weapons: "Although Saddam clearly assigned a high value to the nuclear progress and talent that had been developed up to the 1991 war, the program ended and the intellectual capital decayed in the succeeding years."
2. Chemical weapons: "While a small number of old, abandoned chemical munitions have been discovered, ISG judges that Iraq unilaterally destroyed its undeclared chemical weapons stockpile in 1991."
3. Biological weapons: "ISG found no direct evidence that Iraq, after 1996, had plans for a new [biological weapons (BW)] program or was conducting BW-specific work for military purposes. . . . ISG judges that in 1991 and 1992, Iraq appears to have destroyed its undeclared stocks of BW

weapons [*sic*] and probably destroyed remaining holdings of bulk BW agent."[15]

None of the government reviews discussed the issue of how policy makers used the intelligence. And they can only make judgments based on the best information available to them. Nonetheless, the highly circumstantial quality of the evidence available at the time raises significant questions about the case for WMD. The director of the CIA, George Tenet, had told the president and several of his advisers that the case for WMD was a "slam dunk." But well before Tenet gave this assurance, both President Bush and Vice President Dick Cheney had made unequivocal public statements that Saddam possessed WMD. No one can be faulted for finding it plausible to think Saddam might try to acquire and then conceal WMD, but, again, the prewar intelligence supporting this claim did not support the confidence the president and his inner circle conveyed to the public and which we now know was unfounded.[16]

Most important, the invasion was not a measure of last resort. The United States and Britain were already using force in Iraq and had been doing so for some time. In December 1998 Operation Desert Fox launched as a four-day bombing campaign following Iraq's refusal to cooperate with UN weapons inspectors. Especially in the years prior to the Iraq War of 2003, coalition forces regularly used military power to enforce the no-fly zones in northern and southern Iraq. Intent on war, the administration too quickly dismissed the possibility of some measure of lesser force able to isolate and contain the Iraqi threat. In a *New York Times* op-ed piece just days before the invasion began, Michael Walzer argued along these same lines, offering four practical steps:

1. place the entire country under a no-fly zone;
2. impose the "smart sanctions" the administration described prior to 9/11 and insist that other states comply;
3. step up the inspection regimes by sending in more monitors, backing them up with armed soldiers, and sending surveillance planes in without forty-eight hours' notice; and
4. demand that the European nations balking at war join in this vigorous response.[17]

The United States had good reason to lack faith in the UN inspection process under the direction of Hans Blix, but the choice was not between a full invasion and Blix. The Bush administration did not rest its case for war solely on a preventive force rationale, but insofar as it did rely on this argument it failed to make its case under the standard sketched here.

The 9/11 Attacks. It is difficult to identify when the threat that would materialize on September 11 posed an imminent danger. It is even more difficult to believe that preemptive force at that point in time would have allowed the United States to act effectively toward the legitimate end of self-defense. Certainly when the highjackers wrested control of the planes and veered toward their targets, the attack was imminent. Waiting for this point, however, would already have committed the United States to take the first blow: the very act of using preemptive force, even if time allowed, would have meant the certain death of several hundred Americans on board the planes as a result of American firepower. Under Webster's Rule the attack was not imminent in the months of flight training, surveillance, and other logistical preparations the terrorists engaged in in the United States and abroad during 2000 and 2001. The question, then, is whether the standard for just prevention might have sanctioned an earlier use of force that could have sufficiently disrupted the chain of events leading up to 9/11, or, looking forward, might disrupt future attacks, without granting such license that fear becomes the governing norm.

The standard requires sophisticated intelligence about the enemy, which was lacking in the months leading up to September 11. Officials not only lacked intelligence about the coming attack, but in addition they did not have a complete picture of al Qaeda's involvement in previous terrorist attacks against the American military and diplomatic presence outside the United States from 1992 onward. The *9/11 Report,* issued in 2004 by a committee appointed by the president, describes a complex narrative of events leading up to the attacks. In applying the standard for just prevention to these events, one must ask whether given better intelligence the government might have struck the first blow.[18]

As an initial matter, the demand of clear intent is easily satisfied. Bin Laden openly expressed his intent to kill Americans in two separate fatwas, issued in 1996 and in 1998. In both cases, he explicitly called for jihad against Americans on account of the U.S. military presence in Saudi Arabia, the site of Islam's two most holy sites. Bin Laden signed a statement in 1998 declaring, "The ruling to kill the Americans and their allies—civilian and military—is an individual duty for every Muslim who can do it in any country in which it is possible to do it." In an interview in December 1998 Bin Laden confirmed his aim to retaliate for a missile attack by the United States in Afghanistan on August 20, 1998, stressing that his response would take time.[19]

In addition to these open statements, Bin Laden's clear intent to attack American interests was confirmed by intelligence gathered in the late 1990s showing al Qaeda had a military committee planning numerous operations against U.S. interests worldwide, was seeking nuclear material, and had extensive terrorist training camps within Afghanistan. Firm evidence of Bin Laden's direct role in the attacks on the U.S. embassies in Kenya and Tanzania on August 7, 1998, as well as his indirect role in several previous attacks, confirmed the clear intent of Bin Laden and al Qaeda to continue attacking American interests. The success of these attacks, intelligence pointing to attempts by al Qaeda to obtain nuclear materials, and the wide network of financing all suggested al Qaeda had sufficient means to carry out its ends.[20]

In the *9/11 Report* the commission identified at least two missed opportunities that might have informed government officials of the direct preparations underway in the United States and abroad. Nonetheless the government lacked specific knowledge of preparations by al Qaeda for what became the September 11 attacks. As defined earlier, however, the requirements of clear intent and active preparation do not require specific knowledge of the time, place, or method of an attack; rather, strong evidence that the potential aggressor clearly intends to attack the target state and that the aggressor is actively preparing to achieve this end is sufficient.[21]

In the months leading up to September 11, the government had several indications al Qaeda was preparing such an attack. During the summer of 2001, especially in June and July, intelligence officials registered a tremendous spike in reports of a large and near-term attack against the United States, with most signals pointing toward an attack against American interests abroad. Although the terrorists eventually moved the target date back to early September, the intercepted communications related to what would become 9/11. Admittedly, intelligence reports are rarely tidy and come with varying degrees of reliability, but the United States was aware al Qaeda was actively training terrorists in camps throughout Afghanistan at least since the late 1990s. Various forms of intelligence gathering and Bin Laden's own testimony attested to this fact.[22]

As to the magnitude of harm, any intelligence that would have pointed to the kind of devastation caused by the attacks of 9/11 would have satisfied this measure. Several past attacks, moreover, suggested the level of destruction al Qaeda sought to inflict. The attack on the World Trade Center in 1993, organized by the mastermind of the 9/11 attacks, Khalid Sheikh Mohammed, under the direction of Bin Laden, attested to this fact. Other attacks that directly implicated al Qaeda did as well, including the orchestrated attacks on the U.S. embassies in Africa in 1998 that killed 224 people and injured several thousand others, including many Americans.

Lacking direct evidence of the preparations underway for the events of September 11, the intelligence community was strained to make judgments about the probability of an attack. In the months leading up to September 11, however, intelligence from multiple sources affirmed the likelihood of a near-term attack against the United States. As the commission reported, "A terrorist threat advisory distributed in late June indicated a high probability of near-term 'spectacular' terrorist attacks resulting in numerous casualties. Other reports' titles warned, 'Bin Laden Attacks May be Imminent' and 'Bin Laden and Associates Making Near-Term Threats.'"[23]

Although one must avoid projecting insights easily formed in the present into the past, it seems clear that at least some high-level officials had already concluded an attack against the United States was probable. Moreover, the events of 9/11 did not occur in a vacuum. The intelligence community and the principals in charge of protecting the United States did not wake up that morning to learn of a group called al Qaeda. Bin Laden's terrorist organization was indirectly linked to multiple attacks against U.S. interests from 1992 through 1996, a conclusion the CIA was able to draw as early as 1997. Starting with the attacks on the U.S. embassies in Africa in 1998, Bin Laden was directly involved in attacking the United States and its presence abroad. Although it was not until after 9/11 that the United States was able to affirm

Bin Laden's personal involvement in the attack on the *U.S.S. Cole* in the Yemeni port of Aden on October 12, 2000, by mid-November of that year it was clear al Qaeda had carried out the attack. The repeated success of al Qaeda terrorist operations against the United States, joined with Bin Laden's overt aspirations to attack the American homeland, all suggested the probability of a future attack.[24]

If an opportunity had arisen in which the use of preventive force might have sufficiently thwarted the September 11 attacks, the United States would still have to meet the essential requirement of showing armed force was a last resort. Even though most of the primary government officials responsible for decision making in this area did not grasp the gravity of the threat posed by al Qaeda, several efforts were underway to reduce the risk. Beginning in 1998 the government sought to freeze the assets of both al Qaeda and the Taliban, the radical Islamist regime governing Afghanistan at the time. The government also seriously pursued diplomatic efforts. In 1998 the State Department issued a formal warning to the Taliban and the Sudan that the United States would hold them directly responsible for any terrorist attacks on Americans as long as they continued to provide sanctuary to al Qaeda. The United States successfully pushed for multiple Security Council resolutions against Afghanistan, including economic and trade sanctions, as well as an arms embargo against the Taliban. In 2000 a high-level effort sought to persuade Pakistan to use its influence with the Taliban to expel Bin Laden. Exactly a week before the 9/11 attacks, key policy makers approved a draft presidential directive calling for a multiyear effort to "'eliminate the al Qida [sic] network of terrorist groups as a threat to the U.S.'" The plan included stepped-up diplomatic, economic, and law enforcement efforts, and, if necessary, the use of armed force.[25]

The point of this exercise is not to identify a specific point in time when the United States should have used preventive force against Bin Laden and the al Qaeda network. And better intelligence may have led to a response that did not include recourse to armed force. But if the window of opportunity opened, the United States would have had a compelling case for a preventive military strike.

A Failed Nuclear State. My last case is prospective: the possibility that a nuclear-armed state might collapse and enable terrorists to acquire WMD in the ensuing chaos. Consider, for example, a case in which Islamic extremists in Pakistan assassinate the head of state and the country tumbles into anarchy. At least for some time, neither the Pakistan army nor any coalition is able to restore order. Control over the nation's nuclear arsenal is uncertain, and, under the cover of confusion, al Qaeda operatives, perhaps aided by officers in the military who are either sympathetic or willing to take a bribe, acquire one or more nuclear weapons. Although the prospects of a terrorist group producing their own nuclear weapon are slim, a scenario in which terrorists acquire WMD in the context of a failed nuclear state is plausible.[26]

This possibility is a nightmare the United States can never permit to occur, and the pressure for quick and decisive action would be exceedingly high. One option immediately on the table would be some level of preventive military action—one or more surgical strikes or perhaps something more—to destroy the nuclear weapons before they slip into the wrong hands. If the transfer took place, the terrorists and their hideaways would be the next target. The United States would need intelligence as to where the weapons were located and would have to act with immediate haste. Although production facilities are easier to identify, the weapons themselves are small, emit levels of radiation too low for long-range sensors to trace, and are easily transportable.

Might the standard for just prevention permit such an action? It is not difficult to conclude that under the right circumstances the standard would permit a proportional armed response. As we have seen, a strong case for one criterion can make up for a weaker showing in another area, and this is especially true when, as here, the magnitude of harm is extremely high. Strategies of deterrence for the most part place an effective check on nuclear states. As the Cold War shows, the weapons themselves become the means of deterrence, and states often seek them with that aim in mind. In the case of terrorists such a check is gone; their aim in acquiring WMD is to use them. Al Qaeda has left no doubt about its interest in wreaking maximum devastation. Assuming any weapon the organization acquired was operational and the terrorists knew how to deploy it, the probability of some future harm is great.

As stated earlier, the actual or near possession of WMD in the hands of terrorists, for whom such a weapon has no legitimate purpose, satisfies the need to establish active preparation. The question here is whether the United States has sufficient evidence that al Qaeda or some other terrorist organization is near attaining WMD. The crisis would likely ensue with little warning, and intelligence about al Qaeda's attempts to gain control of a nuclear weapon may be incomplete. Given the terrorist organization's express willingness to acquire WMD, its successful track record in carrying out previous attacks, its known and active presence in Pakistan, and especially the immense destruction that would follow, however, intelligence about the specific plans to seize a nuclear weapon may not be necessary.

Finally, to satisfy the standard for just prevention, the response would have to be necessary and proportional to the threat. This scenario presents a good example of when the use of preventive force may be a last resort against a threat not yet imminent. Here not only is al Qaeda not ready to execute a plan that would involve exploding a nuclear weapon in a high population area; it does not even have the weapon yet. Nonetheless, once the terrorist organization attains it the ability of the United States to prevent an attack may be unacceptably low. Stopping the transfer of WMD to terrorists presents a narrow window of opportunity—perhaps the last reasonable alternative—to prevent an exceedingly great harm that has a high probability of taking place. The limited case for preventive force, and especially the demanding requirement of last resort, is much more likely to justify military action against terrorists than states, which are more responsive to strategies of deterrence, denial, or engagement.

Conclusion

IN THE WAKE OF SEPTEMBER 11, PREVENTIVE force—"preemption" in popular discourse—came to symbolize America's quest for security in an insecure world. The terrorist attacks on New York and Washington, D.C., inaugurated a shift toward strategies of prevention at every level, and preventive force became the public face of this transformation. In the day-to-day fight against terrorism preventive force should be a tool rarely used, an option of last resort. By and large, success in this fight will depend on increased intelligence capacity, refined international coordination, tough diplomacy, the normal tools of law enforcement, interruption of the financial streams that fill the coffers of terror, and other means. Nonetheless, the fall of the Twin Towers made it plausible to think that striking the first blow against a less-than-imminent threat could be a last resort to prevent an attack of unacceptable magnitude. Webster's demand for a threat "instant, overwhelming, leaving no choice of means, and no moment for deliberation" could no longer exhaust the cases in which anticipatory force might be necessary. Imminence, we've learned, is no longer a failsafe proxy for necessity.[1]

The task of revision faces immense challenges, but the moral tradition on the just war points a principled way forward. The tradition suggests a framework that limits recourse to force, while recognizing that an absolute commitment to the imminence criterion may fail to provide states the security they require. Over several centuries a standard evolved within the moral tradition, providing a refined measure of just preventive force. While the tradition has less to say about institutional constraints, it provides a set of criteria for decision making. The dangers of a broad unilateral right to strike first coupled with the incentives states have to protect themselves absent UN approval counsels in favor of an incremental approach.

Most important, this account speaks to the neglected but pressing need for moral legitimacy. Talk of preventive war has left many Americans wanting to nod and shake their heads at the same time: in sober recognition of the threats America faces but worried that an open-ended claim to strike first betrays who we claim to be. At some point, the worry goes, what we do in the name of security undermines the very values for which we stand—a point Kubrick drove home in the ridiculous character of General Turgidson.

The moral tradition on the just war speaks to this worry. From Augustine forward the tradition rejected the pacifist claim that murder and war are morally indistinguishable. But it also rejected the realist claim that ethics end where force begins. Rooted in a notion of the moral equality of persons, the tradition recognized the occasional need and even responsibility to use force under narrow constraints on its occasion and conduct. Taking into account multiple considerations, rejecting the widespread notion that fear alone was sufficient cause, and demanding such an act always be a measure of last resort, the moral tradition carved out a narrow space for preventive force. Although Webster's Rule has served us well, from the beginning his demand for an instant threat ran counter to the tradition's consistent affirmation that states are not subject to the imminence requirement. The affinity between the moral tradition and America's self-understanding suggests the tradition can point a way forward that does not leave a nation that is dedicated to Lincoln's proposition bearing the mark of Cain.

Americans were right to question the seemingly boundless Bush Doctrine, but the limited case for preventive force I have described does not pit us against our best traditions and leave us liable for the infamy Roosevelt ascribed to the bombing of Pearl Harbor. For much of the past six decades it made sense to accept a rule that assumed anticipatory force would only be a last resort against an imminent threat. Although tempted by the prospect of a quick solution to the Soviet menace, Americans were right to reject a preventive first strike in the late 1940s and early 1950s. Fear alone is never sufficient, and strategies of deterrence and containment proved reasonable alternatives to preventive war. Likewise, Kennedy's blockade proved a reasonable alternative to bombing and invading Cuba. As we saw earlier, however, it was the nation's conviction that striking first should always be a last resort that carried the moral weight in these decisions—not an unyielding commitment to imminence. As NSC 68, the Cold War blueprint, perceptively concluded in ruling out a preventive attack against Russia, "Many [Americans] would doubt that it was a 'just war' and that all reasonable possibilities for a peaceful settlement had been explored in good faith." The use of force, especially a first strike, is a "last resort for a free society." The framework I sketched in chapter 8 preserves this conviction but recognizes that against the new threat of global terrorism the point of last resort may arrive prior to the point of imminence.[2]

In 1791 the American-born painter Benjamin West completed *The Expulsion of Adam and Eve from Paradise*. Unlike several of his earlier works exalting the heights of human virtue in Greek and Roman history, *Expulsion* depicts a tragic fall. The Archangel Michael casts the couple from the Garden. Adam covers his face. Eve begs forgiveness. In the faint background, an eagle lunges toward a white-plumed bird and terror-stricken horses run from a lion fast in pursuit. Minus the radiance of Michael, the colors are grim and the land barren.

The sober existence West portrays is the world of Augustine and the world to which the moral tradition on the just war speaks. A world in which evil is real and must sometimes be checked with force. Despite Augustine's often dour reading of history, his is not a world devoid of human flourishing. But it depends on earthly peace, Augustine's term for a minimal social order. Earthly peace is a vital but fragile good, threatened by the same propensities that drove Adam and Eve from paradise. In this world, perfect security is an illusion. As Augustine puts it, "So great is the mutability of human affairs that no people is ever granted a security so great that it need never fear incursions hostile to this life." And yet achieving earthly peace is the cardinal task of government. Those entrusted with securing the nation rarely have perfect information, but what Augustine calls "the claims of human society" compel them to act. Under these conditions, the moral tradition provides a framework for using force—even striking the first blow if necessary—that reconciles the demands of morality with the dangers of a fallen world.[3]

NOTES

Introduction

1. "War Room," *Dr. Strangelove*, DVD, directed by Stanley Kubrick (1964; Culver City, Calif.: Sony Pictures, 2004).
2. Dwight Eisenhower, "Transcript of the President's News Conference on Foreign and Domestic Matters," *New York Times*, March 5, 1959; and "The First Blow?" *Time* (March 16, 1959).
3. Elihu Root, "The Real Monroe Doctrine," *American Journal of International Law* 8 (July 1914): 432.
4. National Security Council, *National Security Strategy of the United States of America* (September 2002).
5. James M. Lindsay and Ivo H. Daalder, "Shooting First: The Preemptive War Doctrine Has Met an Early Death in Iraq," *Los Angeles Times*, May 30, 2004, and Editorial, *New York Times*, September 12, 2004.
6. Joseph Nye, *Soft Power: The Means to Success in World Politics* (New York: Public Affairs, 2004), 6; Niccolò Machiavelli, *The Prince*, ed. Quentin Skinner, trans. Russell Price (Cambridge: Cambridge University Press, 1998), 62; and John L. Gaddis, *The Cold War: A New History* (New York: Penguin Press, 2005), 171.
7. Michael Walzer, "The Triumph of Just War Theory (and the Dangers of Success)," *Social Research* 69 (winter 2002): 931.

Chapter 1. The Turn Toward Prevention

1. For general background on the *Caroline* episode, *see* Andrew Drew, *A Narrative of the Capture and Destruction of the Steamer 'Caroline'* (London: Spottiswoode, 1864); Kenneth R. Stevens, *Border Diplomacy: The* Caroline *and McLeod Affairs in Anglo-American–Canadian Relations, 1837–1842* (Tuscaloosa: University of Alabama Press, 1989); Howard Jones, *To the Webster-Ashburton Treaty: A Study in Anglo-*

American Relations, 1783–1843 (Chapel Hill: University of North Carolina Press, 1977); John E. Noyes, "The *Caroline*: International Law Limits on Resort to Force," in *International Law Stories,* ed. John E. Noyes, Laura A. Dickinson, and Mark W. Janis, 263–307 (New York: Foundation Press, 2007); and Robert Jennings, "The *Caroline* and *McLeod* Cases," *American Journal of International Law* 32 (January 1938): 82–99.

2. Robert Kagan, *Dangerous Nation: America's Place in the World from Its Earliest Days to the Dawn of the Twentieth Century* (New York: Alfred A. Knopf, 2006), 133–37; and Samuel F. Bemis, *John Quincy Adams and the Foundations of American Foreign Policy* (New York: W. W. Norton, 1949), 300–316.

3. Bemis, *John Quincy Adams,* 412–15; and Erasmus, "Have We Any Reason to Expect a War with England?" *Boston Recorder,* December 24, 1841.

4. *New York Herald,* January 15, 1841.

5. "Very Late and Most Important from Buffalo and Navy Island," *New York Herald,* January 3, 1838; and "The Crisis of Affairs Between the US and Great Britain," *New York Herald,* January 4, 1838.

6. "Highly Important from the West—Further Accounts from Navy Island—War with England," *New York Herald,* January 5, 1838; "The British Outrage," *Daily Herald and Gazette,* January 4, 1838; and "Affairs in Canada," *Niles National Register,* January 6, 1838.

7. President, Proclamation, January 5, 1838, in *A Compilation of the Messages and Papers of the Presidents—Martin Van Buren,* ed. J. D. Richardson (Charleston, S.C.: BiblioBazaar, 2007), 279–80; and Letter to Congress, January 5, 1838, in ibid., 138.

8. For background on Webster, *see* Maurice G. Baxter, *One and Inseparable: Daniel Webster and the Union* (Cambridge: Harvard University Press, 1984); and Robert V. Remini, *Daniel Webster: The Man and His Time* (New York: W. W. Norton, 1997).

9. *The Times* (London), March 18, 1841.

10. *Remedial Justice Act, Stats at Large of USA* 5 (1850): 539–40; Henry Fox to Daniel Webster, March 12, 1841, in *British and Foreign State Papers, 1840–41* (London: H.M.S.O., 1857), 29:1126–29.

11. Daniel Webster to Henry Fox, April 24, 1841, in *British and Foreign State Papers, 1840–1841* (London: H.M.S.O, 1857), 29:1137–38.

12. Lord Ashburton to Daniel Webster, July 28, 1842, in *British and Foreign State Papers, 1841–1842* (London: H.M.S.O., 1858), 30:195; ibid., 199; Daniel Webster to Lord Ashburton, August 6, 1842, in ibid., 201–02.

13. *See* Ian Brownlie, *International Law and the Use of Force by States* (Oxford: Clarendon Press, 1963), 19–49; and Noyes, "The *Caroline,*" 263–307; and Timothy G. Kearley, "Raising the Caroline," *Wisconsin International Law Journal* 17 (summer 1999): 325–46.

14. President, Proclamation, January 5, 1838, in *Compilation—Martin Van Buren,* 280; and Webster to Fox, April 24, 1841, in *British and Foreign State Papers,* 30:1137. From 1841 to 1914, the *Caroline* incident received only passing reference, primarily in the limited context of justifiable violations of neutrality for the sake of "self-

preservation." *See* Daniel Gardner, *A Treatise on International* (Troy, N.Y.: Press of N. Tuttle, 1844), 202; Robert Phillimore, *Commentaries Upon International Law* (Philadelphia: T. and J. W. Johnson, 1854–61), 184–85; H. W. Halleck, *International Law* (New York: D. Van Nostrand, 1861), 520–22; Theodore Woolsey, *Introduction to the Study of International Law*, 5th ed. (New York: Charles Scribner's Sons, 1878), 291; T. J. Lawrence, *Principles of International Law*, 4th ed. (Boston: D. C. Heath, 1910), 609–10; and Lassa Oppenheim, *International Law: A Treatise* (New York: Longmans, Green, 1905), 2:187.

15. *See* Brownlie, *International Law and the Use of Force*, 51–111; Stanimir A. Alexandrov, *Self-Defense Against the Use of Force in International Law* (Boston: Kluwer Law International, 1996), 29–76; and C. H. M. Waldock, "The Regulation of the Use of Force by Individual States in International Law," *Recueil Des Cours* 81 (1952-II): 469–86.

16. General introductions to the use of force under the UN Charter include Anthony C. Arend and Robert J. Beck, *International Law and the Use of Force: Beyond the U.N. Charter Paradigm* (New York: Routledge, 1993); Yoram Dinstein, *War, Aggression, and Self-Defence*, 4th ed. (Cambridge: Cambridge University Press, 2005); Thomas M. Franck, *Recourse to Force* (New York: Cambridge University Press, 2002); and Christine Gray, *International Law and the Use of Force*, 2d ed. (Oxford: Oxford University Press, 2004). For the legitimacy of preventive force under Art. 39, *see* Judith Gardam, *Necessity, Proportionality and the Use of Force by States* (Cambridge: Cambridge University Press, 2004), 188–212; and Dinstein, *War, Aggression and Self-Defence*, 280. For an overview of UN Security Council actions under Chapter VII, *see* Gray, *International Law*, 195–251.

17. International Court of Justice, *Case Concerning Military and Paramilitary Activities in and against Nicaragua*, 1986 *ICJ Reports* 14, 94. For an overview of this debate, *see* Franck, *Recourse to Force*, 97–108; Gray, *International Law*, 129–33; and Oscar Schachter, "International Law: The Right of States to Use Armed Force," *Michigan Law Review* 82 (April 1984): 1633–35; and Dinstein, *War, Aggression and Self-Defence*, 182–87.

18. International Military Tribunal (Nuremberg), Judgment and Sentences, October 1, 1946, reprinted in *American Journal of International Law* 41 (January 1947): 205.

19. S.C. Res. 233 (1967); S.C. Res. 234 (1967); S.C. Res. 236 (1967); and S.C. Res. 242 (1967).

20. Israel's official justification for the raid appeared in a document issued by the Israeli government subsequent to the attack. Government of Israel, Ministry of Foreign Affairs, *The Iraqi Nuclear Threat—Why Israel Had to Act* (Jerusalem, 1981); S.C. Res. 487 (1981) (condemning the action); UN SCOR, 36th Sess., 2288th mtg., UN Doc. S/PV.2288 (1981) (Kirkpatrick); and UN SCOR, 36th Sess., 2282th mtg., UN Doc. S/PV.2282 (1981) (Otunnu and Parsons). For an overview of the legal issues, *see* Thomas W. Mallison and Sally V. Mallison, "The Israeli Aerial Attack of June 7, 1981, Upon the Iraqi Nuclear Reactor: Aggression or Self-Defense?" *Vanderbilt Journal of Transnational Law* 15 (summer 1982): 417–46.

21. George H. W. Bush, Letter to the Speaker of the House of Representatives on U.S.

Military Action in Panama, December 21, 1989, in *Public Papers of George Bush* (Washington: Government Printing Office, 1990), 2:1734; and William J. Clinton, Letter to Congressional Leaders Reporting on Military Action against Terrorist Sites in Afghanistan and Sudan, August 21, 1998, in *Public Papers of William J. Clinton* (Washington: U.S. Government Printing Office, 2000), 2:1464.

22. International Court of Justice, *Legality of the Threat or Use of Nuclear Weapons, 1996 ICJ Reports* 226, 245. Commentators have recognized these norms as valid principles of customary law. *See* Florentino P. Feliciano and Myres S. McDougal, *Law and Minimum World Public Order* (New Haven: Yale University Press, 1961), 218–44; Schachter, "International Law," 1635–38; and Gardam, *Necessity, Proportionality and the Use of Force by States.*

23. Roberto Ago, *Addendum to the Eighth Report on State Responsibility,* in *Yearbook of the International Law Commission* (Part I 1980), 69; and Lawrence Freedman, "Prevention, not Preemption," *Washington Quarterly* 26 (spring 2003): 106.

24. Webster to Fox, April 24, 1841, in *British and Foreign State Papers,* 30:1137.

25. *See* Yoram Dinstein, "Implementing Limitations on the Use of Force: The Doctrine of Proportionality and Necessity," *American Society of International Law Proceedings* 86 (1992): 57.

26. Ago, *Addendum to the Eighth Report on State Responsibility,* 69.

27. Robert Dallek, *Franklin D. Roosevelt and American Foreign Policy, 1932–1945* (New York: Oxford University Press, 1979), 85–86, 147–48, 256–57. For a description of the shift Roosevelt inaugurated, *see* John L. Gaddis, *Surprise, Security, and the American Experience* (Cambridge: Harvard University Press, 2004), 35–67.

28. U.S. Commission on National Security/21st Century, *New World Coming: American Security in the 21st Century* (1999); and Eric Lipton, "U.S. Lists Possible Terror Attacks and Likely Toll," *New York Times,* March 16, 2005. For an account of the religious ideology shaping the new terrorist threat, *see* Mary Habeck, *Knowing the Enemy: Jihadist Ideology and the War on Terror* (New Haven: Yale University Press, 2006).

29. Several writings by Gaddis on Cold War strategies and the shifts underway since 9/11 are helpful. *See* John L. Gaddis, *Strategies of Containment: A Critical Appraisal of American National Security Policy During the Cold War,* rev. and exp. ed. (New York: Oxford University Press, 2005), 24–52; Gaddis, *Surprise,* 68–113; Gaddis, "A Grand Strategy of Transformation," *Foreign Policy* (November/December 2002): 50–57; and Gaddis, "Grand Strategy in the Second Term," *Foreign Affairs* 84 (January/February 2005): 2–15.

30. National Security Council, *National Security Strategy of the United States of America* (September 2002). In addition to this document, the primary contributions to the Bush Doctrine include George W. Bush, "State of the Union Address" (January 29, 2002); George W. Bush, "Commencement Address" (U.S. Military Academy, West Point, June 7, 2002); Dick Cheney, "Address at the VFW 103rd National Convention" (Nashville, August 26, 2002); George W. Bush, "Remarks at the U.N. General Assembly" (New York, September 12, 2002); Donald Rumsfeld, "Prepared Testimony by U.S. Secretary of Defense Donald H. Rumsfeld" (Senate

Armed Services Comm., Washington, September 19, 2002); Condoleezza Rice, "Remarks on the President's National Security Strategy" (Waldorf-Astoria Hotel, New York, October 1, 2002); George W. Bush, "Remarks by the President on Iraq" (Cincinnati Museum Center, Cincinnati, October 7, 2002); William H. Taft, "Old Rules, New Threats" (Memorandum to Members of the ASIL–CFR Roundtable, November 18, 2002); Paul Wolfowitz, "Remarks before the International Institute for Strategic Studies" (London, December 2, 2002); National Security Council, *National Strategy to Combat Weapons of Mass Destruction* (December 2002); National Security Council, *National Strategy for Combating Terrorism* (February 2003); William H. Taft, "Preemption, Iraq, and International Law," *American Journal of International Law* 97 (July 2003): 557–63; William H. Taft, "Preemptive Action in Self-Defense," *American Society of International Law Proceedings* 98 (2004): 331–33; and National Security Council, *National Security Strategy of the United States of America* (March 2006).

31. George W. Bush, interview by Tim Russert, *Meet the Press,* NBC, February 8, 2004; and Elaine Monaghan, "Clinton Planned Attack on Korean Nuclear Reactors," *The Times* (London), December 16, 2002.

Chapter 2. "Against Our Traditions"?

1. For general discussions about the role of anticipatory force in American history, *see* Matthew Flynn, *First Strike: Preemptive War in Modern History* (New York: Routledge, 2008); Scott Silverstone, *Preventive War and American Democracy* (New York: Routledge, 2007); Hew Strachan, "Preemption and Prevention in Historical Perspective," in *Preemption: Military Action and Moral Justification,* ed. Henry Shue and David Rodin, 23–39 (Oxford: Oxford University Press, 2007); and Marc Trachtenberg, "The Bush Strategy in Historical Perspective," in *Nuclear Transformation: The New U.S. Nuclear Doctrine,* ed. James J. Wirtz and Jeffrey A. Larsen, 9–21 (New York: Palgrave Macmillan, 2005).

2. This section draws on Samuel F. Bemis, *John Quincy Adams and the Foundations of American Foreign Policy* (New York: W. W. Norton, 1949), 566–72; John L. Gaddis, *Surprise, Security, and the American Experience* (Cambridge: Harvard University Press, 2004), 7–33; Robert Kagan, *Dangerous Nation: America's Place in the World from Its Earliest Days to the Dawn of the Twentieth Century* (New York: Alfred A. Knopf, 2006), 59, 127–28; and Walter A. McDougall, *Promised Land, Crusader State: The American Encounter with the World since 1776* (New York: Houghton Mifflin, 1997), chapters 1–4.

3. George Washington, "Washington's Farewell Address," September 19, 1796, in *A Sacred Union of Citizens: George Washington's Farewell Address and the American Character,* Patrick J. Garrity and Matthew Spalding (Lanham, Md.: Rowman and Littlefield, 1998), 186.

4. Bemis, *John Quincy Adams,* 302; *see also* William Earl Weeks, "John Quincy Adams's 'Great Gun' and the Rhetoric of American Empire," *Diplomatic History* 14 (January 1990): 25–42.

5. *Resolution Relative to the Occupation of the Floridas by the United States of America,* *Stats at Large of USA* 3 (1846), 471.

6. James Monroe to Andrew Jackson, December 28, 1817, quoted in Weeks, "John Quincy Adams's 'Great Gun,'" 27–28.

7. John Q. Adams to George W. Erving, November 2, 1818, in *American State Papers, Foreign Relations* (Washington: Gales and Seaton, 1834), 4:541, 542.

8. "Case of the Caroline," *Albion,* January 6, 1838; and "Troubles with England," *New-Yorker,* February 6, 1841.

9. James Monroe, "Address to Congress," December 2, 1823, in *The Writings of James Monroe,* ed. Stanislaus M. Hamilton (New York: G. P. Putnam's Sons, 1902), 6:325–41.

10. *See* Frederick Merk, *The Monroe Doctrine and American Expansionism, 1843–1849* (New York: Alfred A. Knopf, 1966); and McDougal, *Promised Land,* 77–78.

11. The following account of U.S. actions in the first two decades of the twentieth century draws substantially on Max Boot, *Savage Wars of Peace: Small Wars and the Rise of American Power* (New York: Basic Books, 2002), 129–81.

12. *See* Edmund Morris, *Theodore Rex* (New York: Random House, 2001), 625; and Boot, *Savage Wars,* 135–36.

13. Theodore Roosevelt, "Address to Congress," December 6, 1904, 58th Cong., 3rd sess., *Congressional Record* 39, pt. 1:19.

14. For an overview of the relevant history, *see* Robert Dallek, *Franklin D. Roosevelt and American Foreign Policy, 1932–1945* (New York: Oxford University Press, 1979), 269–313. For a specific account of the attack on Pearl Harbor, see Henry L. Stimson, "Statement by Henry L. Stimson, Former Secretary of War," before Joint Committee on the Investigation of the Pearl Harbor Attack, *Investigation of the Pearl Harbor Attack* (Washington: U.S. Government Printing Office, 1946), 11:5416–31, 79th Cong., 2d sess., 1946. The changes in U.S. foreign policy following Pearl Harbor are recounted in Gaddis, *Surprise,* 35–67.

15. Dallek, *Franklin D. Roosevelt,* 309.

16. Lester R. Schulz, "Testimony of Commander Lester Robert Schulz, U.S. Navy," before Joint Committee on the Investigation of the Pearl Harbor Attack, *Investigation of the Pearl Harbor Attack* (Washington: U.S. Government Printing Office, 1946), 10:4659–63, 79th Cong., 2d sess., 1946; *see also* Robert E. Sherwood, *Roosevelt and Hopkins: An Intimate History* (New York: Harper, 1950), 426–27.

17. Schulz, "Testimony," 10:4662–63.

18. Stimson, "Statement," 11:5421.

19. Franklin Roosevelt, "Address by the President," December 8, 1941, 77th Cong., 1st sess., *Congressional Record* 87, pt. 9:9519; and Franklin Roosevelt, "The President's Address," *New York Times,* December 10, 1941. For an account of the lasting influence of Pearl Harbor, see Emily S. Rosenberg, *A Date Which Will Live: Pearl Harbor in American Memory* (Durham: Duke University Press, 2003). Hull's interaction with the Japanese envoys is described in R. J. C. Butow, "Marching Off to War on the Wrong Foot: The Final Note Tokyo Did Not Send to Washington," *Pacific Historical Review* 63 (February 1994): 67–79.

20. Editorial, "Decade of Fame and Infamy," *New York Times,* December 7, 1951.
21. For an overview of early developments in the Cold War, *see* John L. Gaddis, *The Cold War: A New History* (New York: Penguin Press, 2005), 5–47.
22. The two best accounts of the preventive war debate from 1945 to 1955 are Russell D. Buhite and W. Christopher Hamel, "War for Peace: The Question of an American Preventive War Against the Soviet Union," *Diplomatic History* 14 (summer 1990): 367–84; and Marc Trachtenberg, "A 'Wasting Asset': American Strategy and the Shifting Nuclear Balance, 1949–1954," in *History and Strategy* (Princeton: Princeton University Press, 1991), 100–152. For an overview of the role nuclear weapons played in the early Cold War, *see* John L. Gaddis, *We Now Know: Rethinking Cold War History* (New York: Oxford University Press, 1997), 85–112.
23. Joseph Stalin, "New Five-Year Plan for Russia," February 9, 1946, in *Vital Speeches of the Day* 12 (March 1, 1946): 300; and Editorial, "Stalin's New Party Line," *New York Times,* February 11, 1946.
24. Memorandum Prepared by the Joint Chiefs of Staff (JCS 1496), March 27, 1946, in *Foreign Relations of the United States, 1946* (Washington: U.S. Government Printing Office, 1972), 1:1162, 1:1163; and Memorandum by the Commanding General, Manhattan Engineer District (Groves), January 2, 1946, in *Foreign Relations of the United States, 1946* (Washington: U.S. Government Printing Office, 1972), 1:1198.
25. "'Shoot First,' Arnold Declares on Defense," *New York Times,* January 14, 1946; and "Eaker Sets 4 Lines for Preparedness," *New York Times,* November 21, 1946.
26. Bertrand Russell, "The Atomic Bomb and the Prevention of War," *Bulletin of the Atomic Scientists* 2 (October 1, 1946); and "Russell Urges West to Fight Russia Now," *New York Times,* November 21, 1948.
27. James Burnham, *The Struggle for the World* (New York: John Day, 1947).
28. William L. Laurence, "Vast Power Source in Atomic Energy Opened by Science," *New York Times,* May 5, 1940; William L. Laurence, "The Atom Gives Up," *Saturday Evening Post* 213 (May 5, 1940); and William L. Laurence, "How Soon Will Russia Have the A-Bomb?" *Saturday Evening Post* 221 (November 6, 1948). Gaddis argues that Laurence's articles may have alerted the Soviets to the potential of atomic energy. *See* Gaddis, *We Now Know,* 92.
29. Winston Churchill, "Iron Curtain Address," March 5, 1946, in *Never Give In: The Best of Winston Churchill's Speeches,* ed. Winston S. Churchill (New York: Hyperion, 2003), 413–24; Ambassador in the United Kingdom (Douglas) to the Under Secretary of State (Lovett), April 17, 1948, *Foreign Relations of the United States, 1948* (Washington: U.S. Government Printing Office, 1974), 3:90; Winston Churchill, "United We Stand Secure," March 31, 1949, *Vital Speeches of the Day* 15 (April 1, 1949): 380; and Joseph Alsop and Stewart Alsop, "Mr. Churchill's Riddle," *Washington Post,* April 4, 1949. For background on the Fulton speech, *see* Fraser J. Harbutt, *Iron Curtain: Churchill, America, and the Origins of the Cold War* (New York: Oxford University Press, 1988), 159–208.
30. Walter Lippmann, "Soviet–American Military Ideas," *Washington Post,* March 21, 1946; "Atom Scientists Give Warning That World Control Is 'Imperative,'" *New*

York Times, June 30, 1947; "Atomic Scientists Urge World State," *New York Times*, April 12, 1948; "Catholics Say Evil Dims Peace Lights," *New York Times*, November 15, 1946; "Methodists Assail Hysteria for War," *New York Times*, May 1, 1948; and Gallup Organization, Gallup Polls #378 (September 11, 1946), #458 (July 7, 1950), #536 (August 24, 1954), http://institution.gallup.com. U.S. officials were monitoring public perceptions of a preventive war against Russia as well. A memorandum of June 1951 by the public liaison officer reported that in October 1950, 80 percent of Americans opposed a preventive war against Russia. *See* Memorandum by Mr. Walter P. Schwinn, Public Liaison Officer, June 5, 1951, in *Foreign Relations of the United States, 1951* (Washington: U.S. Government Printing Office, 1980), 1:90–91.

31. Henry Wallace, "Text of Secretary Wallace's Letter to President Truman on U.S. Foreign Policy," *New York Times*, September 18, 1946; "War Chiefs Deny Russia Attack Plans," *Los Angeles Times*, September 19, 1946; and "Truman Silences Wallace Until After Paris Parley," *New York Times*, September 19, 1946.

32. Henry L. Stimson, "The Challenge to Americans," *Foreign Affairs* 26 (October 1947): 9.

33. John Foster Dulles, "Not War, Not Peace," January 17, 1948, *Vital Speeches of the Day* 14 (February 15, 1948): 271, 273.

34. James B. Conant, "Force and Freedom," *Atlantic Monthly* (January 1949): 19–22; James B. Conant, "The Paradox of Force and Freedom," *Washington Post*, January 9, 1949.

35. "The Thunderclap," *Time*, October 3, 1949.

36. "Matthews Bids U.S. Wage 'Aggression for Peace,'" *Christian Science Monitor*, August 26, 1950; Francis P. Matthews, "Aggressors for Peace," August 25, 1950, *Vital Speeches of the Day* 16 (September 15, 1950): 730, 731, 732.

37. For Wedemeyer's comments, *see* Russell D. Buhite and W. Christopher Hamel, "War for Peace," *Diplomatic History* 14 (summer 1990): 377; Hanson W. Baldwin, "War of Prevention," *New York Times*, September 1, 1950; Holmes Alexander, "That Matthews Speech Was a Trial Balloon," *Los Angeles Times*, September 4, 1950; John G. Norris, "Air College Head Suspended for 'Preventive War' Remarks," *Washington Post*, September 2, 1950; for comments by McLellan, *see* "Both Parties Back Truman Arms Call," *New York Times*, September 3, 1950; and "Sen. Russell Says Americans Should Ponder Preventive War," *Washington Post*, September 15, 1950.

38. "Sec. Matthews Rebuked for War Speech," *Washington Post*, August 27, 1950; "Acheson Rules Out 'Preventive War,'" *New York Times*, June 14, 1950; Memorandum of Conversation of August 10 Between the Secretary of State and Various Members of Congress, in *Foreign Relations of the United States, 1950* (Washington: U.S. Government Printing Office, 1977), 1:200; and Robert F. Whitney, "Jessup Abhors Idea of Bombing Russia," *New York Times*, August 28, 1950.

39. Harry Truman, "Text of Truman's 'Report to Nation' on Korea War," *New York Times*, September 2, 1950; Harry Truman, *Memoirs.* Vol. 1: *Year of Decisions* (New York: Doubleday, 1955), 383; John G. Norris, "Air College Head Suspended for

'Preventive War' Remarks," *Washington Post,* September 2, 1950; and Stewart Alsop, "The Code of Harry Truman," *Washington Post,* September 15, 1950.

40. A Report to the President Pursuant to the President's Directive of January 31, 1950 (NSC 68), in *Foreign Relations of the United States, 1950* (Washington: U.S. Government Printing Office, 1977), 1:235–92. For a reprinted copy of NSC 68, background, and wide variety of commentary, *see* Ernest R. May, ed., *American Cold War Strategy: Interpreting NSC 68* (Boston: Beford/St. Martin's, 1993). *See also* John L. Gaddis, *Strategies of Containment: A Critical Appraisal of American National Security Policy During the Cold War,* rev. and exp. ed. (New York: Oxford University Press, 2005), 87–124; and Trachtenberg, "A 'Wasting Asset,'" 107–15.

41. NSC 68, *Foreign Relations of the United States, 1950,* 1:238, 243, 242–43.

42. Ibid., 1:281–82.

43. "Acheson Raps War Talk as 'Terrible Error,'" *Los Angeles Times,* October 9, 1950; Walter H. Waggoner, "Acheson Stresses Moral Purposes," *New York Times,* November 10, 1950; C. L. Sulzberger, "Acheson Says NATO Rejects Idea of a Preventive War," *New York Times,* February 21, 1952; George Dugan, "Church Unit Backs Use of Atom Bomb," *New York Times,* November 28, 1950; and "Churchmen Back Policies, Dun Reports," *Washington Post,* August 30, 1951.

44. Memorandum by the Policy Planning Staff to the Secretary of State, October 16, 1951, in *Foreign Relations of the United States, 1951* (Washington: U.S. Government Printing Office, 1980), 1:224; and Henry Kissinger, "Military Policy and Defense of the 'Grey Areas,'" *Foreign Affairs* 33 (April 1955): 416.

45. John F. Dulles, "Text of Secretary Dulles' Warning Against Communist Encirclement of the West," *New York Times,* January 28, 1953; John F. Dulles, "Policy for Security and Peace," *Foreign Affairs* 32 (April 1954): 353; Walter H. Waggoner, "Dulles Rules Out Preventive War," *New York Times,* November 10, 1954; and Memorandum of Discussion at the 229th Meeting of the National Security Council, Tuesday, December 21, 1954, in *Foreign Relations of the United States, 1952–1954* (Washington: U.S. Government Printing Office, 1984), 2:832.

46. "Eisenhower Hints at Preventive War," *Los Angeles Times,* October 20, 1950; Dwight Eisenhower, "Text of Address by Eisenhower," *Los Angeles Times,* June 24, 1952; Dwight Eisenhower, "Transcript of President Eisenhower's Press Conference on Foreign and Home Affairs," *New York Times,* August 12, 1954; and Memorandum by the President to the Secretary of State, Denver, September 8, 1953, in *Foreign Relations of the United States, 1951* (Washington: U.S. Government Printing Office, 1984), 2:461. Robert H. Ferrell, ed., *The Eisenhower Diaries* (New York: W. W. Norton, 1981), 312.

47. For a short introduction to the Cuban missile crisis, *see* Gaddis, *We Now Know,* 260–80. Transcripts of many of the sessions in which President Kennedy and his advisers discussed the crisis are available in Ernest R. May and Philip D. Zelikow, *The Kennedy Tapes: Inside the White House During the Cuban Missile Crisis* (Cambridge: Belnap Press, 1997). Further background and a narrative based on the transcripts is found in Sheldon M. Stern, *The Week the World Stood Still: Inside the Secret Cuban Missile Crisis* (Stanford: Stanford University Press, 2005).

48. May and Zelikow, *Kennedy Tapes,* 54 (Rusk), 57–58 (McNamara), 58 (Taylor), 122 (full invasion), 73 (McNamara). For comments suggesting that JFK favored air strikes during the first few days of deliberation, *see* ibid., 70–72, 94–95. His changing view is perhaps first signaled in his comment on p. 97 where he begins to think more about the consequences of an air strike and how the Soviet Union might respond.

49. Ibid., 86 (blockade proposal). For examples of McNamara's two questions, *see* ibid., 96–99, 112–15, 157, 162; ibid., 96–97 (consequences quote), 157 (alternatives quote), 113–14 (McNamara's reluctance to argue for the blockade plan at this time).

50. Ibid., 115 (Ball); and Position of [Under Secretary of State] George W. Ball, October 18, 1962, in *The Cuban Missile Crisis, 1962: A National Security Archive Documents Reader,* ed. Laurence Chang and Peter Kornbluh (New York: New Press, 1992), 121. For a further account of Ball's position, *see* George W. Ball, *The Past Has Another Pattern: Memoirs* (New York: W. W. Norton, 1982), 291–92.

51. May and Zelikow, *Kennedy Tapes,* 143 (Ball to full committee), 148 (JFK), 149 (RFK), 171–72 (JFK).

52. Record of Meeting, Washington, October 19, 1962, 11 a.m. at the State Department, in *Foreign Relations of the United States, 1961–1963* (Washington: U.S. Government Printing Office, 1997), 11:119. For more on RFK's role during the crisis, *see* Arthur M. Schlesinger, Jr., *Robert Kennedy and His Times* (Boston: Houghton Mifflin, 1978), 499–532. *See also* Robert Kennedy, *Thirteen Days: A Memoir of the Cuban Missile Crisis* (New York: W. W. Norton, 1968).

53. George W. Ball, *The Past,* 291; Theodore C. Sorensen, *Kennedy* (New York: Harper and Row, 1965), 684.

54. May and Zelikow, *Kennedy Tapes,* 194 (McNamara), 196 (RFK), 198 (Rusk).

55. Ibid., 200–02 (JFK's decisions), 237–38 (JFK not ruling out preventive force for the future), 230 (JFK on Pearl Harbor).

56. Ibid., 275–81.

57. Schlesinger, *Robert Kennedy,* 508; Dean Acheson, "Dean Acheson's Version of Robert Kennedy's Version of the Cuban Missile Affair," *Esquire* (February 1969): 76.

58. May and Zelikow, *Kennedy Tapes,* 88.

59. Ibid., 170.

60. Ibid., 277.

61. Ibid., 229 (RFK conclusion, Rusk). *See also* Abram Chayes, Memorandum for the Attorney General Re. Legality under International Law of Remedial Action Against Use of Cuba as a Missile Base by the Soviet Union, in *The Cuban Missile Crisis* (New York: Oxford University Press, 1974), 108–16.

62. On the Kennedy administration's interest in taking action against China, *see* William Burr and Jeffrey T. Richelson, "Whether to 'Strangle the Baby in the Cradle': The United States and the Chinese Nuclear Program, 1960–1964," *International Security* 25 (winter 2000/2001): 54–99.

Chapter 3. Just War at Home in America

1. Tertullian, *On Idolatry*, trans. S. Thelwall, Ante-Nicene Fathers, vol. 3 (Edinburgh: T&T Clark; Grand Rapids: Eerdmans, 1976), 3:73; *see also* Tertullian, *The Chaplet*, trans. S. Thelwall, Ante-Nicene Fathers, vol. 3 (Edinburgh: T&T Clark; Grand Rapids: Eerdmans, 1976), 3:99–100.

2. David R. Mapel, "Realism and the Ethics of War and Peace," in *The Ethics of War and Peace*, ed. Terry Nardin, 54–77 (Princeton: Princeton University Press, 1996); Jeff McMahan, "Realism, Morality, and War," in *The Ethics of War and Peace*, ed. Terry Nardin, 78–92 (Princeton: Princeton University Press, 1996); Steven Forde, "Classical Realism," in *Traditions of International Ethics*, ed. Terry Nardin and David R. Mapel, 62–84 (Cambridge: Cambridge University Press, 1992); and Jack Donnelly, "Twentieth-Century Realism," in *Traditions of International Ethics*, ed. Terry Nardin and David R. Mapel, 85–111 (Cambridge: Cambridge University Press, 1992).

3. Thuc., *History of the Peloponnesian War*, trans. Rex Warner (New York: Penguin Classics, 1972), 402.

4. Michael Walzer describes the tradition in similar terms. *See* Michael Walzer, *Just and Unjust Wars: A Moral Argument with Historical Illustrations*, 3d ed. (New York: Basic Books, 2002), 11–19.

5. For a historical survey of the just war tradition, *see* James T. Johnson, *Ideology, Reason, and the Limitation of War* (Princeton: Princeton University Press, 1975); James T. Johnson, *Just War Tradition and the Restraint of War* (Princeton: Princeton University Press, 1981); Frederick Russell, *The Just War in the Middle Ages* (Cambridge: Cambridge University Press, 1975); William O'Brien, *The Conduct of Just and Limited War* (New York: Praeger, 1981); and Henrik Syse and Gregory M. Reichberg, eds., *Ethics, Nationalism, and Just War: Medieval and Contemporary Perspectives* (Washington: Catholic University Press, 2007), part 1, "The Medieval Roots of Just War."

6. Pl. *Laws* 1.628; Pl. *Republic* 5.471; Arist. *Politics* 1255a3–1255b; Cic. *On Duties* 1.34–36, 38. The *fetials* are discussed in Alan Watson, *International Law in Archaic Rome: War and Religion* (Baltimore: Johns Hopkins University Press, 1993), 10; John Rich, *Declaring War in the Roman Republic in the Period of Transmarine Expansion* (Brussels: Latomus, 1976); and Thomas Wiedemann, "The Fetiales: A Reconsideration," *Classical Quarterly* 36 (1986): 478–90. For discussion of the influence of Roman law on the moral tradition, *see* Russell, *The Just War*, 4–5, 40–41.

7. The latter's primary writings on war include: Augustine, *Reply to Faustus, the Manichaean*, trans. Richard Stothert, Nicene and Post-Nicene Fathers 1, vol. 4 (Edinburgh: T&T Clark; Grand Rapids: Eerdmans, 1993), bk. 22; Augustine, *Sermon 302*, trans. Edmund Hill, in *Sermons 273–305A*, vol. 8, The Works of St. Augustine 3 (Hyde Park, N.Y.: New City Press, 1994); Augustine, *Letter 138, to Marcellinus*, trans. J. G. Cunningham, Nicene and Post-Nicene Fathers 1, vol. 1 (Edinburgh: T&T Clark; Grand Rapids: Eerdmans, 1979); Augustine, *City of God*, trans. R. W. Dyson (New York: Cambridge University Press, 1998), passim; Augustine, *Let-*

ter 189, to Boniface, trans. J. G. Cunningham, Nicene and Post-Nicene Fathers I, vol. I (Edinburgh: T&T Clark; Grand Rapids: Eerdmans, 1979); and Augustine, *Letter 229, to Darius,* trans. J. G. Cunningham, Nicene and Post-Nicene Fathers I, vol. I (Edinburgh: T&T Clark; Grand Rapids: Eerdmans, 1979).

8. Gratian, *Decretum* (Causa 23), trans. Peter Haggenmacher and Robert Andrews, in *The Ethics of War: Classic and Contemporary Readings,* ed. Gregory M. Reichberg, Henrik Syse, and Endre Begby (Oxford: Blackwell, 2006); Thomas Aquinas, *Summa Theologica,* trans. Fathers of the English Dominican Province (New York: Benziger Brothers, 1948), II.II.40.1. For an overview of Gratian's contribution and other developments in the tradition between Augustine and Aquinas, *see* Russell, *The Just War.* In addition to II.II.40.1, other important texts in Aquinas's *Summa* include II.II.64.7 ("Whether it is lawful to kill a man in self-defense?") and II.II.184.3 ("Whether a religious order can be directed to soldiering?"). In *De Regimine Principium,* Aquinas provides his most complete statement about the sources and ends of political community. Thomas Aquinas, *De Regimine Principum,* ed. and trans. R. W. Dyson, in *St. Thomas: Political Writings* (Cambridge: Cambridge University Press, 2002), 5–52.

9. *See* part 2 for a discussion of the named writers and their relevant primary texts. Various works have addressed the moral tradition and its contribution to the development of international law. For a general treatment of the subject, *see* William O'Brien, "Just War Doctrine's Complementary Role in the International Law of War," in *Legal and Moral Constraints in Low-Intensity Conflicts,* ed. by Albert R. Coll et al., 181-204 (Newport: Naval War College, 1995); William O'Brien, "The International Law of War as Related to the Western Just War Tradition," in *Just War and Jihad,* ed. John Kelsay and James T. Johnson, 163–94 (Westport, Conn.: Greenwood Press, 1991); and James T. Johnson, "Historical Roots and Sources of the Just War Tradition," in *Just War and Jihad,* ed. John Kelsay and James Turner Johnson, 3–30 (Westport, Conn.: Greenwood Press, 1991). Early attention to this subject arose between the two world wars, when several books touching on the subject appeared, including Alfred Vanderpol, *La Doctrine Scholastique du Droit de Guerre* (Paris: A. Pedone, 1919); James Brown Scott, *The Spanish Origin of International Law* (Oxford: Clarendon Press, 1934); John Eppstein, *The Catholic Tradition of the Law of Nations* (Washington: Catholic Association for International Peace, 1935); and the Carnegie Institute series Classics of International Law, which included all the major primary texts starting with Francisco de Vitoria in the sixteenth century.

10. For an overview of the criteria, *see* James T. Johnson, *Morality and Contemporary Warfare* (New Haven: Yale University Press, 1999), 27–38; John Finnis, "The Ethics of War and Peace in the Catholic Natural Law Tradition," in *The Ethics of War and Peace: Religious and Secular Perspectives,* ed. Terry Nardin, 15–28 (Princeton: Princeton University Press, 1996).

11. August *City of God* 4.4–6; August *Against Faustus* 22.74, quoted in Aquinas *Summa Theologica* II.II.40. For statements on Augustine concerning the aim of peace in war, *see* August *Letter 189;* August *Letter 229.*

12. August *Letter 189*.

13. A Report to the President Pursuant to the President's Directive of January 31, 1950 (NSC 68), in *Foreign Relations of the United States, 1950* (Washington: U.S. Government Printing Office, 1977), 1:281–82.

14. *Time,* December 12, 1960; Murray, "Remarks on the Problem of War," *Theological Studies* 20 (March 1959): 40–61; Paul Ramsey, *War and the Christian Conscience* (Durham: Duke University Press, 1961); Paul Ramsey, *The Just War: Force and Political Responsibility* (New York: Charles Scribner's Sons, 1968). James Turner Johnson, a professor at Rutgers University and a student of Ramsey's, and Jean Bethke Elshtain, a professor at the University of Chicago, are two prominent theological ethicists writing in the tradition today.

15. Walzer, *Just and Unjust Wars,* xix; Michael Walzer, "The Triumph of Just War Theory (and the Dangers of Success)," *Social Research* 69 (Winter 2002): 928.

16. For an example of President Clinton's appeal to the tradition during the Kosovo conflict, *see* John M. Broker, "Conflict in the Balkans," *New York Times,* March 25, 1999. Examples of articles invoking the tradition to assess the invasion of Iraq in 2003 include Keith Anderson, "What Kind of War Is It?" *Times Literary Supplement,* September 21, 2001; William J. Bennett, *Why We Fight: Moral Clarity and the War on Terrorism* (New York: Doubleday, 2002); J. Bottum, "You Say You Want a Just War?" *Weekly Standard,* April 21, 2003; Jean B. Elshtain, *Just War Against Terror: The Burden of American Power in a Violent World* (New York: Basic Books, 2003); Richard Falk, *The Great Terror War* (New York: Olive Branch Press, 2003); William Galston, "Perils of Preemptive War," *American Prospect* (September 23, 2002); Robert P. George, "A Just War in Iraq," *Wall Street Journal,* December 6, 2002; Stanley Hauerwas, "No, This War Would Not be Moral," *Time* (March 3, 2003); John Kelsay, "'Just War': The Details," *Chicago Tribune,* November 10, 2002; Joe Loconte, "Rumsfeld's Just War," *Weekly Standard,* December 24, 2001; Peter Steinfels, "The Just-War Tradition, Its Last-Resort Criterion and the Debate on an Invasion of Iraq," *New York Times,* March 1, 2003; and Michael Walzer, "What a Little War in Iraq Could Do," *New York Times,* March 7, 2003.

17. Michael Novak, "Michael Novak's Speech to the Vatican," *National Review Online* (February 10, 2003), http://www.nationalreview.com/novak/novak021003.asp; George Weigel, "Moral Clarity in a Time of War," *First Things* (January 2003); Rowan Williams, "Just War Revisited," Lecture to the Royal Institute for International Affairs, Chatham House (October 14, 2003), http://www.archbishopof canterbury.org; and Jimmy Carter, "Just War—or a Just War?" *New York Times,* March 9, 2003.

18. For general biographical accounts of Augustine, *see* Peter Brown, *Augustine of Hippo: A Biography* (Boston: Faber and Faber, 1967); and Gary Wills, *Saint Augustine* (London: Phoenix, 2000). Works on Augustine's historical context include Averil Cameron, *The Late Roman Empire AD 284–430* (Cambridge: Harvard University Press, 1993); Hugh Elton, *Warfare in Roman Europe* (Oxford: Clarendon Press, 1996); and Peter Brown, *Religion and Society in the Age of St. Augustine* (London: Faber and Faber, 1972). *See* David G. Hunter, "A Decade of Research on Early

Christians and Military Service," *Religious Studies Review* 18 (1992): 87–94, for a discussion of early Christian views of war prior to Augustine.

19. Augustine describes justice within the created state in *City of God* 9.4, 19.27. He describes the state of war within the self in *City of God* 14.15.

20. August *City of God* 1 (preface), 12.23.

21. August *City of God* 19.13; Augustine, *On Free Will*, trans. John H. S. Burleigh, in *Augustine: Earlier Writings*, Library of Christian Classics (Philadelphia: Westminster Press, 1953), 1.32.

22. Augustine describes humans as naturally sociable in *City of God* 12.28, 14.1. For statements on the origin of the political community, *see City of God* 4.15, 19.15. *See also*, R. A. Markus, *Saeculum: History and Society in the Theology of St. Augustine* (Cambridge: Cambridge University Press, 1970), 197–210; Herbert A. Deane, *The Political and Social Ideas of St. Augustine* (New York: Columbia University Press, 1963), 116–53.

23. Two exceptions to this general neglect are Terry Nardin, "International Political Theory and the Question of Justice," *International Affairs* 82 (May 2006): 449–65 (examining the connections between international justice in the just war tradition and more recent inquiries about international distributive justice); and Jean Elshtain, "International Justice as Equal Regard and the Use of Force," *Ethics and International Affairs* 17 (August 2006): 63–75 (examining the broad concept of justice behind the tradition and using that conception to make a case for humanitarian intervention). More recent attention to international justice, especially as it concerns questions of global distribution, began in earnest with Charles Beitz, *Political Theory and International Relations* (Princeton: Princeton University Press, 1979), and has been followed by a number of other important works, including John Rawls, *Law of Peoples* (Cambridge: Harvard University Press, 1999); Martha C. Nussbaum, *Women and Human Development: The Capabilities Approach* (New York: Cambridge University Press, 2000); Martha C. Nussbaum, *Frontiers of Justice* (Cambridge: Cambridge University Press, 2006); Terry Nardin, *Law, Morality, and the Relations of States* (Princeton: Princeton University Press, 1983); Onora O'Neill, *Bounds of Justice* (New York: Cambridge University of Press, 2000); Thomas Pogge, *World Poverty and Human Rights: Cosmopolitan Responsibilities and Reforms* (Cambridge: Polity Press, 2002).

24. Augustine employs the classic definition of justice throughout his writings. *See, e.g.*, Augustine, *Exposition on Book of Psalms*, trans. J. E. Tweed, Nicene and Post-Nicene Fathers 1, vol. 8 (Edinburgh: T&T Clark; Grand Rapids: Eerdmans, 1989), Psalm 84; August *City of God* 19.4, 21; August *On Free Will* 1.15; and Augustine, *On Christian Doctrine*, trans. D. W. Robertson, Jr. (New York: Macmillan, 1958), 1.22. For other examples of Augustine's interpretation of the fourfold classic virtues, *see* Augustine, *Of the Morals of the Catholic Church*, trans. Richard Stothert, Nicene and Post-Nicene Fathers 1, vol. 4 (Edinburgh: T&T Clark; Grand Rapids: Eerdmans, 1996), chap. 15; and August *City of God* 19.4.

25. August *City of God* 19.23; *see* ibid., 19.21–27, for Augustine's rejection of Cicero's definition of a commonwealth and his alternative account.

26. August *Of the Morals of the Catholic Church* chap. 26.

27. August *On Christian Doctrine* 1.30, 32; 1.28; Augustine, *Against Lying,* trans. H. Browne, Nicene and Post-Nicene Fathers 1, vol. 3 (Edinburgh: T&T Clark; Grand Rapids: Eerdmans, 1993), sec. 2; Augustine, *Letter 290, To Proba,* trans. J. G. Cunningham, Nicene and Post-Nicene Fathers 1, vol. 1 (Edinburgh: T&T Clark; Grand Rapids: Eerdmans, 1979).

28. August *City of God* 12.22. *See also* 12.23, 28, 14.1, 19.12, 15. Although Augustine offers a justification for slavery, unlike Aristotle he does not base it on a natural hierarchy; he describes it rather as a punishment of humanity because of sin. *Compare* Arist. *Politics* 1254a18–1255a2 and August *City of God* 19.15. For present purposes I take no position on the more basic issue concerning the ontological grounding of justice, that is, whether Augustine grounds justice in a conception of right order, the inherent rights of persons, or some other theory. I am, however, sympathetic with Nicholas Wolterstorff's conclusion that the Christian scriptures and the Church Fathers, who gave birth to the moral tradition, recognized something like the inherent worth of persons based on the presence of the imago dei, even though the vocabulary of rights would not appear until much later. *See* Nicholas Wolterstorff, *Justice: Rights and Wrongs* (Princeton: Princeton University Press, 2008), 60. *See also* David Little, "A Christian Perspective on Human Rights," in *Human Rights in Africa,* ed. Abdullahi Ahmed An-Na'im and Francis Deng, 59–103 (Washington: Brookings Institution, 1990).

29. Jean Elshtain observes that the account of justice latent in the just war tradition resembles claims undergirding the contemporary human rights movement: "Just war argument and universal human rights are not only not incompatible, they can and should be placed within the same framework." Elshtain, "International Justice as Equal Regard," 66. For an extended historical and philosophical argument that reaches a similar conclusion, *see* Wolterstorff, *Justice.*

30. For passages in which Augustine suggests war can be an act of love for the neighbor, *see* Augustine, *Letter 47, to Publicola,* trans. J. G. Cunningham, Nicene and Post-Nicene Fathers 1, vol. 1 (Edinburgh: T&T Clark; Grand Rapids: Eerdmans, 1979) ("When, however, men are prevented . . . from doing wrong, it may be said that a real service is done to themselves. The precept, 'Resist not evil,' was given to prevent us from taking pleasure in revenge . . . but not to make us neglect the duty of restraining men from sin"); August *Letter 138, to Marcellinus* (comparing the just use of force to a father disciplining his son in love and concluding, "If the commonwealth observe the precepts of the Christian religion, even its wars themselves will not be carried on without the benevolent design that, after the resisting nations have been conquered, provision may be more easily made for enjoying in peace the mutual bond of piety and justice"); Augustine, *Commentary on the Lord's Sermon on the Mount,* trans. William Findlay, Nicene and Post-Nicene Fathers 1, vol. 6 (Edinburgh: T&T Clark; Grand Rapids: Eerdmans, 1974), chap. 20 ("But no one is fit for inflicting this punishment except the man who, by the greatness of his love, has overcome that hatred wherewith those are wont to be inflamed who wish to avenge themselves").

31. The best description of colonial America as a society of largely unquestioned hierarchy and dependency is Gordon Wood, *The Radicalism of the American Revolution* (New York: A. A. Knopf, 1991), esp. chaps. 1–5. I draw on this work here.

32. Ibid., 232–33. For works on the Declaration of Independence, its sources, and its evolving meaning in American society, *see* Carl L. Becker, *The Declaration of Independence: A Study in the History of Political Ideas* (New York: Harcourt Brace, 1922) (the classic study); Gary Wills, *Inventing America: Jefferson's Declaration of Independence* (Garden City, N.Y.: Doubleday, 1978); Pauline Maier, *American Scripture: Making the Declaration of Independence* (New York: Vintage Books, 1998); and David Armitage, *The Declaration of Independence: A Global History* (Cambridge: Harvard University Press, 2007).

33. Thomas Jefferson to Henry Lee, May 8, 1825, in *The Works of Thomas Jefferson*, vol. 12, ed. Paul L. Ford (New York: G. P. Putnam's Sons, 1905), 409; and Maier, *American Scripture*, 47–96, 191–92.

34. Jefferson to Lee, May 8, 1825, in *Works*, 409. For an interpretation of the original meaning of the Declaration of Independence, *see* Maier, *American Scripture*, 123–43.

35. Patrick Henry to Robert Pleasants, January 17, 1773, in *The Evolution of International Human Rights*, 2d ed. (Philadelphia: University of Pennsylvania Press, 2003), 33.

36. *See* Maier, *American Scripture*, 160–92.

37. William L. Garrison, *Boston Courier*, July 9, 1829, quoted in Maier, *American Scripture*, 198; John Q. Adams, *Argument of John Quincy Adams before the Supreme Court of the United States in the Case of United States v. Cinque* (New York: S. W. Benedict, 1841), 8–9; Frederick Douglass, "What to the Slave Is the Fourth of July?" in *The Frederick Douglass Papers: Speeches, Debates, and Interviews, 1847–54*, ed. John W. Blassingame (New Haven: Yale University Press, 1982), 2:359–88; and Paul M. Angle, ed., *The Complete Lincoln–Douglas Debates of 1858* (Chicago: University of Chicago Press, 1991), 379. For accounts of social movements making appeal to the Declaration of Independence, *see* Maier, *American Scriptures*, 197–99; and Armitage, *Declaration*, 94–96.

38. Henry Knox to George Washington, July 7, 1789, in *American State Papers, Indian Affairs* (Washington: Gales and Seaton, 1832), 1:53. For background, *see* Reginald Horsman, *Expansion and American Indian Policy, 1783–1812* (East Lansing: Michigan State University Press, 1967).

39. Report from Henry Knox to George Washington, June 15, 1789, in *American State Papers, Indians Affairs* (Washington: Gales and Seaton, 1832), 1:13.

40. John L. Gaddis, *The Cold War: A New History* (New York: Penguin Press, 2005), 171; Leslie H. Gelb and Justine A. Rosenthal, "The Rise of Ethics in Foreign Policy," *Foreign Affairs* 82 (May/June 2003): 3.

Chapter 4. Early Modern Rivals

1. Few scholars have explored what the just war tradition had to say about preventive force. One who has is Gregory Reichberg, "Preventive War in Classical Just War Theory," *Journal of the History of International Law* 9, no. 1 (2007): 5–34.

2. Augustine, *On Free Will*, trans. John H. S. Burleigh, in *Augustine: Earlier Writings*, Library of Christian Classics (Philadelphia: Westminster Press, 1953), 1.11 (emphasis added); Augustine, *City of God*, trans. R. W. Dyson (New York: Cambridge University Press, 1998), 1.30. For an extended discussion of both of these passages, *see* J. Warren Smith, "Augustine and the Limits of Preemptive and Preventive War," *Journal of Religious Ethics* 35, no. 1 (2007): 141–62. Gratian, *Decretum* (Causa 23), trans. Peter Haggenmacher and Robert Andrews, in *The Ethics of War: Classic and Contemporary Readings*, ed. Gregory M. Reichberg, Henrik Syse, and Endre Begby (Oxford, England: Blackwell, 2006), 110.

3. On the background to the neo-Thomists, *see* J. A. Fernandez-Santamaria, *The State, War and Peace: Spanish Political Thought in the Renaissance 1516–1559* (Cambridge: Cambridge University Press, 1977); Bernice Hamilton, *Political Thought in Sixteenth-Century Spain* (Oxford: Clarendon Press, 1963); James B. Scott, *The Spanish Origin of International Law* (Oxford: Clarendon Press, 1934); Quentin Skinner, *The Foundations of Modern Political Thought*. Vol. 2: *The Reformation* (New York: Cambridge University Press, 1978), 135–72.

4. Francisco de Vitoria to Miguel de Arcos, November 8, 1534, in *Vitoria: Political Writings*, ed. Anthony Pagden and Jeremy Lawrance (New York: Cambridge University Press, 1991), 331.

5. Francisco de Vitoria, *On the American Indians*, in *Vitoria: Political Writings*, ed. Anthony Pagden and Jeremy Lawrance (New York: Cambridge University Press, 1991), 231–92; and Francisco de Vitoria, *On the Law of War*, ibid., 293–327. For further context, *see* Anthony Pagden, *The Fall of Natural Man* (New York: Cambridge University Press, 1982), 27–56.

6. Vitoria rehearses many of these ideas in his commentary on Aquinas's treatise on law. *See* Francisco de Vitoria, *On Law: Lectures on ST I-II.90–105*, in *Vitoria: Political Writings*, ed. Anthony Pagden and Jeremy Lawrance (New York: Cambridge University Press, 1991), 153–204.

7. Francisco de Vitoria, *On Civil Power*, ibid., 3–44. Vitoria, *On the Law of War*, 303–04. Perhaps the most important statement of the neo-Thomist response to Machiavelli and the permissive account of war was Peter Ribadeneira, *Religion and the Virtues of the Christian Prince* (1595).

8. Francisco de Vitoria, *On Homicide and Commentary on Summa theologiae II-II Q. 64*, ed. and trans. John P. Doyle (Milwaukee: Marquette University Press, 1997), 201–03.

9. Vitoria, *Commentary on II.II.64.7*, 201, 202–03.

10. Vitoria, *Commentary on II.64.2*, 143; *cf. Digest* 9.2.45.4. For Augustine and Aquinas on self-defense, *see* Augustine, *Letter 47, to Publicola*, trans. J. G. Cunningham,

Nicene and Post-Nicene Fathers 1, vol. 1 (Edinburgh: T&T Clark; Grand Rapids: Eerdmans, 1979); Thomas Aquinas, *Summa Theologica*, trans. Fathers of the English Dominican Province (New York: Benziger Brothers, 1948), II.II.64.7. Vitoria, *Commentary on II.II.64.7*, 191–93.

11. Vitoria, *Commentary on II.II.64.7*, 203.

12. Ibid.

13. Ibid (emphasis added).

14. Ibid., 234n246; Vitoria, *On the Law of War*, 298 (emphasis added).

15. On the revival of interest in Tacitus, *see* Peter Burke, "Tacitism, Skepticism, and Reason of State," in *The Cambridge History of Political Thought 1450–1700*, ed. J. H. Burns and Mark Goldie, 479–98(New York: Cambridge University Press, 1991); Skinner, *The Foundations of Modern Political Thought. Vol. 1: The Renaissance*, 244–62; Giovanni Botero, *The Reason of State*, trans. P. J. Waley and D. P. Waley (New Haven: Yale University Press, 1956), xiii.

16. *See* Nicolai Rubinstein, "Italian Political Thought, 1450–1530," in *The Cambridge History of Political Thought, 1450–1700*, ed. J. H Burns and Mark Goldie, 30–65 (Cambridge: Cambridge University Press, 1991).

17. Niccolò Machiavelli, *The Prince*, ed. Quentin Skinner, trans. Russell Price (Cambridge: Cambridge University Press, 1998), 55, 59, 55.

18. Ibid., 10–11, 11.

19. Ibid., 62.

20. Alberico Gentili, *On the Law of War*, trans. Gordon J. Laing, Classics of International Law (Oxford: Clarendon Press, 1925), 1.1.10.

21. Ibid., 1.7.54, 1.7.53, 1.3.23 ("Whereas there are two modes of contention, one by argument and the other by force, one should not resort to the latter if it is possible to use the former. The necessity which justifies war . . . arises when one is driven to arms as the last resort").

22. Vitoria, *On the Indians*, 155; and Vitoria, *On the Law of War*, 302, 312.

23. Gentili, *On the Law of War*, 1.14.97, 1.14.98.

24. Ibid., 1.14.99, 1.14.100.

25. Ibid., 1.14.104, 1.14.101, 1.14.106. For a history of the "balance of power" idea, *see* Evan Luard, *The Balance of Power: The System of International Relations 1648–1815* (London: Macmillan, 1992), 1–7; Michael Sheehan, *Balance of Power: History and Theory* (New York: Routledge, 1996), 29–36.

26. Alberico Gentili, *On Embassies*, trans. Gordon J. Laing, Classics of International Law (1924; reprint, Buffalo: William S. Hein, 1995), 156.

27. Francis Bacon, *Considerations Touching a War with Spain*, in *The Works of Francis Bacon*, ed. Basil Montagu (Philadelphia: A. Hart, 1852), 2:202, 2:208, 2:205.

Chapter 5. Anticipation in a State of Nature

1. Hugo Grotius, *On the Law of War and Peace*, trans. Francis W. Kelsey, Classics of International Law (1950; reprint, Buffalo: William S. Hein, 1995), 2.1.17. Borschberg concludes that Vitoria is the single most important influence on Grotius. *See*

Peter Borschberg, "Hugo Grotius: A Profile of His Life, Works, and Legacy," in *Commentarius in Theses XI* (Berne: Peter Lang, 1994), 48n145. In Grotius's early and short *Commentarius in Theses XI,* he cites Vitoria twelve times, more than any other person. Ibid., 48–52. Several passages represent Grotius's rejection of the just fear tradition. *See* Grotius, *On the Law of War,* 2.1.5, 17, 2.22.5. Richard Tuck places Grotius wholly on the side of those espousing a permissive account of war: "The view taken of Grotius in the conventional histories of international law badly misrepresents his real position. Far from being an heir to the tradition of Vitoria and Suarez . . . he was in fact an heir to the tradition Vitoria most mistrusted, that of humanist jurisprudence." Richard Tuck, *The Rights of War and Peace: Political Thought and International Order from Grotius to Kant* (New York: Oxford University Press, 1999), 108. As I argue later in this chapter, I think Grotius and Hobbes share an important starting point that brings the two traditions at this point in time close together on a theoretical plane. Nonetheless, Tuck's conclusion is too sweeping. He bases it primarily on an interpretation of Grotius's view of international punishment and the implications this view has for the treatment of native peoples. *See* Grotius, *On the Law of War,* 2.20.40. However, Tuck gives no attention to Grotius's view of anticipatory force, even though Tuck mentions the issue in regard to other figures he considers. On this subject Grotius is clearly extending the thought of the neo-Thomists.

2. Hedley Bull coined the term "domestic analogy," an idea he explores at length in two essays published in 1966. *See* Hedley Bull, "Society and Anarchy in International Relations," in *Hedley Bull on International Society,* ed. Kai Anderson, 77–94 (New York: Palgrave Publishers, 2000); and Hedley Bull, "The Grotian Conception of International Society," ibid., 95–124. *See also* Michael Walzer, *Just and Unjust Wars: A Moral Argument with Historical Illustrations,* 3d ed. (New York: Basic Books, 2002), 58–59.

3. Grotius, *On the Law of War,* 2.1.5, 2.1.16.

4. Ibid., 2.1.5; and Daniel Webster to Henry Fox, April 24, 1841, in *British and Foreign State Papers, 1841–1842* (London: H.M.S.O, 1858), 30:1137.

5. Grotius, *On the Law of War,* 2.1.5.

6. Francisco de Vitoria, *On Homicide and Commentary on Summa theologiae II-II Q. 64,* ed. and trans. John P. Doyle (Milwaukee: Marquette University Press, 1997), 203; Grotius, *On the Law of War,* 2.1.3 (emphasis added), 2.1.5.

7. *Digest* 43.16.3.9.

8. Gratian, *Decretum* (Causa 23), trans. Peter Haggenmacher and Robert Andrews, in *The Ethics of War: Classic and Contemporary Readings,* ed. Gregory M. Reichberg, Henrik Syse, and Endre Begby (Oxford: Blackwell, 2006), 110. For examples of civil lawyers who invoked the concept of *in continenti, see* Frederick Russell, *The Just War in the Middle Ages* (Cambridge: Cambridge University Press, 1975), 42n11. For a brief description of the incorporation of Roman law into medieval accounts of war and self-defense, *see* ibid., 40–54.

9. Francisco de Vitoria, *On the Law of War,* in *Vitoria: Political Writings,* ed. Anthony Pagden and Jeremy Lawrance (New York: Cambridge University Press, 1991), 300.

Grotius does not use *in continenti,* but the meaning is the same: "Periculum prae-
sens hic requritur, et quasi in puncto" (Present danger is here required, and as if
in a moment). Hugo Grotius, *De Jure Belli et Pacis* (Cambridge: John W. Parker,
1853).

10. Grotius, *On the Law of War,* 2.1.16.

11. Ibid., 2.20.39.

12. Ibid., 2.1.16.

13. For Grotius's understanding of punishment, *see On the Law of War,* 2.20.8–9.

14. Ibid., 2.22.5, 2.1.5, 2.1.17.

15. The transformation in natural law theory in the modern period is described in
Knud Haakonssen, "Divine/Natural Law Theories in Ethics," in *The Cambridge
History of Seventeenth-Century Philosophy,* ed. Daniel Garber and Michael Ayers,
2:1317–57 (New York: Cambridge University Press, 1998), ; T. J. Hochstrasser, *Natural Law Theories in the Early Enlightenment* (Cambridge: Cambridge University
Press, 2000); Richard Tuck, "The 'Modern' Theory of Natural Law," in *The Languages of Political Theory in Early-Modern Europe,* ed. Anthony Pagden, 99–119
(Cambridge: Cambridge University Press, 1987), ; and J. B. Schneewind, *The Invention of Autonomy: A History of Modern Moral Philosophy* (New York: Cambridge
University Press, 1998), 58–81. On the more particular but related issue of the development of natural rights from medieval to modern times, two representative
works are Brian Tierney, *The Idea of Natural Rights* (Grand Rapids, Eerdmans,
2001); and Richard Tuck, *Natural Rights Theories: Their Origin and Development*
(New York: Cambridge University Press, 1979).

16. Grotius, *On the Law of War,* Prolegomena, sec. 5. The seminal work on the rise of
skepticism is Richard H. Popkin, *The History of Scepticism,* rev. and exp. ed. (New
York: Oxford University Press, 2003); *see also* Charles Larmore, "Scepticism," in
The Cambridge History of Seventeenth-Century Philosophy, ed. Daniel Garber and
Michael Ayers, 2:1145–1192 (New York: Cambridge University Press, 1998); and
Schneewind, *The Invention of Autonomy,* 42–57.

17. Grotius, *On the Law of War,* 1.1.1. Grotius always referred to his earlier work as *De
Indis,* and not until the nineteenth century did an editor assign it the name *On the
Law of the Prize.* The Dutch East India Company had sought for some time to form
trade routes to Asia, which at that time the Portuguese dominated. In 1603 a captain affiliated with the company seized a Portuguese ship loaded with goods. A
Dutch court held a hearing on the issue and decided the company could keep most
of the profits. Several Mennonite shareholders, however, opposed the decision to
retain the goods as unjust. The company entreated Grotius to write a defense of
the decision and the result was *De Indis,* dealing with the moral and legal status
of prize and booty. He argues that the company has a right to the goods because
it acquired them in a just war according to natural law. Except for a chapter on
maritime law, the apology was not published until 1864. While Hobbes and others following Grotius would not have read it, the prolegomena to this work sheds
much light on the sometimes confusing introduction to his much more widely
read work *On the Law of War and Peace.*

18. Grotius, *On the Law of the Prize (On the Indies)*, trans. Gwladys L. Williams, Classics of International Law (1950; reprint, Buffalo: William S. Hein, 1995), chap. 2, p. 9; Grotius, *On the Law of War*, 1.2.1; Grotius, *On the Indies*, chap. 2, pp. 10, 11.

19. These passages come from Grotius, *On the Indies*, chap. 2, pp. 9–14; Grotius, *On the Law of War*, Prolegomena, sec. 6–8. In his prolegomena to *On the Law of War and Peace*, Grotius begins his response to Carneades, the representative skeptic, with his principle of sociability, without any mention of the prior law of self-preservation. In answering the question "whether it is ever lawful to wage war?" in book 1, chapter 2, however, he begins with the "first principle of nature," self-preservation, and then turns to the second law of sociability. Richard Tuck offers a convincing explanation of the confusion surrounding these laws in the later work, as compared to *On the Indies*, in which Grotius explains both laws. Tuck begins by noting that the second edition of *On the Law of War and Peace*, the edition most often read today, includes a heavily reworked introduction in which sociability is given a much more prominent role than it has in an earlier edition, which is closer to the structure that appears in *On the Indies*. Tuck explains this change in terms of events in Grotius's life. When he rewrote the introduction in December 1631, Tuck argues, Grotius was seeking to return to the Netherlands from exile and wanted his work to be more appealing to the Calvinist culture of his opponents, who were worried about the implications of a system that started with self-interest as its fundamental law. Tuck, *The Rights of War and Peace*, 94–102.

20. *On the Indies*, chap. 2, p. 12.

21. Grotius, *On the Law of War*, Prolegomena, sec. 6–7.

22. Grotius, *On the Indies*, chap. 2, pp. 11, 9, 29.

23. Grotius's account of the state's origin in *On the Law of War and Peace*, Prolegomena, sec. 15–16, is muddled and thin. He offers a much fuller account in *On the Indies*, chap. 2, pp. 19–20.

24. Grotius, *On the Indies*, chap. 2, pp. 27–28; and Grotius, *On the Law of War*, Prolegomena, sec. 26.

25. For a survey of the reactions to Hobbes's ideas by his contemporaries, *see* Samuel I. Mintz, *The Hunting of Leviathan: Seventeenth-Century Reactions to the Materialism an Moral Philosophy of Thomas Hobbes* (London: Cambridge University Press, 1962). For an overview of Hobbes's view of states and their relationship to one another, *see* Charles Beitz, *Political Theory and International Relations* (Princeton: Princeton University Press, 1979), 27–34.

26. Noel Malcolm, "A Summary Biography of Hobbes," in *The Cambridge Companion to Hobbes*, ed. Tom Sorell, 19 (New York: Cambridge University Press, 1996). A copy of *On the Law of War and Peace* was included among the books in the library of a wealthy family Hobbes worked for in the 1620s. A library catalog lists the book in Hobbes's hand. *See* James J. Hamilton, "Hobbes's Study and the Hardwick Library," *Journal of the History of Philosophy* 16 (October 1978): 450. Tuck notes that Hobbes was closely associated with a group in the 1630s known as the Tew Circle, who were enthusiastic readers of Grotius. Richard Tuck, *Philosophy and Government 1572–1651* (Cambridge: Cambridge University Press, 1993), 272, 305.

27. For a helpful overview of Hobbes's moral psychology, *see* Schneewind, *The Invention of Autonomy*, 82–87; and Thomas Hobbes, *Leviathan*, ed. Richard Tuck (New York: Cambridge University Press, 1996), 11.47.

28. Hobbes, *Leviathan*, 11.47.

29. Thomas Hobbes, *On the Citizen*, ed. Richard Tuck and Michael Silverthorne (Cambridge: Cambridge University Press, 1998), Preface, sec. 14; Hobbes, *Leviathan*, 13.63, Introduction, sec. 1.

30. Hobbes, *On the Citizen*, 1.7. For more on Hobbes's materialism, *see* Schneewind, *The Invention of Autonomy*, 88–92.

31. Hobbes, *On the Citizen*, 1.9; and Hobbes, *Leviathan*, 14.64. At one point Hobbes suggests that a very narrow segment of actions could never, on any interpretation, be deemed to contribute to one's self-preservation: "I cannot see what drunkenness or cruelty (which is vengeance without regard to future good) contribute to any man's peace or preservation." Hobbes, *On the Citizen*, 3.27.

32. Hobbes, *Leviathan*, 17.85; *see also* Hobbes, *On the Citizen*, 1.2. Tuck finds a certain minimal sociability in Hobbes, close to Grotius's negative duties. He reasons that recognizing one's right of self-preservation leads one to recognize a similar right on the behalf of others that creates a duty to respect that right. Tuck, *On the Law of War and Peace*, 132.

33. Hobbes, *Leviathan*, 13.62; and Hobbes, *On the Citizen*, 1.3. On leaving the state of nature, *see* ibid., 1.13, 2.3; and Hobbes, *Leviathan*, 14.64–65.

34. Hobbes, *Leviathan*, 13.61; Hobbes, *On the Citizen*, preface, sec. 12; and 1.2. *See also* Hobbes, *Leviathan*, 11.49 ("Feare of oppression, diposeth a man to anticipate, or to seek ayd by society: for there is no other way by which a man can secure his life and liberty.").

35. Hobbes, *On the Citizen*, 13.7.

36. Hobbes, *Leviathan*, 13.63, 15.71; *see also* Hobbes, *On the Citizen*, 1.10. For a description of the same between states, *see* ibid., 28.165.

Chapter 6. Evolution and Eclipse

1. For a historical overview of the balance of power concept, both as an idea and in practice, *see* Evan Luard, *The Balance of Power: The System of International Relations 1648–1815* (London: Macmillan, 1992); and Michael Sheehan, *Balance of Power: History and Theory* (New York: Routledge, 1996).

2. Ronald G. Asch, *The Thirty Years War: The Holy Roman Empire and Europe, 1618–1648* (London: Macmillan, 1997); and Adam Watson, *The Evolution of International Society* (New York: Routledge, 1992), 169–97.

3. Samuel Pufendorf, *On the Duty of Man and Citizen According to Natural Law*, ed. James Tully, trans. Michael Silverthorne (Cambridge: Cambridge University Press, 1991), 2.1.8, 2.1.9; and Samuel Pufendorf, *On the Law of Nature*, trans. C. H. Oldfather and W. A. Oldfather, Classics of International Law (1934; reprint, Buffalo: William S. Hein, 1995), 2.2.4. For secondary sources on Pufendorf's moral the-

ory as it relates to his account of the relations between states, *see* Alfred Dufour, "Pufendorf," in *The Cambridge Dictionary of Political Thought, 1450–1700,* ed. J. H. Burns, 561–68 (Cambridge: Cambridge University Press, 1991); Knud Haakonssen, *Natural Law and Moral Philosophy: From Grotius to the Scottish Enlightenment* (New York: Cambridge University Press, 1996), 35–46; Richard Tuck, *The Rights of War and Peace* (New York: Oxford University Press, 1999), 140–65; and J. B. Schneewind, *The Invention of Autonomy: A History of Modern Moral Philosophy* (New York: Cambridge University Press, 1998), 118–40.

4. Pufendorf, *On the Law of Nature,* 2.3.13, 2.2.3, 2.3.15, 3.3.1, 2.2.3.

5. Ibid., 2.2.9, 2.2.5, 2.2.8.

6. Ibid., 2.2.18.

7. Ibid., 8.6.5, 2.5.6. Pufendorf offers his account of preemption in two main passages: ibid., 2.5.6–9 (individuals), 8.6.1–5 (states).

8. Ibid., 2.5.7, 2.5.8, 2.5.7.

9. Ibid., 2.5.6.

10. Ibid., 8.6.5, 8.6.3.

11. For secondary sources on Vattel's moral and political theory, *see* T. J. Hochstrasser, *Natural Law Theories in the Early Enlightenment* (Cambridge: Cambridge University Press, 2000), 177–83; Tuck, *The Rights of War and Peace,* 191–96; F. S. Ruddy, *International Law in the Enlightenment: The Background of Emmerich de Vattel's 'Le Droit des Gens'* (Dobbs Ferry, N.Y.: Oceana Publications, 1975); Frederick G. Whelan, "Vattel's Doctrine of the State," in *Grotius, Pufendorf and Modern Natural Law,* ed. Knud Haakonssen (Brookfield, Vt.: Ashgate, 1999), 403–06.

12. *See* Emmerich de Vattel, *The Law of Nations or the Principles of Natural Law,* trans. Charles G. Fenwick, Classics of International Law (1916; reprint, Buffalo: William S. Hein, 1995), 1.2.28, Introduction, sec. 10, Introduction, sec. 6.

13. Ibid., 3.3.26. For passages discussing force as a last resort, *see* ibid., 2.18.338–40, 3.3.25, 37.

14. Ibid., 2.14.185, 3.3.42. Other passages on anticipatory force include, ibid., 3.3.42–50, 2.14.184.

15. Ibid., 3.3.44, 3.3.49, 3.3.45. Both Tuck and Hochstrasser overlook these limitations and are unwilling to see Vattel as a transitional figure, simply concluding he gives broad license to attack hegemonic powers. Tuck, *On the Rights of War and Peace,* 193; Hochstrasser, *Natural Law Theories,* 181.

16. Vattel, *The Law of Nations,* 3.3.45.

17. Ibid., 3.12.189. On pre-Westphalian accounts of sovereignty in the moral tradition, *see* James T. Johnson, "Aquinas and Luther on War and Peace: Sovereign Authority and the Use of Armed Force," *Journal of Religious Ethics* 31 (spring 2003): 17n1.

18. Vattel, *The Law of Nations,* 3.12.190.

19. Ibid., 3.12.188.

20. Jean-Jacques Rousseau, *Discourse on the Origin and Foundations of Inequality Among Men,* in *Rousseau: The Discourses and Other Early Political Writings,* ed. and trans. Victor Gourevitch (Cambridge: Cambridge University Press, 1997), 1.5;

Jean-Jacques Rousseau, *The Social Contract*, in *Rousseau: The Social Contract and Other Later Political Writings*, ed. and trans. Victor Gourevitch, (Cambridge: Cambridge University Press, 1997), 1.2.2, 1.8.2.

21. Jean-Jacques Rousseau, *The State of War*, in *Rousseau: The Social Contract and Other Later Political Writings*, ed. and trans. Victor Gourevitch (Cambridge: Cambridge University Press, 1997), sec. 42–43.

22. Rousseau, *The Social Contract*, 6.10 (analogy); Rousseau, *Discourse on Inequality*, 2.34; and Rousseau, *The State of War*, sec. 26–29 (comparison between states and individuals). In an essay of 1756, *A Lasting Peace*, Rousseau restates and criticizes Abbé de Saint Pierre's proposal for international peace, published in the early part of the eighteenth century. A genre of such writings had emerged, of which Kant's *Toward Perpetual Peace* (1795) would become the most well known. Rousseau agreed with Saint Pierre that such a peace required a federated Europe but concluded that only a forceful revolution could bring it about. The end result could never justify the destruction required to reach it. Rousseau, *A Lasting Peace*, trans. C. E. Vaughan (London: Constable, 1917), 112.

23. Jean-Jacques Rousseau, *The Geneva Manuscript*, in *Rousseau: The Social Contract and Other Later Political Writings*, ed. and trans. Victor Gourevitch (Cambridge: Cambridge University Press, 1997), 1.2.14, 1.2.13. For further discussion on the opposition between interest and justice, *see* ibid., 1.2.10.

24. Immanuel Kant, *Religion within the Boundaries of Mere Reason*, ed. and trans. Allen Wood and George Di Giovanni (Cambridge: Cambridge University Press, 1998), 6:93.

25. Immanuel Kant, *Idea for a Universal History with a Cosmopolitan Purpose*, in *Kant: Political Writings*, ed. Hans Reiss, trans. H. B. Nisbet, (Cambridge: Cambridge University Press, 1970), 44.

26. Ibid., 49 (present condition worst), 47, 51 (wars of aggrandizement); and Immanuel Kant, *Conjectures on the Beginning of Human History*, in *Kant: Political Writings*, ed. Hans Reiss, trans. H. B. Nisbet (Cambridge: Cambridge University Press, 1970), 232.

27. Kant, *Religion*, 6:97n. Kant offers his most extended description of this international state of war in his *Metaphysics of Morals*, in *Immanuel Kant: Practical Philosophy*, ed. and trans. Mary J. Gregor (New York: Cambridge University Press, 1996), 6:343–46, 482–84. For a defense of just war theory in Kant's writings, *see* Brian Orend, "Kant's Just War Theory," *Journal of the History of Philosophy* 37 (April 1999): 323–53.

28. Kant, *Metaphysics of Morals*, 6:312; Immanuel Kant, *Toward Perpetual Peace*, in *Immanuel Kant: Practical Philosophy*, ed. and trans. Mary J. Gregor (New York: Cambridge University Press, 1996), 8:346–47, 355.

29. Kant, *Toward Perpetual Peace*, 8:349n.

30. Kant, *Metaphysics of Morals*, 6:307, 346.

31. Clausewitz, *On War*, trans. Michael Howard and Peter Paret (New York: Oxford University Press, 2008), 8.5.

32. William E. Hall, *A Treatise on International Law*, 4th ed. (Oxford: Clarendon Press,

1895), 1–5. Other treatises that represent the changes in the nineteenth and early twentieth centuries include Theodore D. Woolsey, *Introduction to the Study of International Law*, 5th ed. (1879; reprint, Holmes Beach, Fla.: Gaunt, 1998), 1–3; and Lassa Oppenheim, *International Law* (New York: Longmans, Green, 1905), 1:15. Henry Wheaton, *Elements of International Law* (Philadelphia: Carey, Lea and Blanchard, 1836), is a good example of the transition from natural law theory to positivism.

33. Hall, *International Law*, 5. Most scholars of international law rejected the concept of a state of nature as a tool for discerning a natural law but still accepted the concept as a model of interstate relations. For a helpful overview of international law and state practice as it concerned the use of force during this period, *see* Ian Brownlie, *International Law and the Use of Force by States* (Oxford: Clarendon Press, 1963), 19–50; and Judith Gardam, *Necessity, Proportionality and the Use of Force by States* (Cambridge: Cambridge University Press, 2004), 1–27.

34. Hall, *International Law*, 19, 50.

35. Ibid., 45, 281.

36. Ibid., 47, 297–98.

37. Ibid., 64–65; T. J. Lawrence, *The Principles of International Law*, 4th ed. (Boston: D. C. Heath, 1910), 333–34.

Chapter 7. Behind Webster's Rule

1. Hugo Grotius, *On the Law of War and Peace*, trans. Francis W. Kelsey, Classics of International Law (1950; reprint, Buffalo: William S. Hein, 1995), 2.1.5, 2.1.16.

2. Samuel Pufendorf, *On the Law of Nature*, trans. C. H. Oldfather and W. A. Oldfather, Classics of International Law (1934; reprint, Buffalo: William S. Hein, 1995), 8.6.4–5 (states), 2.5.6 (individuals).

3. William Blackstone, *Commentaries on the Laws of England*, 15th ed. (London: A. Strahan, 1809), 4:183.

4. Ibid., 4:184.

5. Wis. Stat. 939.48(1) (2008). For a summary of self-defense doctrine and a list of state statutory provisions, *see* Wayne R. LaFave, *Substantive Criminal Law*, 2d ed. (Eagan, Minn.: Thomson/West, 2003), 10.4. Representative articles on the imminence criterion in the context of battered women syndrome include Richard Rosen, "On Self-Defense, Imminence, and Women Who Kill Their Batterers," *North Carolina Law Review* 71 (1993): 371–411; V. F. Nourse, "Self-Defense and Subjectivity," *University of Chicago Law Review* 68 (2001): 1235–1308; and Whitley R. P. Kaufman, "Self-Defense, Imminence, and the Battered Woman," *New Criminal Law Review* 10 (2007): 342–69.

6. Several scholars have reached a similar conclusion in the domestic context, discussing the case of the battered spouse. *See* Rosen, "Women Who Kill Their Batterers," 371; Richard Schopp, *Justification Defenses and Just Convictions* (Cambridge: Cambridge University Press, 1998), 101–02; and Shana Wallace, "Beyond Imminence: Evolving International Law and Battered Women's Rights to Self-Defense," *University of Chicago Law Review* 71 (2004): 1749.

7. Grotius, *On the Law of War,* 2.1.5 (emphasis added).

8. Pufendorf, *On the Law of Nature,* 2.5.8.

9. Daniel Webster to Henry Fox, April 24, 1841, in *British and Foreign State Papers, 1841–1842* (London: H.M.S.O, 1858), 30:1137.

10. *See, e.g.,* Stephen Macedo, "Introduction," in *Striking First,* ed. Stephen Macedo (Princeton: Princeton University Press, 2008), xiii–xiv; and Allen Buchanan and Robert O. Keohane, "The Preventive Use of Force: A Cosmopolitan Institutional Proposal," *Ethics and International Affairs* 18, no. 1 (2004): 2.

11. Several early documents from the American Colonization Society are included in the first and only publication of the organization's periodical, *The African Intelligencer* (July 1820). Webster expressed some reservations about the organization in a letter to Justice Joseph Story, August 6, 1822, Washington, D.C., in *The Private Correspondence of Daniel Webster,* ed. Webster Fletcher (Boston: Little, Brown, 1857), 6:320–21.

12. U.S. Constitution, art. I, sec. 9, cl. 1; Act of 1807, *Stats at Large of USA* 2 (March 2, 1807): 426; Act of 1819, *Stats at Large of USA* 3 (March 3, 1819): 510–14, 532–34; and Act of 1820, *Stats at Large of USA* 3 (May 15, 1820): 600–01.

13. Accounts of Stockton's maiden voyage and negotiations in Africa include J. B. Taylor, *Biography of Elder Lott Cary* (Baltimore: Armstrong and Berry, 1837) (appendix); Robert F. Stockton, *A Sketch of the Life of Com. Robert F. Stockton* (New York: Derby and Jackson, 1856), 39–47.

14. The most complete account of the encounter between the *Alligator* and the *Marianna Flora* is found in the opinion issued by the district court after the matter went to trial. *The Marianna Flora* (D. Mass Feb. 9, 1822), *microformed on* U.S. Supreme Court Appellate Case Files (no. 150–62, micro-copy no. 214), *rev'd,* 16 F. Cas. 736 (Cir. Ct., D. Mass. 1822) (no. 9,080), *aff'd,* 24 U.S. 1 (11 Wheat. 1) (1826). *See also, Boston Daily Advertiser,* December 26, 1821, for a contemporary account of the *Marianna Flora*'s arrival at Boston.

15. *The Marianna Flora* (D. Mass Feb. 9, 1822), *microformed on* U.S. Supreme Court Appellate Case Files (no. 150–62, micro-copy no. 214), *rev'd,* 16 F. Cas. 736 (Cir. Ct., D. Mass. 1822) (no. 9,080), *aff'd,* 24 U.S. 1 (11 Wheat. 1) (1826).

16. *The Marianna Flora,* 24 U.S. 1, 15 (11 Wheat. 1) (1826). The text of Blake's and Webster's arguments is taken from the extensive notes of the court reporter, Henry Wheaton, and is not an exact transcription.

17. Ibid., 15–19.

18. Ibid., 16, 17.

19. Ibid., 17, 18 (quoting Pufendorf, *On the Law of Nature,* 2.5.6).

20. Blake borrows from an early eighteenth-century translation of the work. *See* Samuel Pufendorf, *The Law of Nature and Nations,* trans. Basil Kennet (Oxford: L. Lichfield et al., 1703). The Latin phrase is *primus mihi sit ictus expectandus. See* Samuel Pufendorf, *De Jure Naturae et Gentium* (London: Lowe and Brydone, 1688). The Kennet version translates *primus* as an adverb meaning "immediately." The better translation is to read *primus* to mean "first," an adjective modifying "blow" (*ictus*). The sentence should read: "I may expect to receive the first blow."

21. Daniel Webster, *The Papers of Daniel Webster: Correspondence, 1798–1824,* ed. Charles M. Wiltse and Harold D. Moser (Hanover, N.H.: University Press of New England, 1975), 1:17.

Chapter 8. Beyond Webster's Rule

1. A helpful statement of these rationales is Larry Solum, "Procedural Justice," *Southern California Law Review* 78 (2004): 186–89.
2. Michael Bothe, "Terrorism and the Legality of Pre-Emptive Force," *European Journal of International Law* 14 (April 2003): 240 ("The argument which is often heard against recourse to the Security Council as a source of legitimization is that it is all too often blockaded. There is, indeed, a certain balance of power in the Council, a system of checks and balances, designed with some degree of political wisdom by the drafters of the Charter").
3. *See* Michael Reisman and Andrea Armstrong, "The Past and Future of the Claim of Preemptive Self-Defense," *American Journal of International Law* 100 (July 2006): 538–50; National Security Council, *A National Security Strategy for a New Century* (December 1999), 13–15.
4. Paul H. Robinson et al., *Criminal Law Defenses* (St. Paul, Minn.: West, 1984) (updated through 2007), sec. 21, sec. 24.
5. Daniel Webster to Henry Fox, April 24, 1841, in *British and Foreign State Papers, 1841–1842* (London: H.M.S.O, 1858), 30:1137.
6. *See* Oscar Schachter, "The Lawful Use of Force by a State Against Terrorists in Another Country," *Israel Yearbook on Human Rights* 19 (1989): 209–31; and Christine Gray, *International Law and the Use of Force,* 2d ed. (Oxford: Oxford University Press, 2004), 124 (concluding that in state practice necessity and proportionality are often the only factors relied on in deciding the legality of certain actions).
7. The Secretary-General's High-level Panel on Threats, Challenges, and Change, *A More Secure World: Our Shared Responsibility* (2004), 66–67, at http://www.un.org/secureworld. One of the early voices calling for a jurisprudence of prevention after the 9/11 attacks was Alan M. Dershowitz, *Preemption: A Knife That Cuts Both Ways* (New York: W. W. Norton, 2006), 25, 190–250. *See also,* Michael W. Doyle, "Standards," in *Striking First: Preemption and Prevention in International Conflict,* ed. Stephen Macedo, 43–96 (Princeton: Princeton University Press, 2008).
8. Daniel Webster to Henry Fox, April 24, 1841, in *British and Foreign State Papers, 1841–1842* (London: H.M.S.O, 1858), 30:1137.
9. Hugo Grotius, *On the Law of War and Peace,* trans. Francis W. Kelsey, Classics of International Law (1950; reprint, Buffalo: William S. Hein, 1995), 2.22.1.
10. On the applicability of assessing the magnitude of the harm in the case of an actual armed attack, *see, e.g.,* Oscar Schachter, "International Law: The Right of States to Use Armed Force," *Michigan Law Review* 82 (April 1984): 1635.
11. Webster to Fox, 24 April 1841, in *British and Foreign State Papers,* 30:1137.
12. Francisco de Vitoria, *On Homicide and Commentary on Summa theologiae II-II Q.*

64, ed. and trans. John P. Doyle (Milwaukee: Marquette University Press, 1997), 203.

13. For a concise summary of these strategies, which I borrow here, *see* James Steinberg, "The Use of Preventive Force as an Element of U.S. National Strategy," 14–16, a working paper for the Princeton Project on National Security, http://www.princeton.edu/~ppns/papers.html. Discussions of deterrence in the new security context include Lawrence Freedman, *Deterrence* (Cambridge: Polity Press, 2004); and Ian Shapiro, *Containment: Rebuilding a Strategy Against Global Terror* (Princeton: Princeton University Press, 2007).

14. Bob Woodward, *Plan of Attack* (New York: Simon and Schuster, 2004), 320. The formal U.S. justification for the Iraq War of 2003 relied on three Security Council resolutions: S.C. Res. 678 (1990), authorizing the First Gulf War; S.C. Res. 687 (1991), establishing conditions for a cease-fire; and S.C. Res. 1441 (2002), providing Iraq a final opportunity to comply. *See* John Negroponte, "Letter to the President of the Security Council," March 20, 2003.

15. U.S. Central Intelligence Agency, National Intelligence Council, *Iraq's Continuing Program for Weapons of Mass Destruction* (October 2002), http://www.cia.gov/library/reports/general-reports-1/Iraq_Oct_2002.htm; and U.S. Central Intelligence Agency, Iraq Survey Group, *Comprehensive Report on Iraq's Weapons of Mass Destruction,* https://www.cia.gov/library/reports/general-reports-1/iraq_wmd_2004, "Key Findings."

16. Woodward, *Plan of Attack,* 249–50 (Tenet comment); Bob Woodward, *State of Denial* (New York: Simon and Schuster, 2006), 303–04 (Tenet comment); George W. Bush, "Transcript of President's Remarks on Iraq Resolution," *New York Times,* September 27, 2002; Dick Cheney, "In Cheney's Words: The Administration Case for Removing Saddam Hussein," *New York Times,* August 27, 2002; for a description of the circumstantial nature of the evidence, *see* Woodward, *Plan of Attack,* 194–201.

17. Michael Walzer, "What a Little War in Iraq Could Do," *New York Times,* March 7, 2003.

18. The select narrative of events in this section is based on the *9/11 Commission Report.* National Commission on Terrorist Attacks Upon the United States, *The 9/11 Commission Report* (New York: W. W. Norton, 2004).

19. Osama bin Laden, "Jihad against Jews and Crusaders (February 23, 1998)," in *Anti-American Terrorism,* ed. Barry Rubin and Judith C. Rubin (New York: Oxford University Press, 2002), 150; Osama bin Laden, "Interview with Osama bin Laden (December 1998)," ibid., 153.

20. *9/11 Report,* 109, 115.

21. Ibid., 181–82, 266–76.

22. Ibid., 256–60. For Osama bin Laden's own statement, see Osama bin Laden, "Interview with Osama bin Laden (December 1998)," 155.

23. *9/11 Report,* 257.

24. Ibid., 109, 193.

25. Ibid., 204–05.
26. I borrow this example from Michael O'Hanlon, "Dealing with the Collapse of a Nuclear-Armed State: The Cases of North Korea and Pakistan," a working paper for the Princeton Project on National Security, http://www.princeton.edu/~ppns/papers/ohanlon.pdf.

Conclusion

1. Webster to Fox, April 24, 1841, in *British and Foreign State Papers,* 30:1137.
2. A Report to the President Pursuant to the President's Directive of January 31, 1950 (NSC 68), *Foreign Relations of the United States, 1950* (Washington: U.S. Government Printing Office, 1977), 1:243, 1:284.
3. Augustine, *City of God,* trans. R. W. Dyson (New York: Cambridge University Press, 1998), 17.13, 19.6.

INDEX

active preparation, 117, 134, 136, 150, 158, 170–71, 179, 183

al Qaeda, 176–83

Aquinas, Thomas, 78–79, 101–3, 116, 173

atomic bomb. *See* nuclear weapons

Augustine, 7, 77–79, 83–89, 100, 104, 186

Bush Doctrine, 3–4, 33–34, 161, 175, 185

Bush, George W., 33, 82, 175–78

Caroline affair, 11–21, 165

Clausewitz, Carl von, 143–44

Cold War, 30–31, 51–64, 71, 80–81. *See also under* deterrence

Cuban missile crisis, 64–72

Declaration of Independence, 74, 91–93, 202n32

Decretum, 77, 100, 116

democracy, 47, 57, 59, 63, 74, 163

deterrence, 31–33, 72, 174, 182, 185

discrimination, 79, 81

domestic analogy, 113, 120, 133, 205n2

failed nuclear state, 181–83

First Seminole War, 37–40

Gentili, Alberico, 108–111, 127

Grotius, Hugo, 111, 112–23, 128, 150, 152, 205n1, 207n19; *On the Law of War and Peace*, 77–78, 113, 123, 144

Hall, Edward, 143–45

harm. *See* injury

Hobbes, Thomas, 8, 107, 111, 123–28, 146, 208n27

imminence rule. *See* Webster's Rule

in continenti, 115–16, 133, 150

injury, 78, 100, 103–4, 111, 114, 133, 135–37, 171–72. *See also* just cause

intent, certainty of, 105, 117, 134, 136, 150, 168–70

international law, 6, 33, 71, 130, 137, 144–46, 211n33

Iraq War 2003, 6, 82, 164, 173, 175–78, 214n14

jus ad bellum, 28–29, 78

jus gentium. *See* international law

jus in bello, 28–29, 78, 79, 81

just cause, 78, 100, 103–6, 109, 134

just fear tradition, 100, 106–11, 118,
123–28, 138–45, 174
just war tradition, 7, 74–83, 89–96

Kant, Immanuel, 95, 138, 140–43, 146

last resort, 7, 20, 26–28, 76, 79, 80,
82, 159–60, 167, 173–75
law of nations. *See* international law

Machiavelli, Niccolò, 5, 107–8, 111, 127,
146
Manhattan Project, 50, 52, 54, 57
Marianna Flora, case of the, 154–59
Monroe Doctrine, 37, 40–43, 49
moral equality of persons, 90–96, 118,
185
moral tradition. *See* just war tradition

natural law theory, 119–23
necessity. *See* last resort
noncombatant immunity. *See* discrimination
NSC 68, 60–62, 80, 186
nuclear weapons, 30, 49, 49–58, 62,
64, 70–71, 176, 182

pacifism, 75, 76, 80, 84
Pearl Harbor, attack of, 30, 43–50, 66,
69–72, 185
preemptive force, 3, 6, 8, 24–29, 32–
34, 104–5, 162
preventive force, 6, 8, 52–54, 58–59,
63, 94–95, 165–83
probability, 136–37, 172
proportionality, 20, 27–29, 77, 79–82,
172–73

Pufendorf, Samuel, 129–34, 146, 150–
52, 158–59

raison d'état, 106–7, 123
realism, 75, 76, 80, 84, 100
right intention, 77–79, 82
Rousseau, Jean-Jacques, 138–40, 146

self-preservation, law of, 122, 125–27,
132, 135, 138, 144–45
September 11, 2001 attacks, 2–3, 29–
30, 82–83, 164, 178–81
skepticism, 119–23
sociability, law of, 121–22, 126, 128,
138, 140
sovereign authority, 78–79, 127, 137–38
sufficient means, 105, 114, 117, 134, 136,
150, 170

terrorism, threat of, 29–34, 160, 161,
186

UN Charter, 22–27, 81, 160, 163–65;
article 51, 23–24, 49, 165

Vattel, Emmerich de, 78, 134–38, 146
Vitoria, Francisco de, 7, 81, 100–106,
111, 116, 150

weapons of mass destruction (WMD),
30–33, 170, 182, 183
Webster, Daniel, 7, 18–21, 115, 154–59
Webster's Rule, 7, 20, 61, 71–72, 79,
99, 167; *Caroline* affair, 11–21, 165;
necessity, 27, 153, 159–60; post
World War II, 21–26; proportionality,
27–28, 30–34, 35